Put Yourself in Their Shoes
Understanding Teenagers with Attention Deficit Hyperactivity Disorder

Harvey C. Parker, Ph.D.

Specialty Press, Inc.
Plantation, Florida

Specialty Press, Inc.
300 Northwest 70th Avenue, Suite 102
Plantation, Florida 33317
(954) 792-8100 • (800) 233-9273

Printed in the United States of America

ISBN 1-886941-19-X

Library of Congress Cataloging-in-Publication Data

Parker, Harvey C.
        Put yourself in their shoes: understanding teenagers with attention-deficit
hyperactivity disorder / Harvey C. Parker.
                p.   cm.
        Includes bibliographical references and index.
        ISBN 1-886941-19-X (paper: alk. paper)
        1. Attention-deficit disordered youth--Popular works.
2. Attention-deficit disordered youth--Family relationships--Popular works. I. Title
RJ506.H9P38 1999
616.85'89'00835--dc21   98-43908
                                                                                  CIP

*This book is dedicated
to my wife, Roberta, our
children, Michelle and Julia, and
to our parents and grandparents whose wisdom,
kindness, and everlasting love will always be remembered.*

Table of Contents

1 Put Yourself in Their Shoes

Put yourself in the shoes of these adolescents with attention-deficit/hyperactivity disorder (ADHD).

Jeff—age 17

When Jeff was asked what it was like having ADHD he said, "I grew up not realizing I had a problem. I was the kid who was always in trouble. My friends would call me "Zip" because I rushed around so much and I hardly ever sat still. In school, teachers would send conduct notes home practically every day. My parents would react in all sorts of ways, but mostly they seemed worried about me. I can remember wanting very badly not to disappoint them. I left home each morning promising myself I would stay out of trouble. I tried, but the notes kept coming."

Samantha—age 15

Samatha explained her ADHD in this way. "I never had problems with my behavior. I was quiet in school and pretty much followed the rules. My biggest problem was paying attention. I would be the last one finished and I had a hard time studying for tests. It seemed to take all night to get my homework done. I found out I had ADHD when I was 13. I still didn't believe there was anything wrong with me. After I started taking medicine I saw a big change. I was able to study longer and could concentrate. My grades have gone way up. I guess it did make sense. Something must have been wrong."

Jessica—age 17

My first two years in high school were almost a disaster. I just barely passed. In my junior year I read an article about ADHD in a teen magazine. I recognized myself right away. My parents and I found someone who could help me and now I'm doing better. Before that, things were pretty rough. I thought I would never graduate. Twice a year our entire family would meet and spend the day together. My immediate family, together with my aunts, uncles, and cousins could fill up a small restaurant so we usually had picnics at a park. These times were very special to me. Everyone would fuss over all of us kids and make a big deal out of even our smallest accomplishments. When you know people care about you like this it makes you stronger."

Elliott—age 14

Elliott said he spends all his time thinking about golf. He practices everyday after school at the driving range near his house. In the past year he has become a golf fanatic. No problem concentrating there! Yet, put him in school and the lights go out. He has never been able to pay attention in class or keep track of his work. He has never read a book cover to cover—except golf magazines, of course!

Rob—age 18

Rob is a risk-taker. He was diagnosed with ADHD at age seven. He said, "When I was six, I climbed to the top of a 30-foot tree and jumped cannon-ball style into a lake. Now I'm 18 and my father says I hold the world's record for visits to the emergency room." Rob is extremely popular at school and is a star player for his high school basketball team.

Janet—age 17

Janet takes risks of another kind. She's been using drugs steadily throughout high school. Her friends tell her she has a problem, but Janet won't listen.

Carl—age 15

Carl's teachers always said he could do better if he would just try and pay attention. He was never able to succeed in school even when he put his mind to it. He was diagnosed with ADHD a few months ago and started to take medication. His schoolwork turned around, and Carl is looking forward to improving his grades.

ADHD—A Problem with Self-Regulation

People with ADHD, like those described above, often have problems regulating their attention, impulses, and motor activity. While we are always easily able to regulate many things in our environment, regulating ourselves is not always so simple. We control an air conditioner by lowering or raising the temperature on a thermostat. We slow down a car by releasing the pressure on the accelerator pedal. We enter numbers on a panel to control the cooking time or heat intensity of a microwave oven. We use a remote control to lower the volume of a television set. Regulation of these devices is made easy for us by switches, pedals, panels, or buttons.

People don't have switches, pedals, panels, or buttons for regulating their attentiveness, impulsiveness, or activity. If we did, perhaps ADHD would not exist. Unfortunately, the process of self-regulation—willfully controlling our behavior—is more complicated. The brain is responsible for self-regulation—planning, organizing, and carrying out complex behavior. These are called "executive functions" of the brain. They develop from birth through childhood. During this time, we develop language to communicate, memory to recall events, a sense of time to comprehend the concept of past and future, visualization to keep things in mind, and other skills that enable us to regulate our behavior. Executive functions are carried out in the front part of the brain in an area called the orbital-frontal cortex. This part of the brain is not as active in people with ADHD.

To stay properly "on course" throughout the day, we must all make choices about our behavior. When driving, the choice to speed competes with the option to obey the speed limit. In school, daydreaming competes with paying attention to the teacher.

Self-regulation is *not* always just a matter of choice

Self-regulation involves making choices of how we will respond to situations in our life. But is regulating our behavior simply a matter of choice? And once the choice is made to regulate, is it just a question of willpower? No. The capacity for self-regulation, like most other human traits, varies from individual to individual. To some extent, differences in our ability to self-regulate may be inherited in much the same way as we inherit height, hair color, or intelligence.

Problems with self-regulation exist in varying degrees in everyone. Many people have experienced times when they had trouble concentrating. Sometimes it's because we're tired, bored, hungry, or distracted. We've all had periods of hyperactivity or impulsivity where we couldn't contain our behavior or we acted too quickly without weighing the consequences of our actions. Does this mean we all have ADHD? Of course not. It means that problems with self-regulation are familiar to all of us from time to time.

Inattention

Problems with inattention can stem from difficulties with self-regulation. When we are asked to read a chapter in a book and pay attention to the material being read, the words on the page compete with internal and external events (thoughts, noise in background, music playing) for our attention. Attention paid to the reading selection is the result of a self-directed process. This process involves a repeated cycle of focusing, inhibiting (not allowing your attention to get diverted), and refocusing. Whichever stimulus captures our attention has a great deal to do with our interests at the time in addition to our ability to focus. For those with ADHD, somewhere in this cycle of focusing, inhibiting, and refocusing their attention gets diverted—most likely due to poor inhibition of behavior.

**People with ADHD have trouble
sustaining their attention to a task.**

Adolescents with ADHD frequently have trouble sustaining attention to tasks. They make careless mistakes in schoolwork, work, or other activities. They don't seem to listen when spoken to directly. They don't finish schoolwork, chores at home, or responsibilities in the workplace. They have particular difficulty with tasks that are tedious, boring, repetitive, and uninteresting. People with ADHD do better when large tasks are broken down into smaller ones, when frequent supervision is provided to remind them to refocus their attention, when work breaks are available so that attentional demands are reduced, and when they are working on tasks that are novel and interesting.

Assign an ADHD adolescent a chapter to read in a world history book and watch as his attention drifts after a page or two. However, give him a favorite magazine to read, and he may be able to read it cover to cover. Effort to pay attention can usually be sustained longer for enjoyable activities—playing video games, watching television, listening to music, reading an interesting book, or annoying the heck out of a little brother or sister. Attention is less likely to shift if the material being presented is novel or unusual. Dr. Sydney Zentall and her colleagues at Purdue University have demonstrated that teachers can make work assignments more interesting to ADHD students by adding novelty to the assignment. Adolescents with ADHD may benefit from the opportunities they have for movement and stimulation throughout the school day as they change classes every period in middle and high school. They don't have to remain at one desk, with one teacher, for hours at a time.

Impulsivity

Problems with impulsivity also stem from difficulties with self-regulation. Impulsivity refers to the person's inability to regulate emotions and behavior. Adolescents who are impulsive often blurt out answers before questions have been completed. They often have difficulty waiting their turn and constantly interrupt conversations, activities, and games. Impulsive teenagers act quickly, without giving sufficient forethought to the consequences of their behavior. The comic strip character, Dennis the Menace, often thought of as the epitome of impulsivity, described his impulsivity in this way:

**"By the time I think about
doing something, I've already done it."**

Impulsivity probably causes the most problems for people with ADHD. In addition to blurting out, interrupting, and intruding on others, highly impulsive people have a tendency to engage in activities without considering consequences. Some of these activities can be high risk ones which can have serious consequences. According to research done by Dr. Russell A. Barkley of The University of Massachusetts Medical Center, impulsive adolescents are more likely to:

- have automobile crashes
- get traffic citations
- smoke cigarettes and use alcohol
- have unprotected sex

The 15-year-old ADHD boy who brought samples of his parents' prescription medications to school to give out to his friends could not offer any plausible reason for his behavior. "I don't know why I did it ... I wasn't thinking," was all he could say. As we talked about the behaviors that had gotten him in trouble in the past few months, he began to realize that he often did not think about the consequences of his actions.

Impulsivity puts ADHD adolescents at greater risk much of the time. We need to teach impulsive ADHD adolescents to evaluate their behavior carefully and to think twice before acting in a potentially dangerous way.

Hyperactivity

Of all the characteristics of ADHD, hyperactivity seems to be the one most likely to improve with time. Young hyperactive children can be continuously moving. Stay around them for awhile and you'll be exhausted by their constant activity. However, as hyperactive children mature into adolescence, they typically show less hyperactivity. Restless, fidgety behavior takes its place and can be seen in tapping fingers, moving arms and legs, or excessive talking. Subjective feelings of restlessness make it difficulty for adolescents with ADHD to stay seated for long periods of time.

Other Common Characteristics of Teenagers with ADHD

Overarousal

Overarousal refers to the inability to modulate emotions or physical activity. Adolescents with ADHD often react strongly to situations or events that would normally not produce such an intense response in others. For example, they may become extremely excited at the prospect of an upcoming trip to the point that they talk about it incessantly. They may dread an upcoming test and lose sleep over it because they anticipate a poor grade. A disagreement with another family member might lead to a major argument because of heightened emotions and poor self-control.

Adolescents with ADHD have a tendency to wear their emotions on their sleeve. They may not be able to contain their exuberance, disappointment, anger, or worry. This can make them stand out among their peers who might be more quiet about their feelings.

Disorganization

Difficulty organizing tasks and activities can be a big problem for some adolescents with ADHD. They often lose things necessary for tasks such as school assignments, pencils, books, or tools. They are forgetful in daily activities such as keeping appointments, remembering to do things, or recalling instructions or information presented in school. Messy rooms, misplaced homework, overdue projects, lost school books, cars that look lived in, and school lockers filled with clutter are typical examples of adolescent ADHD disorganization. Even the best, state-of-the-art looseleaf notebook, equipped with dividers, compartments, folders, and everything but a personal secretary, may not succeed in keeping an ADHD student organized.

A little disorganization may not greatly impair performance, especially if you don't have a lot of things to manage. But for adolescents who must handle a heavy schedule at school, meet responsibilities at home, and maybe even perform well at a part-time job, even a little disorganization can lead to disaster. ADHD teens with many responsibilities may benefit from training in time management, use of appointment books, writing "do lists," scheduling long-term projects, and study strategies to stay organized.

Immediate Gratification

People with ADHD are motivated by the moment.

When faced with the choice of either studying for a test or shopping with a friend, many adolescents would weigh the pros and cons of each option. Their decision would be based on both reason and emotion. For the adolescent with ADHD, reason often takes a back seat to emotion in decision-making, especially if there is opportunity for immediate reward.

Impulsivity makes it difficult for the adolescent to delay gratification and wait for a payoff sometime in the future. To help with this, long tasks may need to be broken down into short ones. Short-term goals should be established. Feedback about behavior should be frequent and positive. This will help the adolescent stay on task and persist in his effort to achieve.

Irritable Mood and Low Frustration Tolerance

Most teenagers lack patience with their parents and teachers. They can become irritable, moody, and frustrated with little provocation. Sometimes a parent risks their life just by walking into their son's or daughter's room to say "good morning."

ADHD can cause the adolescent to be more irritable and moody. They may get upset easily and often far out of proportion for the situation. Talking to them during or immediately following an emotional episode is often unproductive as they have trouble calming themselves.

They rarely perceive themselves as the cause of a problem but are more likely to feel like the victim. Psychologists call this "external locus of control." Because ADHD adolescents often perceive a problem to be the fault of others rather than themselves, it is difficult to persuade them to take responsibility for their behavior.

Adolescents with ADHD have "external locus of control." They often perceive a problem to be the fault of others rather than themselves.

It is often more productive to let time pass after an emotional outburst and later, when things have calmed down, try to discuss the situation with your son or daughter. In a later chapter, we will discuss communication styles between parents and teens that could enhance meaningful discussion.

Inconsistency in Performance

The behavior and performance of adolescents with ADHD is often unpredictable and erratic.

For example, a student with ADHD may work steadily to complete assignments all morning only to drift off into oblivion during afternoon classes. He may stick to a story writing task and compose a creative composition in class one week, yet have trouble staying on task the very next week doing a similar assignment.

Your daughter might come home one day and busily start straightening up her room, nearly throwing out everything in sight, only to have the room looking like a disaster area a few days later. Mood and behavior can change rapidly (e.g., one minute helpful and the next oppositional and defiant).

When a person with ADHD is able to maintain self-control or pay attention in one situation and not in another, you might suspect that he may have more control over his behavior than he really has. "If he can do it now, why couldn't he do it before?" you wonder. One of the most consistent things about the behavior of those with ADHD is their inconsistency. When activities are structured, when motivation is maximized, and when immediate feedback about performance is available people with ADHD usually do best.

Academic and Social Problems

Many teenagers with ADHD suffer indignity and embarrassment in school because they can't perform as well as their classmates. Difficulties with concentration, organization, and learning result in school underachievement and failure. Problems handling responsibility or behaving appropriately often cause disagreements. Parents become uncertain and confused about how to handle these problems, even when their kids are young. When these problems continue into adolescence, where life is more complicated and the consequences of failure are more serious, parents often are desperate for answers.

ADHD is Not Just Found in Kids

We used to think that kids would outgrow most of the symptoms of ADHD by the time they were teenagers, but now we know adolescents and adults can also suffer from ADHD. Their lives will be made more difficult by this disorder. They will have more problems in school. They will have more trouble making and keeping friends than others in their social group. They may not reach the same level in their schooling, jobs, or careers as they might have had ADHD not been a factor in their life. For some, ADHD will contribute to delinquency, substance abuse, or even criminal behavior. Having ADHD can be serious business. If you are a parent, a teacher, or a caregiver to adolescents with ADHD, it is important to learn about this disorder.

ADHD is a Hidden Disability

Disabilities such as paralysis or total blindness or deafness are obvious to others. However, some physical or mental impairments are not readily apparent. These are referred to as hidden disabilities. They include such conditions as learning disabilities, diabetes, epilepsy, poor vision or hearing, and allergy.

ADHD is also often referred to as a hidden disability. Its symptoms may not always be obvious. Those with ADHD may look fine in many situations. However, under certain conditions, they may be unable to maintain the self-control, attention, or necessary activity level to learn, execute tasks, or behave appropriately.

Many of the more than four million students with disabilities enrolled in public elementary and secondary schools in the United States have hidden disabilities. Forty-three percent are learning disabled, 8 percent are emotionally/behaviorally disturbed, and 1 percent have other health impairments. Students with ADHD are most likely scattered across all three of these groups.

Research Abounds on ADHD

ADHD has been extensively studied for more than 50 years.

With more precise technology to study brain function, research has given us a greater appreciation for the neurobiological basis of ADHD. Studies involving molecular genetics have provided us with mounting evidence to support the theory that ADHD is a genetic disorder. It is not primarily caused by parental neglect, lack of love, or inadequate discipline.

We have learned ADHD is most likely part of a family of disorders and that people with ADHD often have accompanying problems with learning, mood, and behavior that need to be considered in treatment.

Pharmaceutical companies have developed new medications to help manage ADHD symptoms. A number of medications have withstood the scrutiny of years of scientific research. The safety and effectiveness of many of these medications in treating those with ADHD has been well documented.

Educators understand the importance of providing assistance to children and adolescents with ADHD in school. Research has shown us that students with ADHD are more apt to perform poorly in school and are at greater risk for failure. Teachers can use special strategies and accommodations in school to help those with ADHD succeed.

The true benefactors of this abundant research are the children with ADHD and their families. The quality of their lives has been enhanced by the knowledge we have about ADHD and effective methods of treatment.

Public Policy and ADHD

ADHD can significantly impair a person's ability to function. Public schools are now required to provide special education and related services to students with ADHD who demonstrate a need for such assistance. Employers must also consider the needs of those with ADHD who require accommodations in the workplace. Such programs may "even the playing field" for those disabled by ADHD who are seeking to compete with non-disabled people in school, in the workplace, or elsewhere.

Information and Support is Available

Information to help those with ADHD and their family is readily available. Organizations like Children and Adults with Attention Deficit Disorders (CH.A.D.D.), the Learning Disability Association (LDA) and the Attention Deficit Disorder Association (ADDA) provide valuable information about ADHD and related problems to the public. Parents can participate in these organizations and obtain much needed support. There are dozens of publications about ADHD in bookstores, libraries and on the Internet. The A.D.D. WareHouse publishes and distributes a large assortment of books, videos, and training and assessment products on ADHD and related problems. To contact these organizations refer to the appendix for more information.

Is ADHD a New Disorder?

ADHD is not a new disorder. Pediatricians, clinical psychologists, psychiatrists, and neurologists have been diagnosing and treating children and adolescents with ADHD for dozens of years. In fact, nearly half of the patients seen for treatment in child mental health clinics are referred for problems related to inattention, hyperactivity, or impulsivity—the core symptoms of ADHD.

Dr. George Still, a British physician, was one of the first people to write about children with problems of hyperactivity and poor self-control. In the early 1900s he described them as having a defect in moral control or Still's disease. There have been many names applied to this condition. Throughout the past several decades children with ADHD symptoms have received a diagnosis of postencephalitic disorder, hyperkinesis, minimal brain damage, minimal brain dysfunction, hyperkinetic reaction of childhood, attention deficit disorder with or without hyperactivity, and attention-deficit/hyperactivity disorder.

ADHD Name Changes Since 1902
Still's disease
postencephalitic disorder
hyperkinesis
minimal brain damage
minimal brain dysfunction
hyperkinetic reaction of childhood
attention deficit disorder
attention-deficit/hyperactivity disorder

The different names for ADHD reflect our evolving knowledge of this disorder. In 1980, the name of the disorder was changed from hyperkinetic reaction of childhood to attention deficit disorder (ADD). ADD included three subtypes (with hyperactivity, without hyperactivity, and residual type). In 1987, the disorder was renamed attention-deficit/hyperactivity disorder (ADHD).

How Common is ADHD?

Most experts agree that approximately 3-5 percent of the population of children in the United States have ADHD. To some extent, this is an arbitrary amount because it depends on how ADHD is defined, the age of the population studied, and the measures used for evaluation. Individual symptoms of ADHD can be found in many normal children. One survey of a sample of children done by Dr. John Werry and Dr. Herbert Quay, noted ADHD researchers, found teachers rated 30 percent of the boys and 12 percent of the girls as overactive, 49 percent of the boys and 27 percent of the girls as restless, and 43 percent of the boys and 25 percent of the girls as having short attention spans. This has led some critics to suggest that since these symptoms are so prevalent in children, ADHD should not be classified as a disorder. They fail to consider that for a child to be diagnosed as ADHD, they must exhibit several symptoms of inattention or hyperactivity-impulsivity "often," from an early age, persistently over time, and these symptoms must lead to significant impairment in at least two settings (e.g., home, school, work, community). When all of these criteria are considered, ADHD occurs in about 3 - 5 percent of children.

Children with ADHD have been found in every country which has studied ADHD.

Dr. Russell A. Barkely (1998), Director of Psychology and Professor of Psychiatry and Neurology at the University of Massachusetts Medical Center in Worcester, Massachusetts, reviewed several studies done in other countries of the prevalence of ADHD. He concluded that ADHD is a worldwide problem. Children with ADHD have been identified in every country in which ADHD has been studied. Prevalence rates vary from one country to another because of the way the researchers defined ADHD and measured it, characteristics of the population studied, or because of absolute differences in the amount of ADHD that exists in the country studied. For example, in those studies reviewed, rates of ADHD in New Zealand ranged from 2 - 6.7 percent, in Germany 8.7 percent, in Japan 7.7 percent, and in China 8.9 percent.

Three Types of ADHD

The *Diagnostic and Statistical Manual of Mental Disorders (DSM IV)*, published by the American Psychiatric Association in 1994, provides clinicians with the criteria that need to be met to diagnose mental disorders. According to the DSM IV, to receive a diagnosis of ADHD a person must exhibit a certain number of behavioral characteristics reflecting either inattention, hyperactivity-impulsivity, or both for at least six months to a degree that is "maladaptive and inconsistent with developmental level." These behavioral characteristics must have begun prior to age seven, must be evident in two or more settings (home, school, work, community), and must not be due to any other mental disorder such as mood disorder, anxiety, etc.

These criteria were field tested by the DSM IV committee studying ADHD, and they determined that children and adolescents with these behavioral characteristics fell into one of three types. Some showed predominant symptoms of hyperactivity-impulsivity, some showed predominant symptoms of inattention alone, and some showed symptoms of both inattention and hyperactivity-impulsivity combined.

Three Types of ADHD

- Predominant symptoms of inattention
- Predominant symptoms of hyperactivity-impulsivity
- Combined symptoms of inattention and hyperactivity-impulsivity

Attention-deficit/hyperactivity disorder (ADHD) is the technically correct term for this disorder as listed in the DSM IV. The term attention deficit disorder (ADD) was used in a previous edition of the manual published in 1980. For more than 10 years, ADD and ADHD have been used synonymously in public policy and in publications.

DSM IV Symptoms of ADHD

ADHD—predominantly inattentive type refers to people who exhibit signs of inattention and do not show signs of hyperactivity-impulsivity. The following behaviors are frequently seen in people with this type of ADHD.

Inattention

    a.   often fails to give close attention to details or makes careless mistakes in schoolwork, work, or other activities

    b.   often has difficulty sustaining attention in tasks or play activities

    c.   often does not seem to listen when spoken to directly

    d.   often does not follow through on instructions and fails to finish schoolwork, chores, or duties in the workplace (not due to oppositional behavior or failure to understand instructions)

    e.   often has difficulty organizing tasks and activities

    f.   often avoids, dislikes, or is reluctant to engage in tasks that require sustained mental effort (such as schoolwork or homework)

    g.   often loses things necessary for tasks or activities (e.g., toys, school assignments, pencils, books, or tools)

    h.   is often easily distracted by extraneous stimuli

    i.   is often forgetful in daily activities

ADHD—predominantly hyperactive-impulsive type refers to people who exhibit signs of hyperactivity and impulsivity and do not show signs of inattention. The following behaviors are frequently seen in people with this type of ADHD.

Hyperactivity

    a.   often fidgets with hands or feet or squirms in seat

    b.   often leaves seat in classroom or in other situations in which remaining seated is expected

    c.   often runs about or climbs excessively in situations in which it is inappropriate (in adolescents or adults, may be limited to subjective feelings of restlessness)

    d.   often has difficulty playing or engaging in leisure activities quietly

Note: From American Psychiatric Association (1994). *Diagnostic and Statistical Manual of Mental Disorders. Fourth Edition.* Washington, D.C.: Author. Copyright 1994 by the American Psychiatric Association. Reprinted by permission.

e.   is often "on the go" or often acts as if "driven by a motor"
f.   often talks excessively

Impulsivity

g.   often blurts out answers before questions have been completed
h.   often has difficulty awaiting turn
i.   often interrupts or intrudes on others (e.g., butts into conversations or games)

ADHD—combined type refers to people who exhibit signs of both inattention and hyperactivity-impulsivity.

How the Types of ADHD Compare

We can compare the three types of ADHD in terms of prevalence, associated problems, impact on academic performance, intelligence, achievement, age of onset, and whether males or females are more likely to be in one or another type.

Prevalence

Within the general population, children with ADHD—inattentive type outnumber those with the combined type or the hyperactive-impulsive type. However, children with the combined type are more commonly referred to clinics for treatment of ADHD over the other two types. Dr. Stephen Faraone and his colleagues at Massachusetts General Hospital evaluated 301 children with ADHD that were referred to their program for treatment. Of this group, 61 percent had a diagnosis of ADHD—combined type, 30 percent had a diagnosis of ADHD—inattentive type, and 9 percent had a diagnosis of ADHD—hyperactive-impulsive type.

Occurrence of Associated Problems

These same researchers found that children with the combined type of ADHD are more likely to have problems with behavior than children with either of the other two types. Those in the combined type are at greater risk for associated problems like oppositional defiant disorder, conduct disorder, tics, and bipolar disorder. These are called co-occurring or co-morbid conditions because they are frequently associated with ADHD. They will be discussed in more detail in the next chapter.

Academic Functioning

Children with ADHD—inattentive type show many symptoms of inattention and few symptoms of hyperactivity-impulsivity. In school these children are described as daydreamy and "in a fog." They frequently need reminders to stay focused on a task to completion. They may be under active rather than over active, and they often are sluggish and complete tasks after others. Even motor activities that don't require a great deal of concentration, like getting ready in the morning, picking up their room, or taking the garbage out, may take longer to complete than average. Because they are sluggish and excessively daydreamy, these children may miss out on learning activities and opportunities to interact. They may be more reluctant to initiate social contact, and they may be more passive than others. They tend to make a greater number of errors on academic tasks or tasks that require sustained concentration because they have difficulty staying focused and outputting a consistent amount of energy to complete the task.

ADHD—inattentive type
less aggressive, less impulsive,
sluggish, lethargic

Intelligence and Achievement

Children in each of the ADHD types show more impairment that non-ADHD children on measures of intellectual functioning and academic achievement. Children with either the combined or inattentive type are at greater risk for problems in school. Those with the combined type are also more likely to be put into special education classes. As compared to children who are inattentive alone, those in the combined group tend to be identified sooner because of their behavioral and social problems resulting from impulsivity and poor self-control.

People with ADHD—inattentive type
are usually identified later than those with
ADHD—hyperactive-impulsive type

Gender Differences and Age of Onset

ADHD symptoms of hyperactivity and impulsivity occur about three times more often in boys than in girls. There is an even distribution of ADHD, inattentive type across the sexes.

There are differences in the age of onset of each type of ADHD. The hyperactive-impulsive type has an earlier onset with many children being identified in preschool, kindergarten, and first or second grade. ADHD–inattentive type, however, tends to have a later onset. The majority of these individuals are identified in the intermediate elementary grades or even later.

This may be due to a number of reasons. First, problems with self-control are more easily noticed at younger ages than problems with inattention. Even at age two children who are very hyperactive, impulsive, demanding, and fussy stand out. Children who are quiet and passive don't. Second, young children are not required to pay attention for long when they are in preschool or in the primary grades. Often it isn't until second or third grade that more seatwork is given, and the child must complete papers that require extended time. While teachers of primary age children may be concerned about the inattentive child who is having trouble completing work or learning, they may not consider the problem to be serious until the child goes on to third, fourth, or fifth grade.

Treatment Issues

We don't know as much about treating people with ADHD–inattentive type as we do those with the combined or hyperactive-impulsive types. We know that all three types respond to stimulant medication. This improves attention and has additional benefits with regard to behavior, eye-hand coordination, and short-term memory. Approximately 90 percent of ADHD adolescents with either combined or hyperactive-impulsive type will have a positive response to stimulants. Only about 30 percent of the inattentive ADHD teenagers have such a robust positive response. When they do, they may be able to benefit from lower doses of medication than those who are hyperactive and impulsive.

The most important issue affecting treatment of children and adolescents who have different types of ADHD is the presence of associated disorders. For example, disruptive behavior in the form of opposition, defiance, and rule-breaking occurs more frequently in adolescents who exhibit signs of hyperactivity and inpulsivity as opposed to inattention alone. Problems related to associated disorders will be more fully discussed in the following chapter.

Summary

Put yourself in the shoes of an adolescent with ADHD and you will probably find that life can be pretty tough. ADHD affects people in many ways. Conflicts at home, problems in school performance, social difficulties with peers, and a host of other problems such as low self-esteem and discouragement are frequently found in those with ADHD.

There are three types of ADHD. The inattentive type, hyperactive-impulsive type, and combined type which has characteristics of inattention as well as hyperactivity and impulsivity. ADHD is no longer considered a disorder that just affects children. Adolescents and adults can also be diagnosed with ADHD. Characteristics of the disorder—inattention, hyperactivity, and impulsivity—are found in all people. Only when these characteristics are present to a severe degree and impair functioning in more than one setting do we consider the diagnosis of ADHD. Advances in brain and genetic research provide evidence to support ADHD as a neurobiological disorder with a genetic basis. ADHD has been found to be present in all countries throughout the world where investigators have studied the disorder.

2 Associated Problems

As if ADHD weren't enough of a problem in and of itself, adolescents with ADHD typically also have other behavioral, emotional, or learning disorders as well. The most common of these are oppositional defiant disorder, conduct disorder, depression, and anxiety. Other disorders which can co-occur with ADHD are learning disabilities, speech and language problems, fine-motor incoordination, motor tics, and Tourette's syndrome. Obviously, the presence of these co-occurring problems complicates the diagnosis and treatment of adolescents with ADHD.

Oppositional Defiant Disorder

For as long as the Nelsons could remember, Jack was always a strong-willed child. His grandfather used to call him the "mule" because there would be no way you could stop him once he made up his mind to do something. Any attempt to persuade him would be met with a temper outburst or argument which would cause havoc within the family.

Up to 40 percent of children and as many as 65 percent of adolescents with ADHD exhibit such degrees of stubborness and noncompliance they fall into a category of disruptive behavior disorder known as *oppositional defiant disorder*. Children and teens with oppositional defiant disorder are described by their parents as difficult to manage. They may exhibit frequent temper outbursts. They can be strong-willed and argumentative with adults. They may actively defy or refuse adult requests or rules and they often blame others for their own mistakes. They are touchy or easily annoyed by others, angry and resentful, spiteful, and may swear or use obscene language.

**Up to 65 percent of adolescents with ADHD
exhibit oppositional behavior.**

To be diagnosed as having oppositional defiant disorder, the adolescent must have a pattern of negative, hositle, and defiant behavior which lasts at least six months. The behavior pattern must cause significant impairment in social, academic, or occupational functioning. During this time at least four of the behavioral characteristics listed below must be present.

Characteristics of oppositional defiant disorder:
(1)   often loses temper
(2)   often argues with adults
(3)   often actively defies or refuses to comply with adults' requests or rules
(4)   often deliberately annoys people
(5)   often blames others for his or her mistakes or misbehavior
(6)   is often touchy or easily annoyed by others
(7)   is often angry and resentful
(8)   is often spiteful or vindictive

Adolescents with oppositional defiant disorder can have a devastating effect on their family. Parents get fatigued under the constant pressure of trying to manage their oppositional teen's behavior. Communication between parent and teen usually is quite negative and coercive. The parents yell a great deal and the adolescent continuously defies them. This pattern of defiance may have go on for many years, disturbing everyone in the family.

As you can imagine, when ADHD and oppositional defiant disorder co-occur, the problems can multiply. If the adolescent with ADHD is treated early there is a good chance symptoms of defiance will improve. Parents can learn behavior management strategies to cope better with the defiant teenager. Medications to treat the ADHD can also improve compliance. Educational interventions to treat the ADHD can relieve school pressures resulting in improvements in attitude and behavior.

Conduct Disorder

Conduct disorder co-occurs with ADHD in about 30 percent of children and adolescents referred for treatment. Adolescents with conduct disorder may exhibit behavior which is characterized by aggression to people and animals, destruction of property, deceitfulness or theft, and serious violation of rules.

**Thirty percent of adolescents with ADHD
also have signs of a conduct disorder.**

To be diagnosed as having conduct disorder, the adolescent must have a pattern of behavior in which the basic rights of others or major social norms or rules are violated. There must be the presence of at least three of the following characteristics within the past year with at least one characteristic present in the last six months.

Characteristics of conduct disorder:
Aggression to people and animals
  (1) often bullies, threatens, or intimidates others
  (2) often initiates physical fights
  (3) has used a weapon that can cause serious physical harm to others (e.g., a bat, brick, broken bottle, knife, gun)
  (4) has been physically cruel to people
  (5) has been physically cruel to animals
  (6) has stolen while confronting a victim (e.g., mugging, purse snatching, extortion, armed robbery
  (7) has forced someone into sexual activity

Destruction of property
  (8) has deliberately engaged in fire setting with the intention of causing serious damage
  (9) has deliberately destroyed others' property (other than by fire setting)

Deceitfulness or theft
  (10) has broken into someone else's house, building, or car
  (11) often lies to obtain goods or favors or to avoid obligations (i.e., "cons" others)
  (12) has stolen items of nontrivial value without confronting a victim (e.g., shoplifting, but without breaking and entering; forgery)

Serious violations of rules
  (13) often stays out at night despite parental prohibition, beginning before age 13 years
  (14) has run away from home overnight at least twice while living in parental or parental surrogate home (or once without returning for a lengthy period)
  (15) often truant from school, beginning before age 13 years

The severity of conduct disorder ranges from mild to severe based on the number of symptoms demonstrated and the degree of harm rendered to person or property. There are two broad groups of adolescents with conduct disorder. In one group are adolescents who had an early onset of symptoms of conduct disorder. Those in this group developed symptoms before age 10. They are more likely to have antisocial behavior problems throughout life. In the second group are adolescents who had a later onset of symptoms of conduct disorder. Those in this group developed symptoms after the age of 10. Their antisocial problems are not as chronic and persistent and are not likely to continue beyond adolescence.

As with oppositional defiant disorder, when ADHD and conduct disorder co-occur, problems can multiply. Early intervention is extremely important to prevent serious antisocial behavior, substance abuse, and potential delinquency. Parents will benefit from learning behavior management strategies. Treatment with medication can improve symptoms of aggression, defiance, and irritability as well as targeting ADHD symptoms. Educational interventions can reduce stress on the adolescent and may make school a more positive experience.

Depression

Teens with ADHD may be at greater risk for developing depressive disorders than non-ADHD adolescents. It is estimated that as many as 30 percent of ADHD adolescents develop symptoms of depression.

One type of depression children or adolescents may develop is known as *dysthymia*. Adolescents with dysthymia have low mood most of the day, more often than not, for at least one year. Their low mood may take the form of irritability. In addition, they may have symptoms of poor appetite or overeating, insomnia or hypersomnia, low energy, low self-esteem, poor concentration, and feelings of hopelessness.

Another type of depression adolescents may develop is known as *major depression*. Those with major depression have depressed mood most of the day nearly every day for at least two weeks. Other symptoms include deriving little or no pleasure from activities; significant weight loss when not dieting or less weight gain than expected; insomnia or hypersomnia nearly every day; low energy; feelings of worthlessness or inappropriate guilt nearly every day; diminished ability to think, concentrate, or make decisions; and recurrent thoughts of death.

Dr. Joseph Biederman, a child and adolescent psychiatrist, and his colleagues at Massachusetts General Hospital found that having ADHD increases the risk for developing manic-depressive illness, also known as *bipolar disorder*. Eleven percent of the children with ADHD they studied had bipolar disorder at the start of their study and an additional 12 percent developed bipolar disorder four years later. Children with bipolar disorder have frequent and rapid dramatic shifts of mood including elation, depression, irritability, and anger. At times they may have an exaggerated positive view of themselves, believing they are right and others wrong. Their speech may become "pressured" marked by intense rapid talking and accompanied by "racing thoughts" they cannot control.

**Depression is found in
30 percent of adolescents with ADHD.**

In addition to the symptoms noted above, a family history of bipolar disorder, severe symptoms of ADHD, oppositional disorder, and conduct disorder are markers that could signal the presence of bipolar disorder.

Anxiety Disorders

Adolescents with ADHD are more likely to have anxiety related disorders than those not affected by ADHD. Two types of anxiety disorders that occur in adolescents are *separation anxiety disorder* and *overanxious disorder*.

To be diagnosed as having separation anxiety disorder, the adolescent must have the following characteristics for more than four weeks.

Characteristics of separation anxiety disorder:
(1)	recurrent, excessive distress when separated from home or a major attachment figure (i.e., parent or other relative) occurs or is anticipated
(2)	persistent and excessive worry about losing, or about possible harm befalling, major attachment figures
(3)	persistent and excessive worry that an untoward event will lead to separation from a major attachment figure (e.g., getting lost or being kidnapped)
(4)	persistent reluctance or refusal to go to school or elsewhere because of fear of separation
(5)	persistently and excessively fearful or reluctant to be alone without major attachment figures at home or without significant adults in other settings
(6)	persistent reluctance or refusal to go to sleep without being near a major attachment figure or to sleep away from home
(7)	repeated nightmares involving the theme of separation
(8)	repeated complaints of physical symptoms (such as headaches, stomachaches, nausea, or vomiting) when separation from major attachment figures occurs or is anticipated

Overanxious disorder of childhood may exist if there is excessive anxiety and worry about a number of events or activities (such as school) occurring more days than not for at least six months. The child or adolescent with this type of anxiety disorder finds it difficult to control worrying and may have some of the following additional symptoms: restlessness or feeling keyed up or on edge; becoming easily fatigued; difficulty concentrating or their mind going blank; irritability; muscle tension; and a sleep disturbance that can cause difficulty falling asleep, staying asleep, or having a restful sleep.

Treatment for adolescents with ADHD, who also have an anxiety disorder, must address both conditions. These teens need support, reassurance, and encouragement. Antidepressant medications may improve their mood, reduce anxiety, and also help with some ADHD symptoms. Stimulant medications may increase anxiety in some adolescents.

Learning Problems

Learning difficulties in adolescents with ADHD are common. They range from academic performance problems to trouble with learning skills such as reading, math, and use of language. ADHD students may have trouble planning, organizing, and completing work. They may not be able to sustain attention to assignments, they may require more time to complete work, or may be helped by having shorter assignments. They may not read instructions carefully or may make careless errors. They tend to have significant difficulty planning long-term projects, often waiting until the last minute to get work turned in.

**As many as 25 percent of children with ADHD
show signs of a learning disability.**

Up to 25 percent of children with ADHD show evidence of a learning disability. A *learning disability* is a deficit in one or more of the basic psychological processes involved in understanding or using spoken or written language. These problems are often the result of language impairments, perceptual dysfunctions, or disturbances in the way information is processed and expressed in written or oral communications. Learning disabled students may show weaknesses in reading, writing, spelling, or arithmetic skills.

Obsessive-Compulsive Disorder

Approximately 25 percent of people with obsessive-compulsive disorder have ADHD. *Obsessive-compulsive disorder* is characterized by three major characteristics.

Characteristics of obsessive-compulsive disorder:
(1)   intrusive, forceful, and repetitive thoughts, images, or sounds that are lodged in one's mind and cannot be willfully eliminated
(2)   compulsions to perform motor or mental acts
(3)   excessive and recurrent doubting about matters of either major or minor importance

The obsessions or compulsions cause marked distress, are time consuming, and significantly interfere with normal functioning.

Examples of obsessive or compulsive behavior in adolescents may include: over-concern with cleanliness; repeated hand washing; unusual or overly rigid eating habits; excessive concern about the tidiness of their room and their belongings; compulsion to place items around the house in a particular way; repeated checking if something is on or off, locked or unlocked; ritualistic counting; or repetition of a series of acts before moving on to something else.

Jack Nicholson did a wonderful job of portraying a person with obsessive-compulsive disorder in the award-winning movie, *As Good As It Gets!*

Treatment for obsessive-compulsive disorder usually involves a combination of medication and behavior therapy. When ADHD is also present, the treatment can become much more complicated. Multiple medications may be prescribed to treat both disorders.

Asperger's Disorder

Asperger's Disorder is an impairment in social interaction, which was first described in the 1940s. Children and adolescents with Asperger's have impaired social interactions and unusual patterns of communication and behavior.

When communicating, they exhibit some of the following symptoms: a marked impairment in nonverbal behaviors used to communicate with others such as eye contact, facial expression, body postures, and gestures; failure to develop friendships appropriate to one's age and development; failure to seek out others to communicate; and lack of social reciprocity when interacting with others. Those affected by Asperger's seem uninterested in social interaction. In contrast, the ADHD child's social behavior is affected by impulsivity and failure to read social cues because they are not concentrating on the reactions of others.

Those with Asperger's also exhibit unusual behavior patterns including preoccupation with a specific interest; inflexible adherence to specific routines or rituals; repetitive motor mannerisms (such as hand or finger flapping or twisting or whole body movements); preoccupation with parts of objects.

Asperger's disorder is rare and is not frequently seen in those with ADHD. However, some people with Asperger's also have problems with hyperactivity, impulsivity, and inattention. For some, this may be caused by the Asperger's itself, while others may have a co-diagnosis of ADHD.

Speech and Language Problems

Adolescents with ADHD tend to have a greater amount of speech and language problems than those not affected by ADHD. Young ADHD children are more likely to have delays in normal speech development, problems with articulation of sounds, and sequencing thoughts. As they get older, problems with organizing and planning what to say are more frequent.

Problems with language can also lead to difficulties with written expression, reading fluency, and comprehension.

Sensory and Motor Problems

Hearing and vision problems are not more prevalent in ADHD adolescents than they are within the general adolescent population. Neither are there extraordinary delays in the motor development of young ADHD children. However, perhaps as many as 50 percent of ADHD children are reported to have problems with motor coordination, especially on tasks requiring fine-motor coordination. Adolescents with ADHD are often noted to have problems with handwriting.

**About 50 percent of children with ADHD
have problems with motor coordination.**

Social Adjustment Problems

It is estimated that more than 50 percent of teens with ADHD have some type of social relationship problems. Observers report hyperactive children to be much more aggressive, disruptive, bossy, noisy, intrusive, and inappropriate socially. They experience high rates of social rejection from peers. They tend to have an external locus of control moreso than non-ADHD children. That is, they are more likely to view events that happen to them as not being their fault, and they may blame others too quickly. These traits probably follow them through their teen years.

Those with ADHD—inattentive type may have different social problems. These adolescents are by nature more passive, quiet and non-competitive than their peers. While they are better accepted by peers than those children with ADHD who are hyperactive and impulsive, they often remain on the outskirts of social relationships. They can be quiet and shy, which keeps them from initiating interaction with others.

Transient Tics

Transient tics are sudden, repetitive, and involuntary movements of muscles. Vocal tics involve muscles that control speech and cause involuntary sounds such as coughing, throat clearing, sniffing, making loud sounds, grunting, or calling out words. Motor tics involve other muscles and can occur in any part of the body. Some examples of motor tics are eye blinking, shoulder shrugging, facial grimacing, head jerking, and a variety of hand movements. Tics that are less common involve self-injurious behavior such as hitting or biting oneself and coprolalia (involuntary use of profane words or gestures). When these types of tics occur many times a day, nearly every day for at least four weeks, but for no longer than 12 consecutive months, the child may have a transient tic disorder.

It is estimated that 10 percent of children and adolescents with ADHD will develop a transient tic disorder. Others may develop a tic disorder that is associated with the use of stimulant medication.

Chronic Tics and Tourette's Syndrome

A child who has either a motor or a vocal tic (but not both), which occurs many times a day, nearly every day, for a period of at least one year (without stopping for more than three months), may be diagnosed as having a chronic tic disorder. *Tourette's syndrome* is a chronic tic disorder characterized by both multiple motor tics and one or more vocal tics, although not necessarily concurrent. These tics are more severe than the simple, transient motor tics described earlier. They occur many times a day, nearly every day or intermittently throughout a period of more than one year. They involve the head and frequently other parts of the body such as the torso, arms, and legs. Vocal tics may include the production of sounds like clucking, grunting, yelping, barking, snorting, and coughing. Utterances of obscenities, coprolalia, are rare and occur in about 10 percent of children with Tourette's.

Dr. David Comings and Dr. Brenda Comings, of the City of Hope Medical Center in Duarte California, studied 130 patients with Tourette's. They found that more than half of them had ADHD. Stimulants should be used cautiously with children who have chronic tic disorder or Tourette's syndrome and ADHD.

Cigarette Smoking and Substance Use Disorder

Adolescents who smoke cigarettes have a five times greater likelihood of using drugs than non-smokers. Studies by Dr. Joseph Biederman and his colleagues at Massachusetts General Hospital, found ADHD subjects were more likely to be smokers (19 percent in the ADHD group vs 10 percent in a normal control group), and they started smoking at an earlier age.

These investigators also found cigarette smoking increases in subjects with ADHD as the number of comorbid disorders they have increases. The rate of cigarette smoking was 10 percent in ADHD subjects with no comorbid disorders, 21 percent in those with one comorbid disorder, 35 percent in those with two comorbid disorders, and 40 percent when ADHD and three other disorders (depression, anxiety, and conduct disorder) were present.

**ADHD alone does not
increase the likelihood of substance abuse.**

Several studies looking at the comorbidity of substance use disorder and ADHD in adolescence indicated that the presence of ADHD alone does not increase the risk of developing a substance use disorder. However, ADHD plus conduct disorder does.

Sleep Problems

Excessive movement during sleep, once thought to be a characteristic of those with ADHD, is no longer one of the criteria used in considering a diagnosis. However, research conducted on the sleep behavior of children with ADHD consistently notes that parents report greater sleep problems in ADHD children than in non-ADHD children. These reports indicate that more than 50 percent of ADHD children need more time to fall asleep, nearly 40 percent may have problems with frequent night wakings, and more than half have trouble waking in the morning.

Summary

Adolescents with ADHD frequently have co-occurring problems. Disorders involving disruptive behavior such as oppositional defiant disorder and conduct disorder are the most common co-occurring conditions. In addition, a significant number of children and adolescents with ADHD also suffer from mood disorders such as depression and anxiety. Learning problems associated with speech and language disorders, problems with reading, mathematics, and writing, as well as school performance problems are common. Problems with fine-motor incoordination, simple motor tics, chronic tics, and Tourette's syndrome are associated with ADHD. While ADHD children and adolescents are at no greater risk for developing disorders such as obsessive-compulsive disorder or Asperger's disorder, a significant number of children with these conditions do have ADHD.

It is the exception rather than the rule if an adolescent with ADHD doesn't have any co-occurring problems. Professionals assessing children and adolescents for ADHD should look for the presence of these other conditions.

3   A Closer Look at Teenagers with ADHD

"Who would have guessed how Jeff turned out?" thought Mrs. Roberson as she beamed with pride while watching her son receive his high school diploma. Jeff's parents breathed a sigh of relief as he walked off the stage. Trying to catch a glimpse of his parents, he smiled proudly. Jeff, his parents, and teachers knew the extra effort he made to graduate.

Jeff's story is similar to many of those told by parents of children with ADHD. Jeff was diagnosed early, at age six. An evaluation done by the psychologist indicated he had signs of ADHD. Jeff's mother got a second opinion from his family doctor, and Jeff started treatment before the school year concluded.

Mrs. Roberson reflected on the past as she watched her son graduate from high school. She recalled the countless trips to school to talk to his teachers about his behavior, work, and attitude. Things would go up and down in elementary school. Sometimes Jeff would be "on a roll," the medication would be working great, and his attention and focus were fine. At other times, he'd fall apart. A visit to the psychologist to get him back on track with a behavior management program or an adjustment in his medication would be all he needed. The amount of time, care, and attention Jeff needed to manage his ADHD seemed endless.

When Jeff began middle school, his parents crossed their fingers and hoped for the best. They couldn't imagine how things would work at school when there were five or more teachers to conference with rather than just one or two. Sure enough, things seemed to worsen each year through middle school and high school. But he finally made it—with the help of some really dedicated teachers and a wonderful guidance counselor. Jeff, of course, gets most of the credit. He tried to settle down and work in his junior and senior year. And now the payoff had arrived—graduation! As Jeff grasped his diploma, Mrs. Roberson felt a heavy weight lifting from her shoulders. Jeff made it! For now, at least , they were safe.

Jeff had just turned 14 when I started counseling him. At that time, his life seemed quite chaotic. He had managed to alienate his mother and stepfather with whom he lived, his older brother couldn't stand him and neither could most of his friends. Jeff's teachers were fed up with his "know-it-all attitude" in school. In class he would be out of his seat more than in it. He fidgeted so much one teacher threatened to tie him down. When it came time for him to work quietly at his desk in school, Jeff would be busy talking to another student or showing him something he had found in his backpack. Jeff never seemed to know what he was supposed to do or where he was supposed to be. His sense of organization was non-existent.

Jeff's graduation from high school was indeed a landmark event, and his eventual graduation from college was an added bonus. Jeff certainly gets much of the credit, but it was a team effort. His parents stood behind him every step of the way. They never gave up on Jeff, and whenever he needed help, they were there for him.

About a year ago, Jeff, then 24, called me. He had just come back to South Florida to see his family. He had completed an undergraduate degree in computer technology and landed a great job as a software designer for a high tech company in the Silicon Valley. He was quite successful in his work, had made good friends, and was involved in a serious romance.

Jeff's story is a positive one—as are the stories many families of children with ADHD are proud to tell. Often they go through hell and back managing the problems that ADHD and its associated disorders bring. They are tired by years of struggle, but somehow they manage to go on day-to-day to provide the structure, support, supervision, and love their child needs. Below are a few more stories of adolescents and their families who have struggled with ADHD. The names have been changed to protect their confidentiality.

Jason - ADHD—inattentive type with learning disabilities

Roy and Sally Roberts waited until they were settled before having children. Roy, an employee for a major accounting firm, and Sally, a travel agent who specialized in corporate travel, were married five years when their first child, Jason, was born. It was "easy as pie" Sally would tell her family and friends. "From start to finish, Jason's birth was a labor of love!" she said. Sally's and Roy's parents lived close by and spent a great deal of time visiting with their grandson. Jason was a lucky boy. With so many people around to shower him with love and attention, he was sure to grow up safe and secure.

Jason sailed through preschool, kindergarten, and first and second grades without a hitch. "A wonderful little boy," were typical comments offered by teachers at parent-teacher conferences. He finished his work, respected others, and seemed intelligent.

At the start of third grade, Jason's teacher noticed he was having trouble completing tasks. Long after the other students in his class finished their seat work, Jason would be working on his assignment. The teacher mentioned to Mr. and Mrs. Roberts that Jason daydreamed and often had to be reminded to get back on task. She promised the parents she would watch Jason more carefully throughout the year and encourage him to work more quickly.

By the middle of the year, Jason's teacher became more concerned. Not only was Jason having trouble completing his class work, he didn't comprehend written instructions well and had trouble reading as fluently as others. Concerned that Jason may not be ready to handle the independent work that would be required of him in fourth grade, the teacher suggested to Jason's parents that he be referred for an evaluation to determine his learning skills.

The school psychologist met with Jason and completed tests to measure his intellectual ability, academic achievement, and skills such as memory, attention, use of language, and eye-hand coordination. The school social worker met with his parents to obtain Jason's medical history, which included information about Mrs. Roberts' pregnancy and delivery of Jason, his health, and his development socially, emotionally, and academically. Jason's parents and teachers were given a set of questionnaires to complete, which included behavior rating scales.

When the assessment was completed, Jason's parents met with the school's child study team to review the test results. The school determined that Jason had ADHD—predominantly inattentive type along with a learning disability, which affected his use of language and his ability to read and comprehend. The child study team recommended that Jason go into a special class for part of the day to help him with his reading and language. His regular education teacher continued to work with him in other subjects and made accommodations to help him pay attention and reduce pressure to perform.

Jason continued through elementary school and received extra help and attention. In middle school, he was reevaluated and had improved in his academic skills, although he still had trouble attending and completing work. He enrolled in all regular education classes. Jason's parents met with his teachers to request they continue to provide accommodations for him.

Despite the teacher's assistance and understanding, Jason still had problems in middle school, and his parents began investigating the possibility of putting him on medication to improve his attention span. His doctor recommended Ritalin, which Jason began taking twice a day in seventh grade. Everyone immediately noticed an improvement. His teachers continued to make accommodations and kept his parents informed of any changes in behavior or problems.

Jesse - ADHD—combined type with depression

Jesse, an 18-year-old, dropped out of high school in his junior year. He was delivering pizza part-time. He came for an evaluation at the request of his parents, who wanted him to consider a future career and hoped he would return to school.

Jesse provided a history that depicted a young man who had academic problems in school and family problems at home. He was comfortable in his present job, remarking that there was no stress or pressure, and the money he earned was enough. He had no lofty plans for the future and didn't see himself ever returning to school. Jesse said some of his worst moments in life were in the classroom where he could never sit still or concentrate on what his teachers were saying. In elementary and middle school, his teachers would interpret his lack of attention as defiance, and he would frequently get in trouble with his parents for poor school performance. In high school his teachers left him alone, and he left them alone. He often sat for hours in class doing nothing,

Jesse's parents completed questionnaires and rating scales to provide a complete picture of Jesse as a child. His parents reported a lengthy history of extreme hyperactivity and impulsive behavior. From the time Jesse first entered preschool, he had trouble sitting still in class, controlling his mood, and following instructions. Similar problems continued in elementary school. Jesse was frequently criticized for behavior problems in class, and his parents were called for numerous parent-teacher conferences. His impulsive behavior was legendary in his small community. Everyone knew Jesse as the nonstop, hyperactive kid who grew up to become a wild, risk-taking teenager.

Recently, Jesse's mood had seemed depressed to his parents. During the past year, he stayed in his room quite often for long periods of time. He made little effort to see his friends, and he was irritable and difficult to get along with at home. Given his recent mood changes and isolation, his parents were concerned he might be using drugs.

Jesse's evaluation revealed that he had ADHD—combined type. He had problems with hyperactivity and impulsivity in addition to significant difficulty paying attention. His intellectual ability was quite good, scoring nearly within the superior range of intelligence. Basic academic skills were fairly good for his age, but significantly below what would be expected of someone with his intellectual ability. Jesse's performance on computerized tests of impulse control and attention span revealed problems with self-regulation and attention.

During the evaluation, it became clear that Jesse was suffering from depression. His mood was low, he seemed apathetic about his job and his future, he showed little interest in being with friends, eating, or having fun. He was given a diagnosis of ADHD, combined type and depression. He did not admit to any problems with substance abuse.

During the examination, Jesse discussed his own concerns about his future. He obviously agreed with his parents that his present job wasn't going to do for the long haul. He was interested in going back to school to learn a vocation or trade, but was terrified of failure. He admitted to worrying a great deal about his future, but he didn't know how to start preparing for it. He agreed to come for additional counseling to discuss vocational options and to work on his negative self-image. He tried medication to help improve his mood and attention ability.

Jesse eventually went to a vocational-technical school in his community and studied air conditioning and refrigeration. He succeeded with the program, landed a job as soon as he graduated, and has been working ever since.

Tony - ADHD—inattentive type and learning problems

Tony, a 14-year-old, was referred for assessment and treatment by his pediatrician, who was concerned that he might have a learning disability and problems with attention.

Tony's parents described him as a kindhearted, pleasant, and agreeable young man. He was the oldest of their three children, and the most conscientious and responsible. "He only has problems in school," said his parents, who described a lengthy history of academic difficulties since Tony was in elementary school. Tony was in danger of failing three out of five subjects when he came for an evaluation.

Mr. and Mrs. Gordon reported that Tony was the product of a full-term, normal pregnancy and delivery. He was a very healthy baby and showed no signs of developmental problems from infancy through toddlerhood. His motor coordination, speech and language skills, and cognitive ability seemed to develop normally as a youngster. Tony had no history of any serious illnesses, and other than some recurring ear infections in kindergarten, he was healthy growing up. His parents reported that Tony is well-liked in the neighborhood by adults and peers. He has many friends who frequently come to visit because of Tony's collection of radio controlled cars.

Tony's current teachers completed a series of behavior rating scales designed to obtain information about a student's classroom behavior, academic performance, and social and emotional adjustment. Tony's teachers all agreed that he was a pleasant, likeable young man who had serious problems with paying attention, comprehending assignments, and completing work. Written summaries of his school performance by the teachers resulted in comments such as: "Tony just can't seem to keep his mind on anything we do in class." "He has to be reminded to pay attention constantly." "I don't think he really understands some of the work we are doing." None of Tony's current teachers characterized him as having a problem with behavior. Self-control was good, and he showed no evidence of impulsive behavior, hyperactivity, or aggression. Interestingly, his teachers remarked he was a little too quiet and maybe even a bit withdrawn.

Mr. and Mrs. Gordon were not at all surprised by the remarks Tony's teachers made about him. They had heard the same comments many times before from previous teachers. Tony had been tested in third grade for problems with inattention and performance, but the school psychologist could find no evidence of a learning disability or attention problem at the time.

When Tony was re-evaluated, his test results showed that he was of average intelligence. He had scored average on academic tests of arithmetic computation and word recognition, but below average skills in reading comprehension and written language development. Tests measuring perceptual processing revealed problems with auditory short-term memory and fine motor coordination.

Tony was diagnosed as having a learning disability and ADHD— inattentive-type. These problems were explained to Mr. and Mrs. Gordon, and Tony started a multi-modal treatment program. He saw a local educational specialist for help with reading and written language skills. This specialist worked closely with Tony's teachers at school so he could benefit from the supplementary instruction he received. His pediatrician agreed to prescribe Ritalin, which Tony took twice a day to help improve attention span in school and once after school to assist with homework. The school agreed to set up a plan for Tony to receive accommodations in the classroom. Some of these accommodations would reduce the amount of work Tony was assigned and allow more time for him to complete assignments.

Elaine - ADHD—hyperactive-impulsive type with conduct disorder and substance abuse disorder

From the day Elaine was born, her mother sensed she was going to be a handful to raise. "She came out in a hurry and hasn't slowed down since!" exclaimed her mother, who had come for an interview to discuss her 17-year-old daughter. Within the first 10 minutes Mrs. Sorenson mentioned so many problems that Elaine had gotten into, you would have thought she was twice her age.

When she was 10 years old, she was suspended from school for fighting with another student. She ended up hitting a teacher who had tried to break up the brawl. A few months later she got suspended again, this time for smoking in the girl's bathroom. Her attitude in school was disagreeable and obnoxious, both to her fellow students and teachers. By the time she got to high school, she was rude, defiant, and in trouble most of the time. She got into the habit of skipping classes. She and her friends would hang out in someone's car and smoke marijuana. Sometimes they would go back to school in the afternoon and sometimes not. One time they took the car out for a ride and got into an accident. Three people in the other vehicle they crashed into were injured. Elaine and her friends were taken into custody.

A psychoeducational evaluation done by the court indicated that Elaine had a diagnosis of ADHD, conduct disorder and substance abuse disorder. Elaine was ordered by the court to do 200 hours of community service and receive individual and family therapy and treatment for her substance abuse problems. She made it clear from the start that she was not going to be a cooperative patient. Nevertheless, treatment started and focused on family issues with several goals in mind: to encourage Elaine to take responsibility for her substance abuse disorder; to help Elaine and her mother (father was not in the picture) communicate more effectively with one another; to encourage mother to set more effective limits at home; and to assist Elaine in vocational planning. Medical treatment for Elaine's ADHD problems was not initiated until progress in some of these other areas was made.

Elaine attended a 12 step Narcotics Anonymous program and weekly family therapy sessions. She enrolled in a vocational education program to receive training to become a cosmetologist. Her talent in this area was obvious to her instructors who praised her quick ability to learn. Elaine enjoyed the hands-on training and began to show more of an interest in her future. Previous problems with attention span and concentration did not affect her performance as a cosmetologist. She did not have to focus attention for long periods of time and could shift activities with every new client.

As Elaine's interest in her work grew more serious, her negative behavior and fluctuating moods at home lessened. Her self-esteem improved and she took great pleasure in her new found success. She was motivated to complete her vocational training. Problems with substance abuse diminished and Elaine and her mother made strides in their relationship.

Elaine is now 27-years-old. She continues to work as a cosmetologist and has built up a loyal following of clients. She is married and has a three year old daughter whose boundless energy and curiosity keeps her very busy.

Summary

There are many common elements found in families of children and adolescents with ADHD. A close look at these families reveals a lengthy history of adjustment problems at home, in school, and in other settings. The onset of ADHD symptoms is usually noticed early in the child's life and by the time parents seek assistance they and their child are often frustrated and stressed. Fortunately, with greater awareness about ADHD than ever before, children are being identified earlier and help is more available.

A close look at the lives of adolescents with ADHD reveals more than just problems with inattention, impulsivity, or hyperactivity. As indicated in the previous chapter, adolescents with ADHD often have co-occurring problems such as learning difficulties, mood disorders, or behavior disorders. Parents, educators, and health professionals must be aware of the existence of these other problems and provide assistance to the adolescent in areas where help is needed.

While as many as 50% of adolescents with ADHD will continue to be affected by this disorder in adulthood, with the proper support, guidance, and treatment they can lead productive lives.

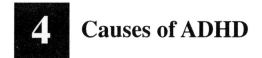 4 Causes of ADHD

We know a great deal more about the causes of ADHD today than we did 10 or 15 years ago. Developments in medical technology have given us better tools to study brain functioning. Advances in the field of genetics have enhanced our understanding of the heritability of ADHD. Just as important, we have a better understanding of the things that do not cause ADHD.

Brain Functioning in ADHD

Scientists who study ADHD agree that it is a neurological disorder. We have suspected this for many years, but we now have much more scientific research, which points us to specific areas of the brain that are involved in ADHD.

The brain has two sides, which we call the right and the left hemispheres. The external surface, called the cortex, includes four lobes: the frontal (in the front), temporal (near the temples), parietal (above the ears), and occipital (in the back). These four lobes control motor activity and sensation. Higher cortical functions, such as thinking, are controlled by the frontal lobe, a region associated with ADHD.

The brain's highly sophisticated communication system is composed of billions of nerve cells called neurons. Each neuron connects with thousands of other neurons, relaying messages that rely on chemical reactions. These chemical reactions occur at sites both inside and outside the neuron in the synapse, or junction, between the cells and are carried out by receptors. Receptors are part of the neuron membrane and have the capacity to recognize a neurotransmitter or a hormone.

When an order or response is chosen, a biochemical reaction takes place to transmit the impulse that carries the order. The order goes through the axon and dendrites of the neuron. This results in an electrical charge that is carried by neurotransmitters to the synapse. Neurotransmitters are chemical substances produced by the body that regulate brain functioning. Medications used to treat ADHD affect neurotransmitter's metabolism and the supply of neurotransmitters in the synapse and the neuron's receptors.

Current research indicates the frontal lobe plays a significant role in ADHD because it is involved in the regulation of behavior, inhibition of impulses, sequential thinking, planning, and organizing. As we said earlier, these higher order cognitive processes are referred to as "executive function." People who have sustained trauma to the frontal lobe from a head injury, tumor, infection, or disease have problems with executive function.

Executive Functions:
regulation of behavior
sequential thinking
planning and organizing

In animal studies, primates who had the frontal lobe of their brain surgically compromised exhibited behaviors seen in people with ADHD. They became more hyperactive, were less able to sustain attention to a task, and showed greater emotional arousal and impulsivity both under controlled conditions and when observed in their natural environment.

However, early researchers studying hyperactive children could find no evidence of a history of brain injury or disease. Therefore, they assumed that these children must have suffered some problems with brain development that were too minor to detect with the available technology. The term *minimal brain dysfunction* was coined in the 1960s to describe these children.

Since that time, scientists have tried to determine the differences in brain functioning that could account for behaviors associated with ADHD. With new technology to study brain functioning, they were able to take a close look at brain chemistry, brain electrical activity and blood flow, and brain anatomy in people with ADHD.

Brain Chemistry

Researchers have discovered that neurotransmitter chemicals in the brain play an important part in regulating behavior and emotions.

Brain chemistry plays an important
role in causing ADHD. Neurotransmitter
chemicals such as dopamine, norepinephrine,
and serotonin may be involved.

They suspect that malfunction of the way certain neurochemical transmitters operate within the frontal lobe of the brain, and elsewhere, may be responsible. Dopamine, norepinephrine, serotonin, and other neurotransmitters may be involved. These suspicions are greatly supported by the effect that medications, which affect these neurotransmitter chemicals, have on the behavior of those with ADHD. For example, stimulants such as methylphenidate and dextroamphetamine increase levels of dopamine, which results in improvement of ADHD symptoms.

Brain Activity and Blood Flow

Studies using electroencephalography (EEG) to study electrical activity in the brain have shown difference in EEG activity, especially in the frontal lobe, in children with ADHD. Similar findings came from studies investigating blood flow in the frontal lobe of ADHD children.

The most publicized study of brain functioning in ADHD children was done in 1990 by Dr. Alan Zametkin, a child and adolescent psychiatrist, and his colleagues at the National Institute of Mental Health. Using a very sensitive procedure known as positron emission tomography (PET scan), Dr. Zametkin compared the brain activity of 25 adults with ADHD to 50 adults without ADHD. His team found that adults with ADHD had less brain activity, particularly in the frontal region. He repeated the study with adolescents and found similar, but less robust results.

Brain Structure

Dr. George Hynd and his colleagues, at the University of Georgia have used magnetic resonance imaging (MRI) technology to study brain structure and anatomy. They have discovered that an important part of the brain, the caudate nucleus, was somewhat larger than expected on one side of the brain than the other in children with ADHD. This is opposite to what is found in non-ADHD children.

Using a larger sample of subjects, researchers at the National Institute of Mental Health also found differrences in the expected size of the caudate nucleous in children with ADHD. Dr. Xavier Castellanos and his associates used quantitative magnetic resonance imaging to study brain structure in 57 boys with ADHD and 55 healthy matched controls, ages 5 to 18 years. Significant differences in brain structure were found between the two groups.

Factors that Could Affect Brain Development

What factors could account for neurological differences in either brain chemistry, brain activity, blood flow, or brain structure between people with ADHD and those without ADHD? The main factors studied to date have been: fetal exposure to toxic substances during pregnancy, exposure to lead, and differences that could be attributed to heredity.

Smoking and Alcohol Use in Pregnancy

Researchers have found an association between mothers who smoked tobacco products or used alcohol during their pregnancy and the development of behavior and learning problems in their children. A similar association between lead exposure and hyperactivity has been found, especially when the lead exposure occurs in the first three years. Nicotine, alcohol, and lead can be toxic to developing brain tissue and may have sustained effects on the behavior of the children exposed to these substances at early ages. However, it is unlikely that such exposure accounts for differences in brain development in the vast majority of children and adolescents with ADHD.

Heredity

Heredity is the most common cause of ADHD, and it most likely accounts for much of the difference in brain development that we see when we compare ADHD children and non-ADHD children. For years we have suspected that heredity plays an important role in ADHD. Most of our information about the inheritability of ADHD comes from family studies, adoption studies, twin studies, and molecular genetic research.

Family Studies

If a trait has a genetic basis we would expect the rate of occurrence to be higher with the biological family members (e.g., brown-eyed people tend to have family members with brown eyes). Dr. Joseph Biederman and his colleagues at the Massachusetts General Hospital have studied families of children with ADHD. They have learned that ADHD runs in families. Family studies of ADHD have found 10 percent to 35 percent of the immediate family members of children with ADHD are likely to have the disorder and 32 percent of siblings of children with ADHD have ADHD themselves. Dr. Biederman's group also found that if a parent has ADHD, there is a 57 percent chance that one of their children will have it.

Adoption Studies

If a trait is genetic, adopted children should resemble their biological relatives more closely than they do their adoptive relatives. Studies conducted by psychiatrist Dr. Dennis Cantwell compared adoptive children with hyperactivity to their adoptive and biological parents. Hyperactive children resembled their biological parents more than they did their adoptive parents with respect to hyperactivity.

Twin Studies

Another way to determine if there is a genetic basis for a disorder is by studying large groups of identical and non-identical twins. Identical twins have the exact same genetic information while non-identical twins do not. Therefore, if a disorder is transmitted genetically, both identical twins should be affected in the same way and the concordance rate—the probability of them both being affected—should be higher than that found in non-identical twins.

There have been several major twin studies in the past few years that provide strong evidence that ADHD is highly heritable. They have had remarkably consistent results in spite of the fact that they were done by different researchers in different parts of the world. In one such study, Dr. Florence Levy and her colleagues studied 1,938 families with twins and siblings in Australia. They found that ADHD has an exceptionally high heritability as compared to other behavioral disorders. They reported an 82 percent concordance rate for ADHD in identical twins as compared to a 38 percent concordance rate for ADHD in non-identical twins.

Molecular Genetic Research

Genetic research in ADHD has taken off in the past five years. This research has focused on specific genes that may be involved in the transmission of ADHD.

For a number of years, Dr. David Comings at the City of Hope in Duarte, California and others have focused on the dopamine type 2 gene, which has been associated with alcoholism, Tourette's syndrome, and ADHD. Dr. Edwin Cook, Dr. Mark Stein, and Dr. Bennett Leventhal in Chicago along with others have studied the role the dopamine transporter gene (DAT1) in children with ADHD.

Recently, the DRD4 repeater gene has been the focus of several other investigators studying ADHD. The DRD4 gets its name of a repeater gene because it repeats its nucleotide sequence along the chromosome. It has also been associated with people who exhibit the personality trait of novelty-seeking behavior. The gene is found in everyone, but it is over-represented in some people with ADHD.

Genetic studies revealed promising results, and we should look for more information about this soon. As we pointed out earlier, inattention, hyperactivity, and impulsivity are characteristic of everyone. They are normal human traits, which taken to the extreme, are considered abnormal. Genetic endowment rather than environmental influence may result in an excessive amount of these behaviors.

Summary

Scientists agree that ADHD is a neurological disorder affecting the frontal area of the brain. This area is responsible for certain executive functions that control the regulation of behavior, thinking, planning, and organizing.

ADHD may be caused by differences in the area of brain chemistry, brain activity and blood flow, or brain structure. Heredity is the most common cause of ADHD. This has been confirmed in studies looking at the rates of occurrence of ADHD within families, studies of adopted ADHD children, and twin studies. Molecular genetic research has focused on the specific gene or genes that may be responsible for characteristics of ADHD.

5 Controversial Treatments for ADHD

Those who suffer from ADHD can choose a number of well established, scientifically proven treatments. These treatments focus on improving difficulties with impulse control, hyperactivity, attention span, organization, academic or work performance, socialization and behavioral compliance. Medications for ADHD, behavior management, parent/teacher/child education, school interventions, and counseling are all accepted and proven treatments that have been repeatedly shown to produce beneficial results for those with ADHD.

There are several other treatments for ADHD which are controversial. Their effectiveness with ADHD has either been disproven or is still unproven. However, these treatments continue to be offered to parents as beneficial. Consumers of ADHD services may be swayed by claims of cure or exaggerated claims of improved functioning supported only by anecdotal reports that lack scientific proof. A discussion of some of thes controversial treatments follows.

EEG Biofeedback

Some proponents of EEG biofeedback claim that they can help those who suffer from ADHD. In theory, improvements in alertness and concentration may result from training people with ADHD to produce a type of brain wave pattern that is inconsistent with inattention and daydreaming. EEG biofeedback measures levels of electrical activity in various regions of the brain. This information is converted into a signal such as a light, a tone, or a video image, which the child can understand. The child is trained to modify this signal by increasing certain brain waves and decreasing others. The training usually involves between 40 and 80 sessions, each lasting at least 40 minutes and held two to three times per week. Educational tutoring and behavior management training are usually provided in sessions along with the EEG biofeedback training.

EEG biofeedback training can cost several thousand dollars. There is no proof that it is an effective treatment for children with ADHD. It has received a great deal of media publicity in the past 10 years. Parents would be advised to wait until more scientific data is available about the efficacy of EEG biofeedback training for treatment of ADHD before relying on this form of therapy.

The Feingold Diet

Dr. Benjamin Feingold's book, *Why Your Child is Hyperactive?*, sparked an interest in the subject of diet and hyperactivity during the 1970s and 1980s. Dr. Feingold, a respected pediatric allergist, claimed that hyperactivity in most children was caused by eating foods that contained artificial colors such as yellow and red food dyes and additives. In his widely read book, he told the stories of children with learning and behavior problems who he observed to dramatically improve when placed on an elimination diet. Dr. Feingold's theory attracted considerable attention. He testified before the Senate Select Committee on Nutrition, appeared on radio and television, and spoke to national groups at conferences. It was at a time when there was a rise in the number of children who were being diagnosed as hyperactive which coincided with the increased use of artificial ingredients added to our food for flavoring, color, and preservative. Thus, the foundation for a plausible explanation was available, and Dr. Feingold received a great deal of support from parents, child care associations, and health professionals. A national organization, the Feingold Association, was formed and still exists today to educate the public about the relationship between diet and behavior.

**ADHD is not
caused by diet!**

The Feingold diet was widely publicized, and parents were more than willing to test out Dr. Feingold's theory. Many parents felt the diet really helped their children, claiming improvements in behavior and mood. However, we know that providing any treatment, even one as innocuous as a sugar pill, can have a strong placebo effect, which can lead to the conclusion that the treatment changed the behavior when it may actually have had no effect. Some parents will see a change for the better because they believe in the treatment. Furthermore, the act of changing a diet, in itself, results in giving the child a great deal of attention, which may modify behavior. Additionally, parents or other caregivers are apt to show approval and gratification when the child's behavior improves, thus unwittingly reinforcing the positive behavior.

Investigators, knowing that claims of treatment effectiveness should only be made after scientifically controlled experiments have been conducted, tested Feingold's theory. Did the Feingold diet affect children's behavior when examined scientifically with controlled experiments? In a review of numerous studies investigating the Feingold diet, psychologists Dr. Kenneth Kavale and Dr. Steven Forness concluded that dietary interventions such as those recommended by Dr. Feingold were not effective treatments for hyperactive children.

Reducing Sugar Intake

Sugar, in the form of glucose, is a source of energy for cell metabolism and is the primary fuel used for brain activity. Sugar has often been linked to behavioral and learning difficulties in children. Parents and teachers will often speculate that children behave worse after ingesting sugar. They see a clear relationship between sugar and behavior.

Scientists, however, have not seen such a clear picture. Scientifically evaluating the influence that sugar has on brain functioning, mood, behavior, and learning is difficult.

In a review of all the studies done to investigate this issue, Dr. Richard Milich at the University of Kentucky found that most studies showed no evidence that intake of sugar had any significant effect on hyperactivity, and for the few studies that did show an effect, sugar was just as likely to improve behavior as it was to worsen it. Dr. C. Keith Conners, an eminent researcher in the field of ADHD, concluded that sugar could either affect a child negatively or positively depending on such factors as age, diet, and individual biological differences in children. Parents should not be inclined to restrict their children's consumption of sugar as a treatment for ADHD.

**Sugar intake does
not cause hyperactivity.**

Megavitamin Therapy

In the 1970s and 1980s claims were made that people with certain psychiatric disorders could be treated with large doses of vitamins or minerals. This was called megavitamin therapy or orthomolecular therapy. Although not produced by the body, vitamins are nutrients that are important to growth and development, including brain functioning. Much of our vitamin intake is through food, but in small amounts. Deficiencies of certain vitamins can lead to disease. For example, an insufficient amount of niacin (vitamin B3) can cause pellagra, and it can also result in depression, memory loss, and can affect mood. Deficiency of vitamin C can lead to the development of scurvy.

We are not sure about the role vitamins play in mental health. Some people may be prescribed much higher doses (megavitamins) of certain vitamins in an effort to prevent or correct an illness or a mental condition. Megavitamin therapy became publicized in the late 1960s when Linus Pauling proposed the use of megadoses of vitamin C as a cure for many illnesses, even the common cold. His work contributed to orthomolecular therapy. Pauling advocated the importance of providing the body with the optimum amounts of vitamins and nutrients for growth and development.

**Megavitamin therapy is
not an effective treatment for ADHD.**

Some proponents of megavitamin therapy and orthomolecular therapy claim that this type of treatment can decrease hyperactivity in children and improve concentration and attention, but the result of scientific studies are disappointing. High doses of vitamins can even be harmful to children. Thus, in treating ADHD when you weigh the benefits and risks of unconventional megavitamin therapy or orthomolecular therapy against traditional therapies (medication, behavior management, etc.), it is apparent that there is no significant benefit to be gained by these unorthodox approaches.

Food Allergies

The notion that ADHD is an allergic reaction that a child can have to ingested food substances or to allergens in the environment was also popular 20-30 years ago and continues to be the subject of ongoing research and publication. This issue is quite different from the concept of sensitivity to additives we addressed earlier. Food allergy refers to an immunologic reaction to ingestion of a food. Food allergy affects from 10 to 15 percent of children and usually results in temporary conditions such as nasal congestion, skin reactions (hives, rashes, eczema), headaches, upset stomach, and asthma. There is very little evidence to indicate that food allergies directly lead to learning or behavior problems in children.

Yeast Build-Up

The assertion that yeast, particularly *candida albicans*, is a major cause of ADHD has long been touted by Dr. William Crook, a pediatrician and allergist in Tennessee. Dr. Crook is a vocal advocate of his theory and continues to publish books and circulate articles about it. Dr. Crook believes that the yeast causes the build up of toxins in the body, which can affect the brain and the nervous system. Excessive build up of yeast can be caused by diet, additives and other chemicals, and it can be reduced by following a low-sugar diet and eliminating certain foods and chemicals. Treatment for candida overgrowth usually includes prescription of an antifungal medication such as Nystatin. Along with the antifungal medication, a diet that eliminates sugar, yeast, and many other foods is an important part of the treatment.

Although Dr. Crook circulates early studies on his theory, there is no scientific evidence supporting the idea that yeast overgrowth is linked to the behavior problems found in children with ADHD.

Vestibular Dysfunction Therapy

Dr. Harold Levinson of Lake Success, New York has written about his theory that ADHD, learning disabilities, and other behavioral and emotional disorders can be due to problems in the body's vestibular system. He recommended the use of anti-motion sickness medications to treat these conditions.

He has written a number of books on his theory, and he explains the success of his treatment by reviewing case studies of individuals. However, he does not cite any controlled scientific studies to prove his theory or treatment

Other Non-Traditional Approaches

There seems to be a proliferation of unproven treatments for ADHD in recent years. Pycnogenol, an anti-oxidant, has been advertised in the past few years as a treatment for ADHD despite a lack of evidence to support these claims. Proponents of antioxidants assert they neutralize unstable, radical oxygen molecules that affect our joint's, skin, and organs and cause problems like depression, Alzheimer's disease, diabetes, and arthritis.

Other claims have been made for such treatments as acupuncture, chiropractic manipulation, and homeopathic remedies. Parents should be cautious about investing their time and money on these treatments because there is no proof they can benefit people with ADHD.

Summary

Over the past 30 years, there have been a number of unsubstantiated theories about the causes of ADHD and related treatments brought to public attention. These presume the cause of ADHD to be related to additives in a person's diet, sugar, lack of enough vitamins and minerals, food allergies, yeast build-up, and problems with the body's vestibular system, which is responsible for our sense of balance. The public is bombarded with anecdotal information to support many of these theories, but none of them have withstood the rigor of scientific scrutiny for us to include them as proven causes of ADHD or proven treatments for this disorder. People with ADHD are best advised to stick to proven treatments involving a multi-modal approach with behavior management, counseling, education, and medication, when indicated

6   Getting a Good Assessment

Before receiving a diagnosis of ADHD, the adolescent should be carefully evaluated. The primary characteristics of ADHD are not difficult for parents to spot at home or for teachers to observe in the classroom. However, not all adolescents who are inattentive, impulsive, or hyperactive have ADHD. These same symptoms can be the result of other factors such as frustration with difficult schoolwork, lack of motivation, emotional concerns, or other medical conditions. A comprehensive assessment by a team of professionals working in conjunction with parents and the adolescent can usually determine whether problems are the result of ADHD or other factors.

When Should You Consider Getting an Assessment for ADHD?

If your teenage son or daughter has had problems in school, at home, or in social activities for at least six months and if these problems appear to be related to inattention, hyperactivity, or impulsivity, you should consider getting an evaluation for ADHD. Use the checklist on the following page to determine if your child is exhibiting symptoms of inattention, hyperactivity, or impulsivity more often than others of the same age.

Put a check next to each statement if your adolescent exhibits this behavior more often than others his or her age.

Symptoms of inattention
_____ fails to give close attention to details or makes careless mistakes in schoolwork, work, or other activities
_____ often has difficulty sustaining attention in tasks or play activities
_____ does not seem to listen when spoken to directly
_____ does not follow instructions and fails to finish schoolwork, chores, or duties in the workplace (not due to oppositional behavior or failure to understand instructions)
_____ has difficulty organizing tasks and activities
_____ avoids, dislikes, or is reluctant to engage in tasks that require sustained mental effort (e.g., schoolwork or homework)
_____ loses things necessary for tasks or activities (e.g., toys, school assignments, pencils, books, or tools)
_____ is easily distracted by extraneous stimuli
_____ is forgetful in daily activities

Symptoms of hyperactivity
_____ fidgets with hands or feet or squirms in seat
_____ leaves seat in classroom or in other situations in which remaining seated is expected
_____ runs about or climbs excessively in situations in which it is inappropriate (in adolescents or adults, may be limited to subjective feelings of restlessness)
_____ has difficulty playing or engaging in leisure activities quietly
_____ is "on the go" or acts as if "driven by a motor"
_____ talks excessively

Symptoms of impulsivity
_____ blurts out answers before questions have been completed
_____ has difficulty awaiting turn
_____ interrupts or intrudes on others (e.g., butts into conversations or games)

The presence of six or more symptoms under the category of inattention or hyperactivity and impulsivity may indicate a problem if they occur frequently.

Who is Qualified to Conduct an ADHD Assessment?

More than one professional is typically involved in the assessment process for ADHD. Physicians, clinical psychologists, school psychologists, clinical social workers, speech-language pathologists, learning specialists, and educators may play an important role in the ADHD evaluation.

Parents usually obtain evaluations for ADHD through their child's school or privately through health care professionals in the community. For parents who are seeking a private evaluation, it is best to find professionals who are knowledgeable about ADHD and who have experience evaluating and treating adolescents. Many parents initially ask their child's pediatrician or family doctor for help. The physician may begin the evaluation and may make a referral to other professionals for their opinions.

If your physician is not familiar with other professionals in the community who are trained to evaluate ADHD, try to find a support group in your community. Children and Adults with Attention Deficit Disorders (CH.A.D.D.), maintains several hundred chapters nationwide. Phone numbers of local chapters are available on the CH.A.D.D. web site (www.chadd.org). Many chapters maintain a listing of professionals in the community who evaluate and treat individuals with ADHD. You can go to a CH.A.D.D. meeting and speak to other parents whose children are being treated. They may give you some additional ideas who you could consult within your community.

It usually makes little difference whether you begin the assessment with your family doctor, a psychologist, social worker, or other medical professional such as a psychiatrist or neurologist. The important thing is to make certain that all aspects of your child's troubles are addressed. Therefore, you will recruit members of your assessment team as they are needed according to the judgement of those evaluating your adolescent. The role of each professional included in the evaluation process is described in the following sections.

The Physician's Role

The physician is usually familiar with your adolescent's medical history and often has some knowledge of the teenager through previous treatment contact. However, your physician may or may not be familiar with the assessment and treatment of adolescents with ADHD. Ask your physician about his experience and training in this area. If you are satisfied he is the right person to do the evaluation—proceed. If not, ask him for a referral to someone trained in the area of ADHD. Your doctor may refer you to a developmental pediatrician (a pediatrician who has special training in the treatment of children with developmental disorders such as ADHD and learning disabilities), a neurologist, or a child and adolescent psychiatrist.

The physician will start by taking a history of the adolescent and your family. Both parents should be present to provide the doctor with information. The history may alert the doctor to health problems, which could account for the development of ADHD symptoms. Information about the pregnancy and delivery including maternal health during pregnancy, use of alcohol, smoking, toxemia or eclampsia, postmaturity of the fetus, and extended labor should be reviewed. Detailed information about the early development of the child, educational progress, and behavior at home, at school, and within the community are essential parts of the history. Furthermore, the doctor should collect information about family relationships with particular concern to any stresses on the child, which could affect behavior and performance.

**The history of the adolescent is an
important part of an ADHD assessment.
medical history
history of development
social and academic performance
adjustment at home
presence of ADHD in other family members
presence of other associated problems**

Routine physical examinations of children with ADHD are often normal, nevertheless they are necessary to rule out the unlikely possibility of there being another medical illness, which could cause ADHD-like symptoms. Vision or hearing deficits should be ruled out. Increased risk of ADHD has been related to a rare genetic disorder—generalized resistance to thyroid hormone. While thyroid dysfunction appears to be more common among children with ADHD, tests to measure thyroid are not typically recommended unless the history or physical examination is suggestive of hypothyroidism or hyperthyroidism, goiter, family history of thyroid disease, or diminished growth velocity. The physician should look out for other medical conditions that might predispose the child to ADHD including fragile X syndrome, fetal alcohol syndrome, and phenylketonuria.

Although no specific laboratory test is available to diagnose ADHD, the physician may want certain laboratory tests done to determine the overall health of the child. Tests such as chromosome studies, electroencephalograms (EEGs), magnetic resonance imaging (MRI), or computerized axial tomograms (CAT scans) are not to be used routinely for evaluation of ADHD.

Child and adolescent psychiatrists and pediatric neurologists, trained in the assessment and treatment of ADHD, may play an important part in identifying this condition as well as other possible related conditions such as learning disabilities, Tourette's syndrome, pervasive developmental disorder, obsessive compulsive disorder, anxiety disorder, depression, or bipolar disorder.

The Psychologist's Role

Often your physician or others will refer you to a psychologist trained to do ADHD assessments and treatment. Not all psychologists are experts in this area so before making an appointment with someone, check their background, training, and experience. You can do this by directly questioning them on the phone. Ask them if they do evaluations for ADHD, how many they do per year, what type of training they received in this area, etc. As we mentioned earlier, you can find the names of psychologists in your community who do such evaluations by meeting other parents at a local support group meeting of CH.A.D.D. or other similar organizations.

The clinical or school psychologist serves an important function on the assessment team. They administer and interpret psychological and educational tests of cognition, perception, and language development (such as intelligence, attention span, visual-motor skills, memory, impulsivity), as well as tests of achievement and social/emotional adjustment. Results of such tests provide important clues as to whether a child's difficulties are related to ADHD and/or other problems with learning, behavior, or emotional adjustment.

Remember, there is no psychological test for ADHD. Even though psychological and educational testing can give you a better picture of your child's strengths and weaknesses, satisfactory performance on these tests does not rule out ADHD.

**There is no psychological test
that can tell us if someone has ADHD.**

Psychologists and other mental health professionals often integrate data collected from parents and teachers who complete behavior rating scales about the adolescent. Most of the rating scales used to assess ADHD provide standardized scores on a number of factors, usually related to attention span, self-control, learning ability, hyperactivity, aggression, social behavior and anxiety. Some of the more popular rating scales used in the assessment of ADHD are:
- Conners Teacher Rating Scale-Revised (CTRS-R)
- Conners Parent Rating Scale-Revised (CPRS-R)
- ADD-H: Comprehensive Rating Scale (Parent and Teacher Forms)
- Conners-Wells' Adolescent Self-Report Scales (CASS)
- Behavioral Assessment System for Children (BASC)
- The Brown Attention Deficit Disorder Scale
- ADHD Symptom Checklist-4 (ADHD-SC4)
- ADHD Rating Scale
- Child Attention Profile (CAP)
- Adolescent Symptom Inventory (ASI)
- Child Behavior Checklist (CBCL)
- Home Situations Questionnaire-Revised (HSQ-R)
- School Situations Questionnaire-Revised (SSQ-R)
- Academic Performance Rating Scale (APRS)

During the course of the evaluation, you will be asked to complete one or more behavior rating scales. It is important for both parents to complete the scales so the psychologist can get a complete picture of the adolescent. Furthermore, one or more behavior rating scales should be given to your child's teachers to complete. Although this may be time consuming in middle and high school, when five or more teachers may be involved, the information is vital for a thorough assessment.

Intelligence Tests

Intelligence tests provide an overall measure of the adolescent's cognitive ability measured by his use of language, reasoning, memory, and perception. The administration of a standardized IQ test is not necessary for every person evaluated for ADHD, although some baseline measurements of cognitive ability should be done.

Intelligence tests will frequently be administered if the psychologist is concerned about the presence of a learning problem or would like to get a more comprehensive idea of the individual's cognitive ability. There are many tests designed to measure intelligence. The ones that are most commonly used for adolescents and young adults are:
- Wechsler Intelligence Scale for Children III (WISC-III)
- Wechsler Adult Intelligence Scale-Revised (WAIS-R)
- Stanford-Binet Intelligence Scale: Fourth Edition

The Wechsler tests provide information about verbal and non-verbal information processing resulting in a verbal I.Q., performance I.Q. and a full scale I.Q. The Stanford-Binet provides scores for verbal reasoning, abstract/visual reasoning, quantitative reasoning, and short-term memory.

**IQ tests tell us about
the individual's strengths and weaknesses in
using language, memory, reasoning, and perception.**

The pattern of scores, which the adolescent receives on the various subtests, may reveal information about the adolescent's ability to use language, memory, perception, and reasoning to communicate and solve problems. Knowing the overall intellectual ability of the person provides a baseline of expected performance. By knowing what the person is mentally capable of, one can make a determination as to whether attention span, achievement skills, and performance in school are above or below what we should be expecting from the person.

Achievement Tests

For those adolescents who are showing signs of academic underachievement or performance problems in school, tests of academic achievement are often incorporated into the ADHD assessment. Many of the problems of adolescents with ADHD relate to school performance and nearly 25 percent of adolescents with ADHD have a co-existing learning disability. Therefore, it is important to examine achievement skills to assess weaknesses that may exist in primary subject areas such as reading, written language, and arithmetic.

There are a number of standardized tests used for this purpose. Among them are:
- Woodcock-Johnson Psychoeducational Test Battery
- Wide Range Achievement Test-Third Edition (WRAT-3)

- Tests of Written Language (TOWL)
- Kaufman ABC (K-ABC)
- Wechsler Individual Achievement Test (WIAT)
- Woodcock Reading Mastery Test
- Key Math Test

Perceptual Tests

Tests which are more specific measures of language, auditory and visual perception, short-term memory, visual-motor skills, impulse control, and other neuropsychological functions can also be an important part of the ADHD assessment. These tests are particularly useful if the adolescent is exhibiting learning problems in school and is suspected of having a learning disability. Some examples of tests of this sort are:
- The Developmental Test of Visual Motor Integration
- Learning Efficiency Test-II (LET-II)
- Wide Range Assessment of Memory and Learning (WRAML)
- Bender Visual Motor Gestalt Test
- Wisconsin Card Sort Test

Computerized Continuous Performance Tests

Computerized tests, known as continuous performance tests (CPTs), are being used by a growing number of professionals to provide further information in the assessment of ADHD. There are several on the market. They all require subjects to respond in specific ways to computer-generated stimuli. The CPTs differ in the type of stimuli presented (letters, numbers, shapes, sounds), the speed and order of presentation, and whether the stimuli are presented visually or auditorily. These tests provide information on such important variables as the individual's attention span, reaction time, and impulse control.

Examples of the more popular computerized continuous performance tests are:
- Gordon Diagnostic System (GDS)
- Tests of Variables of Attention (T.O.V.A.)
- Conners Continuous Performance Test
- Integrated Visual and Auditory Continuous Performance Test (IVA)

Many professionals believe continuous performance tests provide objective information about an individual's ability to maintain attention and control impulsive responding. While there is growing support for the use of such tests, there is also controversy among professionals about the value of continuous performance tests in the assessment of ADHD. Everyone agrees that they should never be the sole measure a clinician uses in an assessment.

The School's Role

Many parents will start the ADHD assessment process with their child's school. Public schools are required by federal law to evaluate students suspected of having a disability (see Chapter 15). The law (Individuals with Disabilities in Education Act) requires schools to follow specific procedures and standards to perform such evaluations. Frequently, the evaluation process is either initiated by the teacher or the parent. A child study team, made up of school personnel such as the guidance counselor, a learning specialist, the principal or his designee, one or more of the student's teachers, or others at the school, will meet to discuss the student. As a first step in the assessment process, the child study team will collect information about the student from his parents and teachers. If this information indicates that the student is showing signs of a disability, further assessment may be done by the school psychologist and other school professionals who need to be part of the assessment team.

Assessments for ADHD should always include information about the student's current and past classroom performance, academic skill strengths and weaknesses, attention span, and other social, emotional, and behavioral characteristics. Such information can be gathered through teacher interviews, review of cumulative records, analysis of test scores, and direct observation of the student in class. The student's adjustment in class should relate to aspects of the instructional environment: the curriculum in which the student is working; teacher expectations for the class and for the individual student; methods of instruction employed by the teacher; incentives for work completion; methods of teacher feedback to students; and comparative performance of other students in the class.

**Teachers play a vital role
in the identification of ADHD students.**

Observational instruments have been developed for the classroom and other school settings. One such instrument, the ADHD School Observation Code Kit (ADHD SOC) by Kenneth Gadow, Joyce Sprafkin, and Edith Nolan, is a simple and effective method to quantify behavioral observations in different school settings.

Once the assessment is completed, you will meet with the child study team to discuss the results. The child study team must consider assessment findings from all other professionals that you provide them. These assessment findings, together with the school's evaluation results, will be considered in determining whether the student has ADHD or any other disability. If the presence of a disability is established and the student needs special education and related services, he may qualify for an Individualized Education Program (IEP). If the child study team determines that the student has a disability but may be better served in the regular education environment, a 504 Plan may be written to provide services and accommodate the student's disability.

If you are dissatisfied with the results of the school's assessment, you should make your concerns known to the school. The school should make every effort to address your concerns and should provide you with a list of procedures you can follow to file a grievance.

The Parents' Role

As the parents, you are important members of the assessment team. Having witnessed your adolescent in a variety of situations over a number of years, you have a unique perspective on your teenager's previous development and current adjustment. This information is usually acquired by interview or through questionnaires. The focus is usually on obtaining overall family history, information about the current family structure and functioning, and documentation about important issues in the adolescent's medical, developmental, social, and academic history. It is important that both parents be involved in the process because each may have a different perspective of the adolescent.

Your role in driving the assessment process is equally important. You should make certain that your child is thoroughly evaluated by knowledgeable professionals. If you have any doubts that an appropriate assessment was done, speak to the professionals involved. Get a second opinion if you are unsure of the findings.

The Adolescent's Role

An interview with the adolescent offers the clinician an opportunity to observe the teenager's behavior first-hand and can yield valuable information about his social and emotional adjustment, feelings about himself and others, and attitudes about school and other aspects of his life.

In comparison to young children, adolescents are better able to tell the clinician if they are having problems with attention span, self-control, restlessness, organization, or other difficulties. They can describe the situations in which such problems most often occur and to what degree they impair functioning. Moreover, adolescents can complete self-report rating scales, which yield quantifiable information about difficulties they are experiencing.

Observations of an adolescent's behavior during interviews, such as their level of activity, attentiveness, or compliance, should not be noted as typical of their behavior in other settings. Normal behavior in a one-on-one setting does not diminish the likelihood of the adolescent having ADHD.

After the Assessment

Ideally, after all the data has been collected, members of the assessment team should collaborate to discuss their findings. In private, community-based assessments, such collaboration is usually done through phone calls from one professional to another or by sending reports of findings. Rarely do all the members of the community-based assessment team meet together with the parents or adolescent to discuss their findings. In school-based assessments, members of the assessment team usually do come together with the parents and adolescent to discuss their findings.

Ideally, assessment data should lead to a thorough understanding of the adolescent's strengths and areas of need physically, academically, behaviorally, and emotionally. If a diagnosis of ADHD and/or other disorders is made, treatment planning should include all areas where interventions are recommended. The physician may discuss appropriate medical interventions with the adolescent and parents. The psychologist or other mental health professionals may discuss counseling, behavior modification, or social and study skills training options. The school may set up classroom interventions to accommodate the adolescent's areas of need in school or may provide special education or related services. Some or all members of the assessment team may become part of the treatment team, which is responsible for managing the treatment of the adolescent.

Once the initial assessment is completed and appropriate treatment is instituted, there should be routine follow-up by members of the team to determine how the adolescent is progressing. ADHD, which is a chronic condition, will often require long-term care and monitoring on a regular basis. Parents play a key role in monitoring treatment effectiveness and in encouraging members of the treatment team to collaborate with one another when making decisions.

**Following the assessment,
several members of the assessment
team may become part of the treatment team.**

Evaluating people for ADHD can be a tedious and time-consuming process, especially if your son or daughter is in crisis and needs immediate attention. Get copies of all the evaluations and treatment recommendations made by the professionals involved. Maintain these records carefully because you may need to provide them to other professionals or to schools in the future. Coordination of this information and services, whether it be by you or a professional on your adolescent's team, is no easy task, but the outcome is usually well worth the effort.

Summary

The evaluation of an adolescent for ADHD usually involves more than one professional. Physicians, psychologists, educators, and others may be part of the assessment team responsible for the evaluation. Information about your adolescent's history and current functioning will be obtained from you, your son or daughter, and from past and current teachers. This information may be collected through interviews, completion of standardized scales, psychological or educational testing, direct observation of the adolescent in school, and review of school and health records.

Findings from the assessment should lead to a diagnosis. If ADHD or another condition is diagnosed, appropriate treatments and interventions should be recommended. Some or all of the members of the assessment team may stay involved as providers of treatment. Parents of ADHD teens often have the time-consuming task of monitoring the progress of their adolescent and informing members of the treatment team about the effectiveness of specific interventions.

As a parent, you will have to monitor a variety of treatments your adolescent may receive. The effectiveness of medication, the benefits of special education programs or accommodations provided at school, counseling, etc. should be monitored. These treatment programs may continue for several years. Although it is difficult to track them at first, it becomes second nature after awhile, and it is made easier by competent professionals who are helping your adolescent.

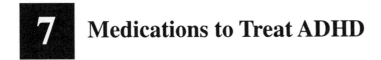

7 Medications to Treat ADHD

Medication has been used to treat ADHD for more than five decades. The research on medical treatments for ADHD is abundant. Numerous scientific studies have been done on thousands of children to investigate the efficacy of stimulant medications. The benefits have carefully been measured against the risks. The conclusion is that many children (50-90 percent) diagnosed with ADHD will be helped by medication. In some cases, medication will be the most effective treatment they will receive.

**Medication is an important part
of treatment for most people with ADHD.
It should not be considered an option of "last resort!"**

The decision to medicate a child with ADHD is no longer reserved for adolescents who are the most severely affected. Medication is no longer an option of "last resort" to be used only when every other option has failed. Medication for many children and adolescents with ADHD may be the first treatment a physician uses, but it should rarely be the only treatment provided. Counseling, educational interventions, and behavior modification are additional treatments that are also recommended.

Prescribing medication to children with ADHD has been a controversial topic in the United States for decades. Over the past 20 years, there have been numerous articles about the stimulant, Ritalin, published in magazines and newspapers. At times journalists have reported sensationalistic stories of Ritalin use and abuse on television and radio. Other times reports and publications offered balanced views on the subject. There have been media reports which were outlandishly slanted against ADHD as a disorder and medication as a treatment. Many parents are unable to differentiate the accurate stories from the inaccurate ones.

**Don't believe everything you
hear about ADHD in the media.
Check out the facts yourself by
asking a health care professional.**

The *Physicians' Desk Reference (PDR)* is a source for information on prescription medication. This book provides facts on each drug including what conditions the drug should be used to treat (indications), when the drug should not be used (contraindications), and any undesirable reactions the drug has been found to have (side effects). The *PDR* may not contain the latest scientific information about a particular drug, even though it is updated annually. Although it does give information about side effects for a drug, it does not tell the frequency of those side effects or the likelihood that a person will experience a side effect. After reading about a drug in the *PDR,* parents occasionally become unduly alarmed about the potential side effects.

If you have any questions about indications, contraindications, or adverse reactions of a particular drug, it is advisable to consult a physician who is knowledgeable about the different medications used to treat ADHD. Pediatricians, neurologists, and child and adolescent psychiatrists are usually familiar with medications to treat ADHD.

Physicians who prescribe medications to treat ADHD need the cooperation of parents and school personnel to ensure that the medication is available and is taken by the adolescent as prescribed. Parents who are biased against medication or those who are uncertain or who have mixed feelings about their child taking ADHD medication may dispense it to the adolescent incorrectly or not give it at all. They may not give the medication regularly as prescribed, causing their child to miss doses or to receive less than an adequate dose.

Parents and school personnel should be responsible for giving medication to the adolescent. Younger adolescents, in particular, should not be responsible for taking their own medication. Some youngsters will forget to take scheduled doses of medication, others may be resistant to taking medication either because they don't like the way it tastes, they have trouble swallowing a pill, or they don't like the way they feel when the medication is working. This can be due to adverse side effects or the medication's primary effect causing them to be more still, more focused, and perhaps more serious-minded. Most adolescents should be able to make their own decisions regarding the use of medication. They will assume responsibility for taking medication and should be able to monitor its effects and report them to health care providers responsible for their treatment.

**Adolescents should be part of
the decision making process regarding
the use of medication to treat their ADHD.**

Parents should be sensitive to how their son or daughter feels about taking medication for ADHD and should respect their wish for privacy if that is what they desire. Open discussions with other immediate family members, extended relatives, friends, and others about the teen's use of medication may be embarrassing and should be avoided. If embarrassed, the adolescent will likely resent taking the medication and may become resistant to continued treatment.

Teachers should also be discreet when reminding a student to take medication in school. A private signal between the teacher and student can be used so attention is not focused on the student. Inadvertent comments can stigmatize the student and cause unnecessary embarrassment. Taking medication is the student's private business, and it should not be made public!

**Taking medication is the student's private
business and should be handled with discretion.**

Medication should never be given without an established system to monitor its effectiveness. The doctor prescribing the medication should obtain information from parents and teachers concerning their observation of any changes in behavior, attentiveness, mood, or physical complaints the adolescent may have while taking medication.

Parents and the adolescent should report information about medication reactions to the physician. They may do so informally or by completing forms such as the Medication Effects Rating Scale (see next page), the Stimulant Side Effects Checklist, the Conners Parent Rating Scale -Revised, or other scales to evaluate behavior. This will give the physician an idea of how well the medication is working and if there are any adverse side effects.

We know that medication effects are the strongest and most observable during structured times when the adolescent is required to be attentive and focused. At home—after school or on weekends—there is little time when the adolescent is required to sit still and attend to seatwork, aside from homework. Therefore, parents may not observe any significant change in the adolescent on medication even though changes are obvious in school.

**Medication effects must be carefully
monitored by teachers and parents. Use of
behavior rating scales is important so the physician
can determine the best dose of medication to prescribe.**

Typically, teachers are the best source of information about medication effects on the student with ADHD. Teachers may report information about the student's reactions to medication informally to the physician or they may complete similar forms as the parents for more systematic data collection. Use of behavior rating scales such as the Conners Teacher Rating Scale-Revised (CTRS-R) or similar scales can be extremely helpful in determining changes in behavior.

Medication Effects Rating Scale

Name_____   Grade_____

Date_____   School_____

Completed By_____   Physician_____

List name(s) of medication student is taking:

MEDICATION(S)	DOSAGE(S)	TIME(S) OF DAY TAKEN	DISPENSED BY
_____	_____	_____	_____
_____	_____	_____	_____
_____	_____	_____	_____

Mark any changes noticed in the following behaviors:

Behavior	Worse	No Change	Improved a Little	Improved a Lot
attention to task	_____	_____	_____	_____
listening to lessons	_____	_____	_____	_____
finishing work	_____	_____	_____	_____
impulsiveness	_____	_____	_____	_____
calling out in class	_____	_____	_____	_____
organization, fine motor	_____	_____	_____	_____
overactivity	_____	_____	_____	_____
restlessness, fidgety	_____	_____	_____	_____
talkativeness	_____	_____	_____	_____
aggressiveness	_____	_____	_____	_____

Mark any side effects noticed by you or mentioned by student:

Side Effects	Comments
appetite loss	_____
insomnia	_____
headaches	_____
stomach aches	_____
seems tired	_____
stares a lot	_____
irritable	_____
vocal or motor tic	_____
sadness	_____
nervousness	_____

The ADHD Monitoring System developed by Dr. David Rabiner is a convenient program that parents can use to carefully monitor how their child is doing at school. By using this program, parents will be able to carefully track their child's progress in school and will be alerted to when any adjustments or modifications to their child's treatment needs to be discussed with their physician.

If an adolescent has been taking medication for ADHD for awhile, it is a good idea to have a no medication trial once in a while in which behavior off medication could be observed by parents and teachers. For example, medication may be discontinued for all or part of the summer on a trial basis if symptoms of ADHD are not severe outside the school setting. Or, if the adolescent's behavior and performance have been stable during the school year, the medication may be discontinued for a time to determine whether medication is still needed. Discontinuing the medication should not be done at the beginning of the school year when teachers are unfamiliar with the student and could not observe any change in behavior or performance.

Stimulants

There have been more than 150 controlled studies on the use of stimulant medications to treat ADHD. The stimulants most frequently used are:methylphenidate (Ritalin), dextroamphetamine (Dexedrine), Adderall, and pemoline (Cylert). Stimulants are the first-line medications used for many people with ADHD. Their effectiveness (at least for the short-term) in treating ADHD has been demonstrated in more than 50 years of clinical use in a large number of patients and in hundreds of studies. Stimulants are the first choice of many clinicians treating ADHD because they work quickly (usually within 30 to 60 minutes), most side effects are mild and reversible, dosing can be modified for optimum results, the effects can be seen within hours, and abuse of stimulants like methylphenidate, pemoline, and Adderall is uncommon.

How do stimulants work in the brain?

Stimulants increase brain activity or arousal. This enables the brain to do a better job of inhibiting behavior and attending to tasks. The stimulants do this by improving the way certain neurotransmitter chemicals work. It is the job of these neurotransmitter chemicals to transmit information within the brain across neurons—nerve cells in the brain. Two neurotransmitter chemicals that are involved in ADHD are dopamine and norepinephrine. When stimulants act on the brain to cause the release of dopamine, for example, the brain is better able to inhibit behavior and maintain attention.

How effective are stimulants?

Although it is often reported that stimulants can be effective 70 percent of the time for ADHD children, one study done by Dr. Josephine Elia and her colleagues at NIMH found that almost all children (96 percent) with ADHD in their sample showed behavioral improvement in response to either methylphenidate or dextroamphetamine. Improvements in behavior and cognition (e.g., attention span) after taking a stimulant may not be exclusive to ADHD children. Normal children will also show similar improvements when taking a stimulant. Thus, improvement in behavior or cognition after taking a stimulant cannot be diagnostic for ADHD.

How do stimulants affect behavior?

In addition to improving hyperactivity, impulsivity, and inattention, stimulants can positively affect academic performance, eye-hand coordination, and social behavior. Teachers often report improvements in the work habits of hyperactive students on stimulant medication. They get their work done quicker, more accurately, and neater than before. They also see a change in social behavior with less interruptions in class and better cooperation with peers and teachers. For some children, stimulant medication reduces aggressive behavior and defiance. The student is more likely to follow instructions and act more respectfully toward the teacher. The table below shows the specific effects documented in groups of ADHD children who responded to stimulant medications.

<u>**Documented Effects of Stimulants on Children with ADHD**</u>
Effects on Motor Activity and Coordination
    Reduced activity level to normal
    Decreased excessive talking and disruption in classroom
    Improved handwriting and neatness of written work
    Improved fine motor control
Cognitive Effects
    Improved attention to tasks
    Reduced distractibility
    Improved short-term memory
    Decreased impulsivity
    Increased academic productivity (i.e., work produced)
    Increased accuracy of academic work
Effects on Social Behavior
    Reduced off-task behavior in classroom
    Decreased anger, better self-control
    Improved participation in organized sports (i.e., baseball)
    Reduced bossy behavior with peers
    Reduced verbal and physical aggression with peers
    Improved peer social status
    Reduced non-compliant, defiant, and oppositional behavior
    Improved parent-child interactions
    Improved teacher-student interactions

The long-term effects of methylphenidate have not been carefully studied, but in a recent study, the behavioral effects of methylphenidate were monitored over a four month period—a relatively short term considering people with ADHD take stimulants for years. Nevertheless, findings from this study showed significant reduction in core symptoms of ADHD (inattention, hyperactivity, impulsivity) and associated problems of aggression and oppositional behavior as measured by teacher ratings.

Predicting Response to a Stimulant

Unfortunately, clinicians are unable to predict how an ADHD adolescent will respond to stimulant medication, which stimulant will be best for a particular adolescent, or what dose would be most beneficial. The physician usually starts by prescribing an initial low dose of one of the stimulants one or two times per day. Reports are obtained from parents, teachers, and the adolescent regarding changes in behavior and the presence of any adverse side effects. Dose may be adjusted weekly until the behavior improves to an acceptable level. Continued monitoring is done for appropriate dosing and management of side effects. Even if a particular stimulant benefits an adolescent, the clinician may try a different stimulant to get a better result. This adjustment process could go on for several weeks or months until the clinician is satisfied that the stimulant chosen, the amount prescribed, and time administered is best for the person.

Determining Which Stimulant to Use First

There is no way for a clinician to predict which stimulant medication to try first with the ADHD adolescent. Ritalin has been the most studied and most commonly used drug for ADHD. It is often the first choice of many physicians. This stimulant has been effective with adolescents and physicians in practice are usually quite familiar with it. Adderall, a newer stimulant, is being used more frequently by physicians.

Ritalin comes in a standard and sustained release form. The standard form comes in 5 mg., 10 mg., and 20 mg. tablets and lasts about four hours. The sustained release form comes in a 20 mg. tablet and lasts about six to eight hours.

Physicians usually start with an initial dose of 5 mg. once a day (usually in the morning) and after a week a second dose (usually at lunchtime) is added. Either dose might be raised by 5 mg. increments over the course of the next few weeks depending on behavioral changes and any reported adverse reactions. There is no evidence that the dose needed will vary with body weight so it is difficult to predict optimum dose. A small child may need the same as an older adolescent or adult.

**Start out with a low dose of
medication. The doctor will adjust
the dose over time based on reports
from teachers, parents, and the adolescent.**

Dexedrine is another frequently prescribed stimulant that has had a long history of efficacy in the treatment of ADHD. Dexedrine comes in 5 mg. tablets and 5 mg., 10 mg., and 15 mg. spansules. Some physicians prefer to prescribe the Dexedrine spansule because it has a longer duration of action than methylphenidate and requires less frequent dosing during the day. The starting dose of Dexedrine is 2.5 to 5 mg. once a day in the morning. A noontime dose may be added, and the dose may be increased as needed. Dexedrine doses are usually about half of the Ritalin dose. Dexedrine also has the advantage of being less expensive than Ritalin.

Adderall, mixed salts of a single-entity amphetamine product, is the newest stimulant on the market for ADHD. Adderall is gaining rapid popularity among clinicians for use with ADHD patients. Adderall comes in 5 mg., 10 mg., 20 mg. and 30 mg. tablets. Adderall has the advantage of working quickly as do other stimulants, but may last longer than standard Ritalin or Dexedrine. Physicians report that children on Adderall may show fewer withdrawal symptoms coming off the medication each day than they do when taking Ritalin or Dexedrine.

Cylert is another stimulant used to treat ADHD. Cylert comes in 18.75 mg., 37.5 mg., and 75 mg. tablets. Cylert requires only once a day dosing in the morning and may last for seven to eight hours or more. The recommended starting dose is 37.5 mg. and it can be gradually increased by 18.75 mg. amounts. The maximum daily recommended dose is 112.5 mg. After long-term use, levels of the medication build up in the bloodstream giving a longer duration of action. Unfortunately, there have been a few reports of chemical hepatitis and liver failure with the use of Cylert. It is not recommended as a first line drug to treat ADHD. The onset of hepatitis cannot be predicted by regular blood tests to evaluate liver function so parents of children taking Cylert should be alert to nausea, vomiting, chronic abdominal distress, lethargy, or jaundice, which could indicate a problem.

Stimulant Use with Adolescents

For many years researchers and clinicians believed that it was unwise to prescribe stimulants to ADHD adolescents because it might suppress growth and would not diminish symptoms of hyperactivity, impulsivity, or attention at this age. There have been many changes in prescription practices for stimulant medication, the most popular of which has been the treatment of adolescents with stimulants.

**Use of stimulants to treat ADHD
in adolescents has increased over the past 10 years.**

In the early 1980s only about 40 percent of ADHD children in elementary school on stimulants continued taking stimulants in secondary school. Ten years later, more than 90 percent of children with ADHD continued to be prescribed stimulants during adolescence. There have only been a handful of published studies investigating the effects of stimulant treatment in adolescents. Those that have been done lead us to expect that stimulant treatments work equally well for ADHD adolescents as they do for ADHD children.

Developing Tolerance

There is no evidence to indicate that children build up a significant tolerance to stimulants even after taking them for years throughout childhood and adolescence. When children move from elementary school to middle school, their school functioning may worsen. Some practitioners assume the adolescents may have developed a tolerance to their medication or may need more medication due to increases in physical size and weight. The physician's response is to prescribe a larger dose or change the medication to find something more effective. It may be better to investigate how accommodations can be made to assist the child in school first before making a change in medication.

Interactions with Other Medications.

It is generally safe to take most other medications while taking stimulants. However, parents should check with a physician to be certain.

Some ADHD children or adolescents who take an antihistamine or a decongestant may become more hyperactive, excitable, and impulsive. The stimulant medication they are taking may seem to have lost its effectiveness. It may be that the antihistamine/decongestant is worsening the ADHD symptoms, and there may not be enough stimulant to control the adolescent's behavior. Or, the antihistamine/decongestant may diminish its effectiveness. In either case, the adolescent may need additional stimulant medication for a short time until he stops taking the other medications.

Stimulant Abuse?

There has been considerable concern in the past few years about the potential for abuse of stimulants, particularly methylphenidate (Ritalin) and dextroamphetamine (Dexedrine). The Drug Enforcement Administration (DEA) classifies all controlled medications as either Schedule I, II, III, IV, or V. The classification of a medication can determine, for example, how much of the medication can be produced in a given year and the types of procedures that need to be followed by physicians for prescribing the medication. The DEA classifies medications based on how likely it is that they will be abused and cause physical or psychological addiction or dependence. Schedule I medications present the highest risk and Schedule V the lowest.

Ritalin is classified as Schedule II. In order for the DEA to classify a medication as Schedule II, the DEA must find that the medication has a high potential for abuse and that abuse of the medication may lead to severe psychological or physical dependence. The DEA believes that Ritalin meets these conditions.

There is little evidence to support any widespread abuse of methylphenidate. There are no cases of methylphenidate abuse or dependence in the over 150 controlled studies of stimulants in children, adolescents, or adults with ADHD. Parents should not be overly concerned that the use of a stimulant medication such as Ritalin for treatment of ADHD would lead to dependence, addiction, or drug abuse. However, misuse/abuse of stimulants can and does occur and parents should be aware of this. There have been isolated reports of elementary and secondary school children giving away or selling stimulants such as Ritalin, reports of diversion of Ritalin into the hands of family members and teachers of children with ADHD, and attempts by people to secure Ritalin through unlawful prescriptions. Parents should maintain possession of any stimulant medication at home and carefully monitor the supply.

Common Side Effects of Stimulants

Common side effects of the stimulants are:
- headaches
- stomachaches
- insomnia
- decreased appetite
- weight loss
- irritability

It is impossible to predict if your teenager will have one of these side effects. For the most part, these side effects are mild, will diminish after a few weeks while medication is continued, or they can be decreased or eliminated by lowering the dose of medication. If a side effect is persistent and uncomfortable, the medication should be stopped and an alternate stimulant considered.

About half of the children started on a stimulant will experience one or more of the common side effects noted above. Interestingly, this same percentage of ADHD children will complain about similar side effects when they take a placebo pill without any active medication. Stomachaches and headaches occur in about one third of children taking a stimulant. Decreased appetite occurs often and usually results in the child eating little for lunch due to the morning dose of medication. If a second or third dose is taken midday or later, this could affect appetite at dinner as well. For most children, however, their appetite returns after school, and they easily make up for the missed lunchtime meal. If appetite suppression is chronic and the weight loss is significant, parents should consult their doctor. Medication dose or timing may need to be modified, nutritional supplements can be added to the diet, or serving a hearty breakfast or late night snack may help.

Infrequent Side Effects of Stimulants

Some of the infrequent side effects that can be caused by stimulant use include rebound effects, difficulty falling asleep, irritable mood, and tics. These side effects have not been well researched in adolescents, but are well understood in children.

Rebound

Some parents report that at the end of the school day, their child becomes more hyperactive, excitable, talkative, and irritable. This phenomena is referred to as "rebound," and it can affect many children with ADHD who take stimulant medication during the school day. When rebound occurs, it usually begins after the last dose of medication is wearing off. Thus, it usually occurs after school in the mid to late afternoon. The doctor may recommend a smaller dose of medication be given or use of another medication to reduce the child's excitability. Sometimes it is easier to take a deep breath during the rebound phase, try to keep your distance from the child, and warn others in the family to do the same. Don't try to get your child to do homework at this time and don't schedule any activities that require calmness, concentration, or persistent effort.

**Rebound effects can occur a few hours
after the last dose of medication was taken.**

Difficulty Falling Asleep

It is not uncommon for children to have difficulty falling asleep. The explanation for sleep difficulty could range from the child not wanting to go to sleep to the child not being able to fall asleep. Parents can try behavior modification approaches to encourage sleep and help the child acquire good sleep habits.

ADHD children taking stimulants who have trouble falling asleep may be experiencing a drug rebound, which makes it difficult for them to quiet down and become restful. In some cases the doctor may recommend reducing the midday dose of medication or may prescribe a small dose of stimulant medication before bedtime. Other medications such as Clonidine or Benadryl may be prescribed to help the child fall asleep.

Irritability

Clinicians and researchers both have noted that stimulant usage in ADHD children may worsen the child's mood. The child may exhibit more frequent temper outbursts, may be more moody, and may become more easily frustrated than usual. His moodiness could lead to much more oppositional behavior at home, greater sibling conflict, and conflicts with peers. Stimulants can also produce dysphoria (sad affect) in some children. If irritability or sadness becomes a concern, the doctor may first try lowering the dose of stimulant, switch to a different stimulant, or may try a different class of medication altogether such as an antidepressant mediation to treat the ADHD and mood problems.

Tics and Tourette's Syndrome

Simple motor tics consist of small, abrupt muscle movements usually around the face and upper body. Common simple motor tics include eye blinking, neck jerking, shoulder shrugging, facial grimacing, and coughing. Common simple vocal tics include throat clearing, grunting, sniffing, and snorting. Stimulants should be used with caution in patients with motor or vocal tics or in patients with a family history of tics.

It is estimated that a little more than half of the ADHD children who start treatment with a stimulant medication will develop a subtle, transient motor or vocal tic. The tic might begin immediately or months after the medication is started. It might disappear on its own while the child is taking stimulants or it might worsen. Many physicians prefer to discontinue or reduce the stimulant medication if tics appear.

**Stimulants such as Ritalin, Adderall,
Dexedrine, and Cylert have been associated
with the occurrence of tics in some children.**

A child who has either a motor or a vocal tic (but not both), which occurs many times a day, nearly every day, for a period of at least one year (without stopping for more than three months), may be diagnosed as having a chronic tic disorder. Tourette's syndrome is a chronic tic disorder characterized by <u>both</u> multiple motor tics and one or more vocal tics. These tics are more severe than the simple motor tics described above. They involve the head and, frequently, other parts of the body such as the torso, arms, and legs. Vocal tics may include the production of sounds like clucking, grunting, yelping, barking, snorting, and coughing. Coprolalia, the utterance of obscenities, is rare and occurs in about 10 percent of children with Tourette's. Stimulants should be used cautiously with children who have chronic tic disorder or Tourette's syndrome and ADHD.

In using stimulants with children with ADHD and tics, clinicians and parents will have to weigh the impairment each of these problems cause for the child and measure the risks and benefits of stimulant treatment. If a child's ADHD severely impairs behavior, socialization, and/or academic performance and the tic does not, stimulants may be beneficial despite the tics. When the risks outweigh the benefits, other classes of medications such as antidepressants or antihypertensives may be used to manage ADHD symptoms with reduced risk of worsening the tics.

Cardiovascular Effects and Seizure Threshold

There has been some speculation and concern that stimulant medications may produce adverse cardiovascular effects in children, particularly with long term use. While stimulants may cause some elevation of the heart rate in some children with ADHD, there is no evidence of any long term cardiovascular effects. Furthermore, there is no evidence that stimulants lower the seizure threshold putting the child at greater risk for having a seizure.

Tricyclic Antidepressants

Tricyclic antidepressants (TCAs) are the next major class of medications, after stimulants, for the treatment of ADHD. Although less well studied than the stimulants, TCAs have been used for several years to treat adolescents with ADHD. They are regarded as second-line medications for ADHD children who have not succeeded with stimulants, for whom stimulants produced unacceptable side effects, or who suffer from other conditions (such as depression, anxiety, Tourette's syndrome, tics) along with ADHD.

TCAs have the additional advantage of longer duration of action (all day) as opposed to four to eight hours common to stimulants. This avoids the troublesome and even embarrassing midday stimulant dose taken at school. Unfortunately, TCAs may not be as effective as the stimulants in improving attention and concentration or reducing hyperactive-impulsive symptoms of ADHD. They also can produce adverse side effects, the most common of which are drowsiness, dry mouth, constipation, and abdominal discomfort. More concern, however, has been expressed at possible adverse cardiac side effects, accidental overdose, and reduced effectiveness over time.

Imipramine (Tofranil), desipramine (Norpramin), and nortriptyline (Elavil) are the three best studied TCAs to treat ADHD.

Imipramine is available in 10 mg., 25 mg., and 50 mg. tablets and is recommended for use in children six years and older. For children weighing under 50 pounds, the starting dose may be 10 mg. in the morning and 10 mg. at bedtime. For children weighing over 50 pounds, the recommended starting dose is 25 mg. in the morning and 25 mg. at bedtime. The dose can be increased every few days until the optimum benefit is reached.

Desipramine is available in 10 mg., 25 mg., 50 mg., 75 mg., and 150 mg. tablets. The starting doses and adjustments are similar to those described for imipramine. Five cases of sudden death during desipramine treatment for ADHD has been reported in the literature. Because of this, there has been a shift to the use of other TCAs, primarily imipramine and nortriptyline, over desipramine for treatment of ADHD in adolescents. Due to concerns about potential cardiac side effects with TCAs in general, TCAs are contraindicated in patients with a history of cardiac disease or arrhythmia or a family history of sudden death, fainting, cardiomyopathy, or early cardiac disease.

**Tricyclic antidepressant medications
may be particularly helpful for adolescents
with ADHD who also have signs of depression.**

Because of their short half-life, stimulants are washed out of the body, or at least substantially reduced, within several hours after the last dose was taken. TCAs, however, have a longer half-life and remain in the bloodstream for a greater period of time. Levels of drugs can build to a point where a toxic amount is present causing irritability, excitability, agitation, anger, aggression, confusion, forgetfulness, or more serious health risks. By drawing blood, levels of the TCA can be measured to determine whether these symptoms are a result of too much medication in the body or other factors related to the patient's illness.

Noradrenergic Agonists

Noradrenergic agonists such as clonidine (Catapres) and guanfacine (Tenex) have been found to be useful in the treatment of ADHD children, especially those who are extremely hyperactive, excitable, impulsive, and defiant. They have less effectiveness in improving attention. They are often the drug of choice in treating hyperactive-impulsive ADHD children with tics or in those children who did not respond to stimulants. Catapres is also prescribed to help children who have difficulty falling asleep and can be a great benefit to children with sleep onset difficulties whether the cause is ADHD overarousal, stimulant medication rebound, or unwillingness to fall asleep.

**Clonidine and Tenex may be
especially helpful for "turbo-charged," very hyperactive
children and adolescents.**

Catapres comes in a tablet form or in a skin patch. In tablet form physicians either prescribe an initial dose of 0.05 mg. at bedtime (to minimize sedation effects), or they may begin with a dose of 0.025 mg. given four times each day. The dose is gradually adjusted over several weeks to 0.15 to 0.3 mg./day in three or four divided doses. The skin patch may be useful to improve compliance and provide more even absorption in the body. The patch comes in a doses of 0.1, 0.2, 0.3 mg./day and may be cut as needed. Once the daily dose has been established with the tablet form, the equivalent patch can be substituted.

It may take a month or so for the effects of Catapres to be seen and even more time for optimal effect to be reached. Sudden discontinuation of clonidine can cause increased hyperactivity, headache, agitation, elevated blood pressure and pulse, and an increase in tics in patients with Tourette's syndrome. Sleepiness, which is the most common side effect of clonidine, gradually decreases after a few weeks. Other side effects may include dry mouth, dizziness, nausea, and light sensitivity. The skin patch can cause a rash.

Tenex is a long-acting noradrenergic agonist similar to clonidine in effect but it has a longer duration of action and less side-effects. It is used with children who cannot tolerate the sedative effects of clonidine or with children for whom the effects of clonidine were too short.

Other Medications

Bupropion (Wellbutrin) is an antidepressant drug that has started being used to treat ADHD. It has not been well studied in this regard. Two studies found it to be effective in reducing symptoms of ADHD. One study compared it to a placebo. In this study, bupropion produced hyperactivity and conduct problems in children who were rated by their teachers and parents. In the second study, comparing the effects of bupropion and methylphenidate, bupropion was equally effective as methylphenidate in producing improvements in behavior and academic performance. Bupropion is administered in two or three daily doses, beginning with a low dose of 37.5 or 50 mg. twice a day and then adjusted over two weeks to a usual maximum of 250 mg./ day in children (300 to 400 mg./day in adolescence). A decrease in seizure threshold is the most serious side effect, which is more likely in patients with eating disorders or in patients taking high doses of buproprion.

Selective serotonin reuptake inhibitors (SSRIs) have not been well studied in the treatment of ADHD. The anecdotal reports from clinicians do not support the use of SSRIs for treatment of ADHD. SSRIs have, however, gained considerable recognition for treatment of depression, anxiety, and obsessive-compulsive disorders.

Selective serotonin reuptake inhibitors (SSRIs) such as fluoxetine (Prozac), sertraline (Zoloft), and paroxetine (Paxil) have not been well studied in treatment of ADHD.

Monoamine Oxidase Inhibitors (MAOIs) have also not been well studied in the treatment of ADHD. Use of this class of medications can be dangerous unless strict dietary precautions are followed. For this reason, they are not typically prescribed for children and adolescents.

Buspirone, an anxiolitic medication, has been used in children and adolescents with anxiety disorders, and researchers have reported significant improvement with it. It has not been well studied in the treatment of ADHD in children, but one recent study of 12 hyperactive children who took buspirone for several weeks showed significant improvement in ADHD symptoms as measured on rating scales completed by their parents. Reported side effects for buspirone are very mild and include nausea, headaches, daytime tiredness, and occasional increase in weight. Further investigation of buspirone is needed before it can be recommended as a treatment for ADHD.

Neuroleptics are not typically used in the treatment of ADHD because of the dulling effect they have on cognitive skills and because of the risk of tardive dyskinesia.

Fenfluramine, benzodiazepines, or lithium are of benefit in other psychiatric disorders but there is no support to their use in the treatment of ADHD.

Is Ritalin Overprescribed in the U.S.?

A feature story in USA Weekend (October 27-29, 1995) was entitled, *The Ritalin Generation*. The author of the article expressed concern as to whether Ritalin was being overprescribed in the U.S. and if it was being used as a "quick fix" by parents and teachers. This is only one of dozens of similar articles that have been printed in newspapers and magazines over the past few years.

The best and most current study on the number of children in the U.S. who are being prescribed Ritalin has been done by Dr. Daniel Safer and his colleagues. Dr. Safer found that approximately 1.5 million children take medication to treat ADHD. This amounts to between 3 and 4 percent of the 40 million school-age children. This seems to be within the range expected since it is conservatively estimated that ADHD probably affects from 3-5 percent of children.

As of 1995, about 1.5 million children were taking medication to treat ADHD.

Experts in the area of ADHD advocate the need for comprehensive assessments before medication is prescribed. A quick interview with the parents and a brief examination of the adolescent does not usually provide enough information to make a diagnosis of ADHD. Doctors should do thorough assessments to assure that only adolescents with a valid diagnosis are being prescribed stimulant medication. This may be idealistic in a world of managed health care where time is limited and authorizations for thorough examinations are often denied by HMOs. However, parents should strive to obtain as complete examination for their son or daughter as they can to make certain of a correct diagnosis before medication is started.

Why is there so much concern about the use of medications to treat ADHD?

We have long believed that family life or other environmental factors are the cause of many behavioral and emotional difficulties in children. Therefore, non-medical treatments were generally accepted to help with such problems. There is a growing body of research that indicates these childhood problems can be due to neurological difficulties, which respond well to medication. It has been difficult for people to accept medical interventions as a primary treatment option for children.

Medications Commonly Used to Treat ADHD

Drug	Dosing	Common Side Effects	Duration of Behavioral Effects	Pros	Precautions
RITALIN® Methylpheni- date Tablets 5 mg. 10 mg. 20 mg.	Start with a morning dose of 5 mg./day and increase by 5 mg. weekly as indicated. Often requires two or three doses each day. Daily dose range 2.5 - 60 mg./day.	Insomnia, decreased appetite, weight loss, headache, irritability, stomachache	3-4 hours	Works quickly (within 30-60 minutes); effective in about 50 percent of adult patients; good safety record	Not recom- mended in patients with marked anxiety, motor tics, family history of Tourette's syndrome, or history of substance abuse.
RITALIN-SR® Methylpheni- date Tablet 20 mg.	Start with a morning dose of 20 mg. and increase by 20 mg. as indicated. Often helps to use short-acting form in morning for quicker action as effect of SR form on behavior may be slower. Doses range up to 60 mg./day.	Insomnia, decreased appetite, weight loss, headache, irritability, stomachache	About 7 hours	Particularly useful for adolescents and adults to avoid needing a noontime time dose; good safety record	Slow onset of action (1-2 hours); not recommended in patients with marked anxiety, motor tics, family history of Tourette's syndrome, or history of substance abuse.
DEXEDRINE® Dextro- amphetamine Tablet 5 mg. Spansules 5 mg. 10 mg. 15 mg.	Start with a morning dose of 2.5 - 5 mg. Increase weekly by 5 mg. as indicated. Tablet form often requires two or three doses each day. Daily dose range, 2.5 - 40 mg./day.	Insomnia, decreased appetite, weight loss, headache, irritability, stomachache	3-4 hours (tablets) 8-10 hours (spansules)	Works quickly (within 30-60 minutes); may avoid noontime dose in spansule form; good safety record	Not recom- mended in patients with marked anxiety, motor tics, family history of Tourette's syndrome, or history of substance abuse.
ADDERALL® Mixed salts of single-entity amphetamine product Tablets 5 mg. 20 mg. 10 mg. 30 mg.	Start with a morning dose of 2.5 mg. for 3-5 year olds. For 6 years and older, start with 5 mg. once or twice daily.	Insomnia, decreased appetite, weight loss, headache, irritability, stomachache	About 3-6 hours	Works quickly (within 30-60 minutes); action may last somewhat longer than other standard stimulants	Use cautiously in patients with marked anxiety, motor tics, or with family history of Tourette's syndrome.

This is not a complete list of medications to treat ADHD. Information presented here is not intended to replace the advice of a physician. © 1998 Harvey C. Parker, Ph.D.

Medications Commonly Used to Treat ADHD

Drug	Dosing	Common Side Effects	Duration of Behavioral Effects	Pros	Precautions
CYLERT® Pemoline Tablets 18.75 mg. 37.5 mg. 75 mg. 37.5 mg. chewable	Start with a dose of 18.75-37.5 mg. and increase up to 112.5 mg. as needed in a single morning dose. 18.75 -112.5 mg./day	Insomnia, agitation, headaches, stomaches, infrequently, abnormal liver function tests have been reported	12-24 hours	Given only once a day	May take 2-4 weeks for clinical response; regular blood tests needed to check liver function.
TOFRANIL® Imipramine Hydrochloride Tablets 10 mg. 25 mg. 50 mg.	For Tofranil and Norpramin: Start with dose of 10 mg. in evening if weight is < 50 lbs. and increase 10 mg. every 305 days as indicated. Start with dose of 25 mg. in evening if weight is > 50 lbs. and increase 25 mg. every 3-5 days as indicated. Given in single or divided doses, morning and evening. Daily dose range 25-200 mg./day. Do not skip days.	Dry mouth, decreased appetite, headache, stomachache, dizziness, constipation, mild tachycardia	12-24 hours	Helpful for ADHD patients with comorbid depression or anxiety; lasts throughout the day	May take 2-4 weeks for clinical response; to detect pre-existing cardiac defect a baseline ECG may be recommended. Discontinue gradually.
NORPRAMIN® Desipramine Hydrochloride 10 mg. 75 mg. 25 mg. 100 mg. 50 mg. 150 mg.		Dry mouth, decreased appetite, headache, stomachache, dizziness, constipation, mild tachycardia	12-24 hours	Helpful for ADHD patients with comorbid depression or anxiety; lasts throughout the day	May take 2-4 weeks for clinical response; to detect pre-existing cardiac defect a baseline ECG may be recommended. Discontinue gradually.
CATAPRES® Clonidine Hydrochloride Tablets 0.1 mg. 0.2 mg. 0.3 mg. Patches TTS-1 TTS-2, TTS-3	Start with dose of .025-.05 mg./day in evening and increase by similar dose every 3-7 days as indicated. Given in divided doses 2-4 times per day.	Sleepiness, hypotension, headache, dizziness, stomachache, nausea, dry mouth, localized skin reactions with patch.	About 3-6 hours (oral form) 5 days (skin patch)	Helpful for ADHD patients with comorbid tic	Sudden discontinuation could result in rebound hypertension. To avoid daytime tiredness, starting dose is given at bedtime and increased slowly.

This is not a complete list of medications to treat ADHD. Information presented here is not intended to replace the advice of a physician. © 1998 Harvey C. Parker, Ph.D.

Special Considerations in Medication Management for Adolescents with ADHD

As we noted earlier, until the mid-1960s, clinical folklore held that stimulant medication would not be effective in adolescence, could worsen symptoms, and may lead to addiction. Even in the past 30 years there has been very little focus on adolescents with ADHD. The vast majority of the scientific literature on ADHD has studied children ages 6 - 12. For example, there have been only six controlled studies of medication usage with ADHD adolescents as compared to more than 150 controlled studies with ADHD children.

The studies done on stimulant medication usage with ADHD adolescents confirm that these medications continue to be effective through this age range. They enable better self control, reduce hyperactivity, and improve attentional focus—just like they do in children. There is no indication that the effect of medication decreases as children become adolescents either because tolerance develops or they grow in size and weight.

When children move from elementary to middle school, where there are greater numbers of teachers and classes to keep track of and more demands are made on their attentional control, their functioning appears to worsen. Practitioners sometimes respond to this by assuming the child is building a tolerance to the medication, and its effects are not as strong or that changes in the child's physical size and weight may require a larger dose.

There is no evidence that stimulant usage in adolescence causes substance abuse or addiction or worsens symptoms of hyperactivity and excitability. Side effects to the stimulant medications are no worse than those found in children. There may be appetite loss, some sleep interference, some reports of stomachaches or headaches, but typically these side effects are not severe enough to stop taking the medication. There used to be concern that the stimulants would reduce growth or slow down the velocity of growth especially if taken during adolescence when growth spurts normally occur. The ultimate height of adolescents is not affected by stimulant use.

Long-acting medications may be used with adolescents to avoid a noontime dose.

Ritalin and Adderall are the most commonly used stimulants for adolescents because they are potentially less likely to be abused than Dexedrine. The doses that adolescents typically need are no different from those required by children. Dosing and scheduling are individual matters and should be determined after medication trials are done. The drug action is short, usually starting within 30-60 minutes after ingestion and lasts about 4-5 hours for the short acting preparations. Many adolescents will not want to go to the school nurse or office to get a noontime dose of medication so longer acting, sustained release preparations or spansules of stimulants are sometimes preferred. Their effectiveness may not always match that of the short acting tablets, but they should be tried to see if a noontime dose can be avoided. Cylert, a longer acting stimulant is preferred by some physicians since it is taken once in the morning and lasts all day. However, Cylert may cause liver disease, and it is not recommended as a first line medication to treat ADHD.

Inadequate prescribing of medication by physicians is frequently a problem found in the treatment of ADHD. As was discussed earlier, physicians should always complete a comprehensive assessment of the patient before prescribing. This may involve a psychological evaluation, educational assessment, or neurological examination in addition to the physician's examination. The physician will be more confident in the diagnosis following a comprehensive evaluation as opposed to a 15 minute interview in the office resulting in a "Let's try Ritalin and see if it works!" approach. If it does work, they may assume the patient has ADHD (not considering that stimulants can also improve attention, impulsivity, or hyperactivity in non-ADHD children and teens). If it doesn't work they may falsely conclude that the patient does not have ADHD or, more correctly they will do a more comprehensive examination of the patient themselves and refer the patient to appropriate specialists or professionals for the proper evaluations.

**A good response to stimulants
does not indicate the adolescent has
ADHD. Most people improve concentration
and attention with stimulants whether they have ADHD or not.**

Physicians may be reluctant to try different medications at different doses with patients who are either nonresponders, whose response to a medication is poor, or who have stopped responding well to a medication after months or years of being a good responder. Physicians should monitor medication effects carefully with weekly visits at first, gradually tapering off to less frequently. The adolescent's response to medication, should be monitored by teacher and/or parent completed rating scales, adolescent self-reports, school performance and grades, etc.Adolescents should always be cautioned about the danger of using alcohol when taking ADHD medication because of the increased risk of enhancing alcohol effects.

The biggest management problem in ADHD adolescent medication use is the reluctance to take the medication and stay on it. Many adolescents will resist taking medication for a number of reasons: they are afraid of the stigma of something being wrong with them; they don't like the way they feel with medication; they lose their appetite; they don't think they need the medication and can help themselves without it. Pediatricians may have a better chance at getting adolescents to comply with taking medication than do psychiatrists because of the stigma associated with going to a psychiatrist.

Summary

Medications are commonly used to treat people of all ages who have ADHD. We used to think ADHD medications were a treatment of last resort, only to be used after other treatments have been tried and failed, or in children and adolescents who are most severely affected, This is no longer the case. The use of medication is common, generally safe, and very effective for the treatment of ADHD. It must, of course, be used with the guidance of a knowledgable physician.

There are several classes of medications used in the treatment of ADHD. Stimulants are the most frequently used and antidepressants and anti-hypertensives are less often prescribed. There have been many controlled studies of stimulants in the treatment of ADHD. These studies confirm their effectiveness in more than 70 percent of children with improvements noted in attention, activity level, impulsivity, work completion in school, and compliant behavior. Antidepressants have been less well studied, but are useful in treating adolescents who do not respond well to the stimulants or who are suffering from depression or low self-esteem in addition to ADHD. The antihypertensive medications have also been less well studied than stimulants and are used to treat those with ADHD who may be very hyperactive, who are aggressive, or who have an accompanying tic disorder. New medications are being tested for treatment of ADHD with some promising results.

When medications are used in treatments, their effects should be monitored carefully. Adjustments in dosage, time taken, or changes in medication type may be made by the physician if problems arise. Parents, teachers, and the adolescent taking the medication should each be responsible for communicating medication effects.

Medication will rarely be the only treatment a child, adolescent, or adult with ADHD receives. A multi-modal treatment program should be considered including counseling, education about ADHD, and school-based or work-based accommodations and interventions.

8 Guiding Your Adolescent

Adolescence is a time of change and transformation. Teenagers are changing physically, sexually, intellectually, and emotionally. These changes are necessary for a successful transition from childhood to adulthood. The span of five or six years of adolescence is a training ground to learn the skills necessary to become an independent, responsible young adult.

Adolescence is a time when teens are trying to discover who they are and how they fit in with everyone else. Looking for confirmation about their identity, teenagers often compare themselves to other teens as a way of guiding their behavior, values, and attitudes. They experiment in many ways—testing out new ways of behaving, dressing, grooming, thinking, and believing. They gradually depend less on family members for guidance and advice. And they take their cue from friends, role models, the media, etc. They frequently withdraw from the family, spend more time by themselves, and establish close relationships with groups of friends.

The job of parents during this transitional phase of development is to guide the adolescent so they will acquire the skills needed to live independently and responsibly. Parents will gradually loosen their control and let their teens experience life more on their own.

Fortunately, most teenagers navigate their way through adolescence quite successfully. They do reasonably well in school, form ongoing relationships, and develop interests that lead them to future education and career choices. Those who do not do well most likely have trouble with school achievement or get into serious trouble involving defiant behavior, repeated lawbreaking, or substance abuse.

Persistence of ADHD into Adolescence

For quite some time, clinicians and researchers failed to realize that ADHD could persist into adolescence. ADHD was thought of as a childhood disorder with symptoms that would diminish over time. As a result, stimulant medication was not recommended during adolescence.

Stimulants were thought to have some potential harmful effects in adolescence because of the concern that they might cause greater hyperactivity or excitability and lead to subsequent substance abuse or addiction.

To complicate things further, health care providers were reluctant to give a diagnosis of ADHD to adolescents. There may have been a bias against the ADHD diagnosis, partly because of the belief that problematic behavior during teenager years could be better attributed to "normal" adolescent rebellion, dysfunctional family interactions, or to lack of motivation to perform responsibly at home or in school.

Long-term studies were done to investigate the persistence of ADHD into adolescence. Gabrielle Weiss and her colleagues tracked about 100 children with ADHD five years after their referral. The youngsters, then 11 to 17 years of age, had improved considerably yet they were still hyperactive, impulsive, inattentive, and had more conduct problems and school performance difficulties than non-ADHD children. Dr. Rachel Gittelman Klein also followed a large group of ADHD children through adolescence. She and her associates found that the rate of persistence of the diagnosis of ADHD during early adolescence (13 to 15 years of age) was high—68 percent. By the time these adolescents reached 16 to 21 years of age, the rate dropped down to 31 percent having the full symptoms of ADHD. Nine percent showed partial symptoms.

The Risks for Adolescents with ADHD

Dr. Russell Barkley and his colleagues compared adolescents with ADHD to a control group of adolescents in a Milwaukee community. They found that adolescents with ADHD were more likely to have oppositional disorder, conduct disorder (truancy, stealing, serious lying, aggression), and substance abuse problems. Many of those who developed conduct disorder go on to have substance use problems and higher rates of suspension or expulsion from school. They were also less competent socially, did less well in school, and had more symptoms of depression.

In following this group of subjects for several more years, Dr. Barkley and his colleagues found that ADHD subjects were more likely to become smokers and engage in more alcohol and drug use than a matched group of control subjects. They had significantly more speeding tickets and automobile crashes. They were at greater risk for HIV and other sexually transmitted diseases since they reported having more unprotected sex. The implications of these findings is that people with ADHD are at greater risk for behaving in ways that can have serious and negative health consequences.

**Follow-up studies show
ADHD behavior puts adolescents
at greater risk for future health problems.**

There have been a number of research studies, which have investigated the course of ADHD adolescents through adulthood, and compared their school achievement, social adjustment, and vocational attainment to groups of non-ADHD controls. Generally, these studies show that people with ADHD complete less formal schooling and have lower ranked jobs than their non-ADHD counterparts. However, having ADHD alone does not predict that a person will develop serious life problems such as academic failure, antisocial behavior, substance abuse, or major psychiatric disorders.

It is when ADHD is combined with other associated problems—conduct disorder in particular—that the course of future development can sour drastically. As we stated earlier, conduct disorder is a condition that can begin in childhood or adolescence. It is characterized by a repetitive and persistent pattern of behavior in which the rights of others are violated and societal norms are disregarded. Adolescents with conduct disorder often act aggressively toward others. They may bully, threaten, or intimidate others. They may be involved in physical fights with or without the use of weapons and may be physically cruel to other people or to animals. In addition, they may have a history of stealing, lying, or destroying other people's property. Furthermore, they often violate parental rules, may have a history of running away from home overnight more than once, and may often be truant from school.

Long-term studies, which followed ADHD adolescents, found that those who had a history of conduct disorder were at the greatest risk for having serious problems with school failure, low occupational attainment, antisocial behavior, and substance abuse. It is the conduct disorder component, not the ADHD, that puts the adolescent at greatest risk for serious problems through life.

Living with an ADHD Teen

Most parents of adolescents with ADHD have plenty of war stories to tell. Living with someone with ADHD, day in and day out, can be exhausting and can take its toll on the adolescent and his family—even in the best of situations. Navigating through the adolescent period with an ADHD teenager is much like walking through a minefield. You can't tell when the next explosion might occur and how much damage could be done. You might get a call from the high school guidance office alerting you that your son or daughter is not completing their work or is failing in several subjects. You might be running to the emergency room every month to take care of an injury that could have been avoided had your child not behaved recklessly. You might be wondering just how high your automobile insurance rates can go if your teenage driver gets one more traffic citation or has another automobile crash.

Seven Principles for Parents of ADHD Teens

The following seven principles of parenting can guide you through the teen years with your ADHD adolescent.

Principle # 1: Provide unconditional love and positive regard.

Obviously, one of the most important things a parent can give their child is unconditional love. Nobody else has the capacity to feel towards your child as you do. Nobody else will care about your child as much as you do. And nobody else's love and caring mean as much to your child as yours does.

Life for kids with ADHD can be tough. Because of their difficulties in school, they face failure and criticism every day from teachers who may not understand them and who are as frustrated with their behavior as you are sometimes. They have a harder time making and keeping friends. Most importantly, they often get similar negative reactions from family members who are just worn out and frustrated because their child just can't seem to get it right.

We know that all this negative feedback has an effect on adolescents with ADHD. Their rate of depression and low self-esteem is much greater than that found in the general population. In a longitudinal study of ADHD children followed from early childhood to adulthood, investigators asked the grown ADHD subjects what made the most positive difference for them in their lives. Their response? Having someone in their life that cared for them and had faith in them. Most likely this person would be a parent, although it could be another relative, a teacher, a friend or a neighbor.

"Having someone that cared about me!" That was the most important thing. Not medicine. Not counseling. Not grades in school.

Loving your child unconditionally means you love him for who he is, not for what he does. You show this unconditional love in your smile, your touch, your looks of concern, your interest, and by giving your time and attention. Your child will sense this and it may very well give him the strength he needs to meet his world each and every day.

Consider the following suggestions when you communicate with your son or daughter.
- Listen to your teenager. Give your child your undivided attention when they have something to say.
- Avoid judging or criticizing. Teens need understanding and guidance. When criticism is necessary, provide it in a constructive way.
- Be courteous and respectful when communicating.
- Express your affection and concern frequently. Tell your child you love them.
- Encourage your teenager to contribute their thoughts and ideas on issues.
- Look for positive accomplisments and offer praise.

In Chapters 9 and 10 we will look at other methods of communicationg and problem-solving which can have a very positive effect on family life.

Principle # 2: Spend enjoyable time with your adolescent.

Child development experts believe giving time to your child impacts his or her development. Spending time and developing a close emotional bond shows your child that you care.

Establishing a close relationship with your son or daughter as they go through their teenage years can be one of the most rewarding experiences in raising a child. You will be able to share their excitement, joy, fear, and frustration as they face new challenges and experience new adventures. It is a thrilling time, and parents should try not to miss it.

Although some teenagers naturally try to distance themselves from their mothers and fathers, parents can do things to close the gap. Try to have some positive time together each week. Find an activity you both enjoy and do it together. Make this special time part of your weekly schedule. One father and son I know went to watch a movie every Wednesday evening. Another mother and son watched their favorite shows on television together a few nights a week. Some parents and teens have mutual interests in sports, and they play sports together or go to sporting events together.

You can't get to know your son or daughter without getting to know their friends as well. Try to make your house open to their friends. Welcome them and make them feel comfortable in your home. Encourage your son or daughter to invite their friends for barbecues, family outings, short trips, etc.

Spend as much time as you can talking with your teenagers—they won't be with you that much longer. By spending time together, you will learn more about what they think, feel and want.

Principle # 3: Become an ADHD expert.

Parents need to learn as much about ADHD as they can. Having knowledge about ADHD, the effect it can have on your child's behavior, socialization, school performance, and home life, will enable you to make the right decisions to best help your son or daughter. Fortunately, a great deal of information about ADHD exists. Books are readily available in national chain stores, through catalogs, and in schools and libraries. Many school districts offer parenting information and programs about ADHD. You can encourage your son or daughter to learn about ADHD as well. Books, videos, and newsletters have been published for children of all ages.

It helps to talk to other parents of ADHD children and teens. As parents we can learn a great deal by sharing experiences with one another. Find a chapter of CH.A.D.D. in your area and try to attend a chapter meeting. They are usually held monthly and feature experts in your community who discuss different aspects of ADHD. A list of CH.A.D.D. chapters can be found on the Internet (www.chadd.org).

Learn about the resources available in your community that provide services to teenagers with ADHD. You will need to know who the ADHD experts are in your area. Knowledge about treating adolescents with ADHD can vary widely among the educational and health care professionals in your community. Find out which ones know the most and have the most experience working with ADHD kids.

Get involved in your child's school. It is frequently at the start of middle school when many children with ADHD begin to have a great deal of trouble in school. As a parent you may have worked closely with your child's elementary school teachers. Maintain this close contact when your child transfers to a secondary school. With more teachers, more classes per day, more assignments to keep track of, and less personal attention given to students with special needs in middle and high school, your help may be needed if your child starts having trouble.

Learn about your child's educational rights. Many students with ADHD will require some special assistance, either in a special education program or by having accommodations provided to him or her in regular education. If your student is having trouble in school, you will need to understand the public school's responsibility to assure that students receive the help they need.

Principle # 4: Model good values.

We must continue to teach our teenagers good values—respect for others, respect for themselves, honesty, responsibility, morality, etc. These high principles in life are important. These principles are taught in school and preached in religious services, but must also be modeled by parents if they are to be incorporated in your child's value system.

Setting a good example for our children by showing them honesty, responsibility, and caring for others will be lessons that they can carry for their entire lives. Children with ADHD aren't generally dishonest, irresponsible, or uncaring. Lying, avoiding responsibility, hurtfulness towards others—those are not on the symptom list for ADHD. But, they are remarkably close to the list of characteristics found in children and teenagers who are diagnosed with social maladjustment and conduct disorder. These are the adolescents who often come to the attention of the juvenile justice system, are suspended or expelled from school, and frequently have serious problems with substance abuse. Interesting, but not surprising, the best predictor of whether a teenager will develop conduct disorder is the presence of conduct disorder or antisocial behavior in his parents.

ADHD adolescents without conduct disorder typically don't have problems this severe. Although as a group they may not do as well educationally and career-wise as others without ADHD, they will generally turn out all right.

The message here is that one of the guiding principles in raising children with ADHD is to be a good example for them to follow. If your teenager doesn't keep his or her room organized, doesn't pay attention in class, or doesn't clean the car out once in a while—don't panic. In the long run these things may not be as important as the type of person he or she is becoming.

Principle # 5: Provide structure at home with clear, consistent rules.

ADHD adolescents need structure—and lots of it. Structure means that parents should clearly spell out how they expect their teenager to act at home and away. We call these house rules and street rules. By having clear sets of rules for the teenager to live by parents set boundaries for behavior.

Many teenagers can impose their own limits on their behavior. They have internalized a sense of what is right and wrong. They can control their behavior, and they behave appropriately. These kids seem to be born with a set of rules and the ability to follow them.

ADHD kids are different. Their main problem is poor self-regulation. They have difficulty inhibiting behavior and that is what gets them in the most trouble. They get stimulated, become overaroused, and out of control. "Managed by the moment" a parent of an ADHD teenager said. Everything else gets shut out.

We can surely provide our ADHD kids with rules about behavior. What we can't give them is the self-control they need to inhibit inappropriate behavior and follow the rules. We can make a rule that they can't use the phone until after their homework is done, but we can't give them the strength to restrain themselves from using the phone and the persistence to concentrate on their homework. Nevertheless, having rules are a good start and an important part of any program to manage the behavior of ADHD teens.

Include your adolescent son or daughter in deciding the rules. The "do it because I said so" approach isn't going to sit well with teens. They want to be heard and they have a right to express their opinion about issues that concern them. By using a democratic process to establish house rules, parents are less likely to make rules that are unrealistic for the adolescent to live by. Through discussion with parents in the rule-making process, teens are better able to see the reasoning behind certain restrictions and expectations. Furthermore, compliance with the rules will most likely be greater since the teenager had a say in constructing them.

Although it is usually better to use a democratic process in establishing house rules and street rules for teenagers, certain rules are going to be nonnegotiable. For instance: no smoking, no drinking alcohol, no using drugs; no violence or cursing; no taking other people's property without asking permission; no staying out past curfew without asking permission; no skipping school; etc. As we said, two sets of rules are useful—house rules and street rules.

Examples of common house rules are:
*   Treat other members of the family with respect.
*   Physical violence or foul language are not permissible any time.
*   Family members are responsible for cleaning their own rooms.
*   Eating is allowed only in the kitchen.
*   No use of the telephone after 10:30 p.m.

Examples of common street rules are:
*   The use of any alcohol or drugs is forbidden.

- You must arrive at school everyday by 7:30 a.m.
- Respect the property of others.
- Show courtesy to others.
- Obey the laws in the community.

Principle # 6: Monitor compliance with rules and check behavior regularly.

Behavior needs to be consistently monitored. Having a set of rules for your teenager to live by is worthless if you are not paying careful attention to whether anyone is following them. It is simply not good enough to wait until a violation of a rule comes to your attention. By then the violation may have gone on for so long that too much damage may have already been done.

For example, if your teenager has had a pattern of not completing homework, you might establish a rule that all homework given that day in school needs to be completed before going out, watching television, using the phone, etc. Once established as a rule, you can't assume that if you don't hear any complaints from school about incomplete homework, all is well. If your teenager is known to have chronic problems with homework completion in the past, parents will have to monitor homework completion daily, whether they hear from the school or not. In fact, for teens who may not be honest about disclosing homework assignments, closer communication with the school may be needed to make sure the student is being truthful. After the teenager has shown consistent improvement in this area over time, less supervision may be appropriate.

Teenagers will balk over such close monitoring and parents may begin to think that nightly conflicts are just not worth the effort. "If he fails he fails!" some exhausted parents will say. But parents shouldn't fall prey to that kind of discouraged thinking. The rule should stand. Frequent monitoring should continue. When the teenager has demonstrated responsible behavior by completing homework, the parent can slowly back off.

Monitor your teenagers' behavior. Check on their whereabouts, what they are doing, when they plan to be at a certain place, what time they will be home, what their friends are like, what their homework is, etc. This is part of the responsibility of being a parent. Teenagers, especially those with ADHD, require this kind of monitoring. Having someone in authority keep an eye on their behavior may reduce impulsivity and may make them think about consequences a little more. Most importantly, it sends a powerful message—you care enough about them to be concerned.

Principle # 7: Inspire confidence as a parent-coach.

Parents who act as coaches rather than critics of their teenager will be able to provide more effective guidance to their child. It is natrual to become defensive and defiant if criticized or judged. Adolescents with ADHD receive a great deal more criticism than the average teenager.

This can lead to feelings of frustration, irritability, resentment, and self-doubt. For this reason, home should be a respite from life's daily pressures. This is especially true if their son's or daughter's problems stem from behavior which their child cannot totally control. If you notice your teenager's problems are mounting try to be a coach rather than a critic. Consider the following points.

1. In general, all kids (and especially those with ADHD) do better when their environment has a lot of structure—frequent monitoring of behavior and feedback.

2. Feedback about behavior is most effective when it is positive and encouraging. Negative feedback, when it must be given, should be communicated without blame or derision. Parents shouldn't emphasize the negative as a first reaction. They should practice positive coaching techniques by giving as much positive reinforcement as possible.

3. While negative consequences for inappropriate behavior are important to discourage the behavior from repeating, the parent-coach seizes every opportunity to build their child's confidence, solidify the parent-child relationship, and motivate their teen to stay on track in the future.

Summary

The job of parents during the period of adolescence is to guide their teenagers so they will acquire the skills needed to one day live independently and responsibly. For the adolescent to learn these skills, parents must gradually loosen their control and let their teens experience life for themselves. Fortunately, most teenagers find their way without running into too much difficulty. Adolescents with ADHD, however, are at greater risk for behaving in ways that can have serious health consequences. They may also experience more difficulty in school, have more automobile crashes, get more traffic citations, and may develop substance abuse problems. Parents living with an ADHD adolescent should be guided by several principles, which may improve the likelihood of positive outcomes and, hopefully, reduce future risks.

1. Provide unconditional love and positive regard.
2. Spend time with your adolescent.
3   Become an ADHD expert.
4. Model good values.
5. Provide structure at home with clear, consistent rules.
6. Monitor compliance with rules and check behavior regularly.
7. Inspire confidence as a parent-coach.

9 Building Communication Skills in Your Family

Good communication skills are vital in a family that hopes to make decisions together, solve problems effectively, and promote a positive sense of well-being among family members. When families are in distress, however, communication is often the first thing to crumble and family members are likely to conflict with one another. Imagine the family as a train and communication as the tracks. How far can the train go if there are breaks in the tracks? How well can families discuss important day-to-day issues, make decisions together, or solve problems that affect one another if communication is poor?

Use of sarcasm, ridicule, name calling, ignoring, making an annoyed face, looking incredulous, snickering, mocking, overgeneralizing, lecturing, not paying attention, interrupting, getting off the topic, ordering, hogging the conversation, threatening, laughing at, and making light of someone's feelings are just a few of the many actions that could interfere with communication. Typically one person's negative action leads to another person's negative reaction and before you know it, an argument erupts, nobody listens to anyone, and positive communication breaks down.

Styles of communication among family members are usually difficult to change. However, with a good effort by everyone, people can begin to communicate with one another in more productive ways. The key is to show respect, patience, understanding, and compassion for one another. Criticism will always block effective communication. Often it is better to say less than more and to do so in a positive way. On the following page is a chart showing behaviors which encourage positive communication and those which cause communication breakdowns. Another copy of this chart can be found in the Appendix for distribution to family members.

Do's and Don'ts of Family Communication
Behaviors Which Build Up or Break Down Communication

<u>**Do**</u>	<u>**Don't**</u>
Wait for the other person to finish speaking	Interrupt
Make brief statements without judging	Lecture, sermonize
Talk in a neutral voice	Talk sarcastically
Make eye contact, acknowledge you are listening by nodding head, etc.	Look away
Sit in a relaxed position	Fidget, move around
Make brief statements, give others a chance to talk	Hog the conversation
Take other people's feeling seriously Recognize other's hurt, pain, anger	Discount feelings
Stay focused on one issue at a time	Change the topic
Make tentative rather than absolute statements, deal with specifics	Overgeneralize, catastrophize, exaggerate
Make suggestions not demands	Give orders or commands
Speak to others in a respectful tone	Call names
Stick with the current issue	Dwell on the past
Stay calm look for solutions	Threaten
Express your feelings to others in an appropriate way	Keep feelings inside
Talk in a neutral voice	Yell or scream

Families whose members have trouble talking with one another can often benefit from communication training. A big part of what therapists do in family therapy is to help family members talk and listen more effectively to one another. The therapist points out negative behaviors such as those above, which cause communication to break down, and suggests positive alternatives. In the following pages are steps you can take to improve communication in your family. Positive communication will make problem-solving with your adolescent more effective.

Three Steps to Improving Communication

1. Identifying Common Mistakes in Family Communication

The goal of this first step is to help family members recognize what builds up or tears down communication in a family. The discussion leader should distribute copies of the Do's and Don'ts of Family Communication chart to each family member (a reproducible copy can be found in the Appendix). Each person should take turns reading aloud three or four Do's with the corresponding Don'ts from the list. After each person has finished reading his portion, family members should evaluate whether any of the Do's and Don'ts relate to the family. Continue taking turns through the entire list, pausing for discussion and evaluation after a portion of the list is read aloud. Family members may point out to one another the mistakes made by themselves and others in communicating. Every effort should be made to keep the discussion constructive.

At the conclusion of the meeting, each family member should pick one or two Do's and Don'ts that they will try to work on when they communicate with others in the coming week.

2. Learning and Practicing Positive Communication Skills

The goal of this meeting is to learn and practice positive communication skills. At the second meeting, the family should refer to the Family Communication list again. Each member should take a turn and discuss the positive communication skill from the Do's and Don'ts list they worked on since the first meeting.

Next, each member should role play a negative and then a positive communication skill using imagined scenarios between family members. For example, an adolescent might play the part of a parent exaggerating or catastrophizing something. Or a parent might play the part of a teenager talking sarcastically to a parent or sibling. Each family member should choose at least one communication skill from the Don't side of the list and act it out. Then they should act out the same situation using a communication skill from the Do side of the list.

Members should pair off for a communication trial. The pair should select a fictitious problem situation for discussion in front of the other family members. Other family members should watch the discussion. Allow the discussion to continue for a few minutes. Each person should have several chances to speak. When the time is up, the other family members can evaluate how well the pair used positive communication skills in their discussion.

At the end of the meeting members should agree to practice positive communication skills with one another over the next several days.

3. Practice Positive Communication Skills with Real Situations

The goal of the third meeting is to practice applying positive communication skills in real-life situations. Each family member should have a copy of the family communication chart shown on the previous page. Each member should take a turn and discuss the positive communication skills they practiced in the past several days.

Members should pair off for a communication trial. The pair should select a real problem situation that occurred this week to discuss in front of the other family members. Other family members should observe the discussion. Allow the discussion to continue for a few minutes. Each person should have had several chances to speak. When the time is up, the other family members can evaluate how well the pair used positive communication skills in their discussion.

At the conclusion of this communication trial, another family member pair should select a second real problem situation that occurred this week. This discussion should also be watched and evaluated by the other members to determine how well the pair used positive communication skills.

Summary

Good communication skills are important in a family especially when there are decisions to be made or problems to be solved. When people are getting along with one another, communication seems to flow smoothly. However, during times of stress, particularly when the stress involves parents and adolescents, family members become short-tempered, argumentative, and defensive. They often communicate with one another in hostile, sarcastic tones, which causes problems rather than solves them.

Each member of the family must try to build their positive communication skills. This can be done at a series of family meetings. Members of the family identify mistakes they make when communicating with one another. Then they learn more positive styles of communication and rehearse them. Role-playing actual situations in the family can help members practice how to speak and how to listen to one another respectfully. With continued practice and a desire to truly respect one another's beliefs and opinions, families can work out any communication difficulties they may have.

10 Problem-Solving Strategies with Adolescents

Adolescents expect their parents and other adults to treat them with more respect than they were given as children. They expect to be given more freedom and opportunity to manage their own lives and will demand that their opinions are heard. Parents who relied primarily on parental authority in the past to discipline will find that once their children begin their passage into adolescence, discipline through power alone will no longer be effective. In fact, it can become quite destructive. The "you will do it or else" parenting approach eventually makes teenagers angry and resentful, breaks down communication, and can result in the teen isolating himself from the family.

Drs. Arthur Robin and Sharon Foster, psychologists who have researched conflict resolution with adolescents, encourage parents of adolescents to use a problem-solving model to resolve parent-adolescent conflict. In doing so family members try to resolve conflict through communication and negotiation. Many families have no formal method of dealing with problem situations. There are several useful steps in the problem-solving process. The following information is intended to train members of your family to use these steps when trying to problem solve.

The five steps in problem-solving are listed below and each step is discussed in the following sections.
1. Identify the problem.
2. Think of plans to solve the problem.
3. Pick the best plan.
4. Try the plan.
5. Evaluate if the plan worked.

To begin the problem solving process, select a time to meet that is convenient for everyone. Avoid any interruptions during the meeting (i.e., phone calls, side discussions with other family members, sound from the television, etc.) so the discussion can flow smoothly.

Select a family member to lead the meeting. The leader should introduce the problem-solving program to other family members. The leader should give a copy of the Problem-Solving Flow Chart (below and in the Appendix) to each family member at the meeting. Using the chart, the leader should lead a discussion of each step of the process as illustrated on the chart. The leader should show everyone the Problem-Solving Worksheet (next page and in the Appendix) that is to be completed during the family meeting.

Use the steps in problem-solving to come up with a plan for the situation described below. Then complete the Problem-Solving Worksheet as you go through the steps to develop your plan.

Sample Problem to Practice On

Janet got her driver's license two months ago. She would like to use the family car at night, but her parents don't think she is ready to drive after dark just yet. Janet and her parents argue about this and seem to get nowhere.

Problem-Solving Flow Chart

The steps listed below will guide you through the problem-solving process. Follow the guidelines listed under each step.

STEP 1: IDENTIFY THE PROBLEM.
   Mother, father, and adolescent should take turns defining the problem as each sees it.
   •   Don't define the problem in an emotional way by blaming, exaggerating, or demeaning others.
   •   Limit your problem definition to just one issue.
STEP 2: THINK OF PLANS TO SOLVE THE PROBLEM.
   Brainstorm ideas to come up with possible plans to solve the problem.
   •   Take turns and think up as many plans as possible—anything goes here.
   •   Don't evaluate any of the plans until everyone has had a chance to share their ideas.
STEP 3: PICK THE BEST PLAN.
   Each person explains how the proposed plan would affect them personally and rates each plan with a plus or minus. Choose the plan with the most consensus.
   •   Be practical and think about how the plan would actually work if you tried it.
   •   Consider how each plan would affect other people's feelings.
   •   Pick the plan that is most agreeable with everyone.
STEP 4: TRY THE PLAN
   Discuss how to put the plan into action and write an "action-plan."
   •   Define the behaviors to be targeted.
   •   Determine consequences (rewards/punishments) and how they will be administered.
   •   Make sure you have a way of keeping track of what is occurring.
STEP 5: EVALUATE IF THE PLAN WORKED.
   Within a week or so, meet again to discuss how the plan worked.
   •   Evaluate if the plan was effective.
   •   Consider if everyone is satisfied with how the plan is working.
   •   If the plan is working well, continue to use it. If the plan is not working well, use the problem solving process to come up with another plan.

Problem-Solving Worksheet

Date:_____

Instructions: Use this form to guide you through the steps of the problem-solving process. Write responses to each step in the spaces provided.

1. Identify the problem. As a family, decide how to define the problem situation and write it down here.

2. Think of plans to solve the problem. Discuss different plans and write a few of them down here.

3. Pick the best plan. As a family, decide which plan is the best one to try.

Plus or Minus Ratings by
Teen   Mother   Father

Plan 1

Plan 2

Plan 3

Plan 4

4. Try the plan. Write down specifically what each member of the family will do to carry out the plan.

5. Evaluate if the plan worked. Write down how the plan worked, what you could do to make it work better, what everyone thought of the plan.

Five Steps to Problem-Solving

1.   Identify the problem.

Try to define the problem by answering the first question, "What is the problem we are having?" Mother, father, and adolescent should take turns defining the problem as they each see it. Defining the problem can be challenging. Several things can go wrong, even in this initial stage. Listening to one another without judging is very important. Be careful not to blame, accuse, or belittle anyone's opinion. Stay on task and discuss one problem only. This is the beginning of the problem-solving process, and it should get off to a good, kind-spirited start.

- Don't define the problem in an emotional way by blaming, exaggerating, or demeaning someone else.
- Limit your problem definition to just one issue. It would be difficult to deal with more than one problem during one family meeting. Select a family member to lead the meeting and to make sure the discussion stays focused on one topic.
- Respect each other's opinions and listen carefully to what each person is saying. Instead of responding to someone else's statement with one of your own, try just restating what that person said to let them know you understand their point of view.

After everyone has spoken, identify what the problem is and write it in the space provided on the Problem-Solving Worksheet.

2.   Think of plans to solve the problem.

Once the problem has been defined, family members should brainstorm possible plans to solve the problem. The meeting leader is responsible for listing these plans on the Problem-Solving Worksheet as members of the group take turns coming up with more. It is important that a plan not be evaluated in discussion until brainstorming is over. Continue to brainstorm until three or four plans are written down.

- Write down as many plans as possible.
- Don't evaluate any of the plans until everyone has shared their ideas.
  Remember, anything goes—so any plan offered should be added to the list.

3.   Pick the best plan.

Family members take turns evaluating each plan. Each person explains how the proposed plan would affect them. Each plan is rated as plus or minus by group members. These ratings are recorded next to the written plan in separate columns of the problem-solving worksheet. Select the plan rated as plus by everyone. If more than one plan was rated plus by everyone, decide to select one or a combination of these plans. If no consensus was reached discuss possible com-

promises from the plans on the list.
- When evaluating a plan, be practical and think how it would actually work if tried.
- Consider how each plan would affect other people's feelings.
- Pick the plan which is most agreeable with everyone.

4. Try the plan.

The goal of this step is to discuss how to put the plan into action and to write an "action plan." When trying to come up with an "action plan," it is best to be specific.
- Define the particular behavior(s) you are trying to work on. Be clear in your definition of terms. For example, if your plan includes the adolescent keeping a "clean" room, does everyone agree what a "clean" room looks like? Or, if the plan states there will be a consequence for "talking back" to a parent, define precisely what is meant by "talking back."
- Determine what consequences (rewards/punishments) will occur following a behavior. Who will administer the consequences, when, and how much or how often.
- Make sure you have a way of documenting what is occurring. For example, you could use a calendar, appointment book, notepaper, or charts to record events on a regular basis.

5. Evaluate if the plan worked.

After about a week of implementing the action plan, the family should meet again to discuss whether the plan was effective and, if not, how it might need to be modified to improve the result.
- Evaluate if the plan was effective.
- Consider if everyone is satisfied with how the plan is working.
- If the plan is working well continue to use it. If the plan is not working well, use the problem-solving process to create another plan.

Try to Solve a Real Problem in Your Family

After you've gone through the problem-solving steps for Janet's driving problem, use the same steps to deal with a real problem in your family. Use the Problem-Solving Worksheet to keep track of the ideas as you go through each step. After you're finished, implement the plan and meet again in a week or so to evaluate the plan.

Problem-Solving Worksheet
Sample for Fictitious Problem

Date:_____

Instructions: Use this form to guide you through the steps of the problem-solving process. Write responses to each step in the spaces provided.

1. Identify the problem. As a family, decide how to define the problem situation and write it down here.

Janet wants to drive the car at night but her parents want her to have more driving experience first.

2. Think of plans to solve the problem. Discuss different plans, and write a few of them down here.

1. Janet can't drive at night until she has 3 months driving experience.

2. Let Janet drive at night around the neighborhood but not further.

3. Janet will practice driving at night with one of the parents in the car. After two weeks, if she is ready, she'll be allowed to drive at night alone.

3. Pick the best plan. As a family, decide which of the plans you have written above is the best one to try.   Plus or Minus Ratings by

	Teen	Mother	Father
Plan 1 *No night time driving for 3 mos.*	minus	minus	plus
Plan 2 *Night time driving locally only.*	minus	plus	plus
Plan 3 *Practice night driving.*	plus	plus	plus

4. Try the plan. Write down specifically what each member of the family will do to carry out the plan.

Janet will practice driving at night with one of her parents in the car at least four times in the next week. The following 2 weeks she will drive at night with her parents to visit her aunt, who lives an hour away, and again to visit a family friend, who also lives an hour away. During this period, Janet will be given additional opportunity to drive at night when she is with one of her parents. At the end of the three week period Janet's parents will review her night driving and will allow her to drive alone at night if they are confident in her ability.

5. Evaluate if the plan worked. Write down how the plan worked, what you could do to make it work better, what everyone thought of the plan.

The plan worked fine. We are comfortable with Janet driving at night by herself.

Troubleshooting the Problem-Solving Process

It is not unusual for a family to have difficulty with the problem-solving process. Below are a list of common problems that families run into while trying to problem-solve.

Communication problems.

Negative rather than positive communication among family members is the main cause for the problem-solving process to fail. It is extremely important for participants to be positive and respectful toward one another when problem solving. Sensitive issues are on the table for discussion and to avoid a flare up of emotions communications should be respectful. Review the chapter on how to build positive family communication skills. Then practice problem-solving with those skills in mind.

Inconsistent implementation.

For a plan to work successfully it has to be implemented consistently. If this is the reason why your plan wasn't working well, identify possible reasons for the inconsistency. Maybe the plan was too inconvenient to implement. Perhaps not everybody agrees with the plan and those who disagree are reluctant to implement it. Could it be that some people just forgot about the plan and went back to their old behavior?

Discuss the possible reasons for inconsistent implementation and make any changes in the plan that are needed so that you can overcome any barriers for next time.

No opportunity to work the plan.

Some action plans don't work because there was no opportunity to implement them. For example, a plan that encouraged an adolescent to come home by 11 p.m. on weekdays and midnight on weekends might not have had to be implemented because the adolescent only went out one night that week.

The problem wasn't clearly defined.

The Scott family created a plan to improve their daughter's homework habits. They decided to limit Allison's use of the phone until all homework and studying was completed. After reviewing the plan the following week, Allison admitted that although she did not use the phone most of the week, she had not completed the majority of the homework assigned to her. Allison realized that she had trouble understanding much of the work assigned to her and that her over use of the phone in the past was just an excuse to avoid difficult work. The family came up with an alternative definition of the problem; Allison was having trouble understanding her homework. They then proceeded to follow the steps to lead to a new action plan that made more sense.

Summary

Adolescents will not accept a "Do it because I said so!" approach to parenting as they might have when they were younger. As they mature, they expect to be treated with respect and courtesy. They want their ideas and opinions to count. This is a good thing. We want our children to grow up to have their own opinion and to think for themselves. Independence should be encouraged provided it is handled responsibly.

Some parents and adolescents will need to learn problem-solving strategies to manage conflicts at home. Problem-solving requires good communication skills among family members and an attitude of respect for one another. There are five steps to problem-solving which the family could learn and practice. Parents are encouraged to use problem-solving to resolve conflicts whenever possible.

11 Using a Home Token Economy to Encourage Behavior Change

A home token economy system can provide families with a positive method to promote behavior change. A token economy system is essentially a contract between the parents and the adolescent stating that if the adolescent behaves in a certain way, the parents will agree to provide certain rewards and/or privileges.

Most child development experts agree that to be effective behavior managers, parents must create an environment within the home in which:

1. expectations about the adolescent's behavior are clearly communicated;
2. motivation is available to encourage the adolescent to meet such expectations; and
3. a system is in place for parents to track the adolescent's behavior and to respond by providing appropriate rewards, privileges, and consequences.

A token economy system satisfies all three of these conditions. As you read the steps in setting up a token economy, you will be required to write down exactly how you expect your teenager to behave, what you will do in response to such behavior, and the benefits or consequences that the teenager will receive for his behavior.

Expectations

To start, you will be asked to examine your adolescent's behavior. Acceptable behaviors are called "Start Behaviors" and unacceptable behaviors are called "Stop Behaviors." Start Behaviors are those behaviors which you expect your adolescent to exhibit more frequently. Likewise, Stop Behaviors are those behaviors which you expect him or her to exhibit less frequently, or not at all. Writing down these expectations so everyone in the family understand exacly what is expected is a very important part of the behavior management program.

Motivation

Motivating your adolescent to behave appropriately by offering incentives for such behavior is another important aspect of the program. Although essential, clear expectations alone often do not produce behavior change. Adolescents may know what their parents expect of them, but don't do what is expected anyway. In this behavior program, your teenager will be given the opportunity to earn points for appropriate behavior, which can be exchanged for rewards and privileges. The adolescent can lose tokens for unacceptable behavior.

Consequences

The behavior management program provides a predetermined consequence for the adolescent's behavior. When using the program, the parent carefully observes the adolescent's behavior, notes the behavior on a chart, and records the number of tokens the adolescent has earned, lost, or spent on rewards and privileges.

Setting Up the Token Economy

The behavior program uses a Home Behavior Chart. The chart has space to record behavior for up to seven days. Each chart is divided into four sections:
1. Start Behaviors
2. Stop Behaviors
3. Rewards and Privileges
4. Total Tokens Remaining

To set up the behavior program, you must first complete each section of the Home Behavior Chart. A sample chart has been included to assist you as you construct the chart for your adolescent. A blank chart can be found in the Appendix and it can be reproduced for your personal use. Use a separate Home Behavior Chart for each child or adolescent in the family who will be involved in the program.

STEP 1: Start Behaviors

Begin by deciding on the behaviors you would like to list in the Start Behaviors section of the Home Behavior Chart. Refer to the sample list of start behaviors below to get an idea of what behaviors you may wish to list in the Start Behaviors section.

This sample list contains common behaviors that have been identified by other parents as desirable. Write down five or six behaviors (from the list or ones that you identified yourself) that you would like to see your adolescent exhibit more often.

Write these in the Start Behaviors section of the Home Behavior Chart. Be sure to include only those behaviors that you are certain your adolescent is capable of doing if prop-

START BEHAVIORS	Value	Su	Mo	Tu	We	Th	Fr	Sa
1 *Wakes up by 7 a.m*	5		5	5	0	5	5	0
2 *Walks dog after school*	5	5	5	5	0	5	5	0
3 *Puts schoolbooks in room*	3		3	3	3	3	3	0
4 *Cleans bedroom by dinnertime*	5	5	5	0	5	5	5	5
5 *Completes h.w. by 10 p.m.*	10	10	10	10	10	10		
6 *Writes phone messages (3x)*	1	3	2	1	3	3	1	
7 **Extra Credit!** *Cleans up yard— mows and trims.*	20	20						20
TOTAL TOKENS EARNED		43	30	24	21	31	19	25

STOP BEHAVIORS	Value	Su	Mo	Tu	We	Th	Fr	Sa
1 *Interrupts others*	5	5		5		5	5	0
2 *Yelling in the house*	5							0
3 *Arguing with parents*	10		10					0
4 *Staying out past curfew*	35							35
5 *No studying or homework*	20					20		0
6								0
7 **Extra Penalty**								
TOTAL TOKENS LOST (Minus)		5	10	5		25	5	35

TOTAL TOKENS AVAILABLE	38	33	32	53	59	78	63

REWARDS/PRIVILEGES	Value	Su	Mo	Tu	We	Th	Fr	Sa
1 *Out on Friday night*	25	25						
2 *Buy a CD at store*	35							
3 *Free make bed pass*	20		20					
4 *Extra 1/2 hr on curfew*	25							
5 *Tickets to ballgame*	75							
6 *Sleep over at friend's*	35							35
7 *Order a pizza*	25							
8								
TOTAL TOKENS SPENT		25	20					35

TOTAL TOKENS REMAINING	13	13	32	53	59	73	28

erly motivated. Avoid listing anything which is vague (e.g., "good attitude," "cooperative," "friendly," etc.). Only list observable and specific behaviors. For those start behaviors which can occur several times a day (e.g., "washes dirty dishes," "walks dog," or "puts garbage in garbage can," etc.), you should put the maximum number of times you will reward the behavior each day in brackets.

Next, assign a token value to each of the behaviors in the Start Behaviors section. The value should be between 1 and 25 tokens. To be effective, token values need to be high enough to encourage the child to display the behavior. Behaviors that are more difficult for the child, or which have more importance to you, should be assigned a higher token value. For instance, "practicing piano for 1/2 hour" or "doing homework for one hour" should probably be worth more than "walking the dog" since these behaviors require more time and effort. It is important to immediately record the appropriate behavior on the chart after the behavior has occurred. In addition, parents should provide verbal praise to the adolescent for the behavior.

Sample Start Behaviors

- awake and out of bed by   o'clock
- walks the dog (3x)
- makes bed
- leaves for school by   o'clock
- practices instrument
- puts dirty clothes in laundry
- mows yard
- starts/finishes homework on time
- studies for 60 minutes
- makes eye contact
- listens the first time asked
- throws out garbage
- uses manners at table
- reads for   minutes
- earns   grade in school
- makes plans with a friend
- washes car

- by   o'clock dresses self
- hangs up wet bathroom towel
- comes to dinner on time
- waters plants
- keeps room neat
- home by 10 p.m. weekdays
- completes chores list
- unloads dishwasher
- picks up laundry at dry cleaners
- in bed by   o'clock
- sets table
- speaks to others politely
- asks permission to borrow
- talks about feelings
- tells the truth
- takes medicine
- practices baseball 15 min. with younger brother

START BEHAVIORS	Value	Su	Mo	Tu	We	Th	Fr	Sa
1 *Wakes up by 7 a.m*	5							
2 *Walks dog after school*	5							
3 *Puts schoolbooks in room*	3							
4 *Cleans bedroom by dinnertime*	5							
5 *Completes h.w. by 10 p.m.*	10							
6 *Writes phone messages (3x)*	1							
7 Extra *Cleans up yard-* **Credit!** *mows and trims.*	20							
TOTAL TOKENS EARNED								

Extra Credit!

There is an additional line called Extra Credit in the Start Behaviors section. The adolescent can earn extra tokens by displaying a behavior that is not listed as a start behavior, but which the parent would like to encourage and reward.

STEP 2: Stop Behaviors

Refer to the list of sample stop behaviors below to get an idea of what behaviors to list in the Stop Behaviors section of the Home Behavior Chart.

This sample list contains common behaviors that have been identified by other parents as undesirable. Choose four to six behaviors from the list. Choose behaviors that you would like to see your adolescent do less often or not at all. Write these behaviors in the Stop Behaviors section of the Home Behavior Chart. Be sure to include only those behaviors which you are certain your adolescent is capable of stopping if properly motivated. Avoid listing vague behaviors (e.g., "moody," "lazy," "immature," etc.). Only list observable and specific behaviors.

Then assign a token value to each of the behaviors in the Stop Behaviors section. The value should be between 5 and 50 tokens. A stop behavior that occurs frequently or has more importance to you should be assigned a higher fine value. The adolescent should receive a fine or loss of tokens whenever s/he exhibits any of the behaviors in the Stop Behaviors section. To be effective, a fine needs to be strong enough to deter the person from displaying the behavior. Parents should immediately record the inappropriate behavior on the chart and should not engage in any verbal arguments or prolonged discussion with the adolescent about the behavior.

There is an additional line called Extra Penalty in the Stop Behavior section. The adolescent can lose tokens by displaying a behavior that is not specifically listed as a stop behavior, but which the parent finds extremely inappropriate and, therefore, worthy of penalizing the child by deducting tokens.

Sample Stop Behaviors

- sleeps past 11 a.m. on weekends
- fights with brother or sister
- whines
- comes home after 10 p.m. weekdays
- uses profane language
- talks back
- ignores parental request
- interrupts
- uses phone more than 2 hours per day
- not ready for school by   o'clock
- does not complete homework
- gets in trouble at school
- leaves bike, etc. outside
- tells parents to "shut up"
- teases younger sister
- messy room
- doesn't put dirty clothes in laundry
- slams doors
- cheats on test

- gives dirty looks
- borrows clothes without asking
- refuses to wake up in morning
- plays stereo too loud
- refuses to eat
- leaves without telling where
- smokes
- lies
- does not study for a test
- tattletales
- makes long distance calls
- gets poor grade in school
- has temper outburst
- refuses to take medicine
- argues with parents
- doesn't make bed
- sneaks food
- argues about a penalty

STOP BEHAVIORS	Value	Su	Mo	Tu	We	Th	Fr	Sa
1 *Interrupts others*	5							
2 *Yelling in the house*	5							
3 *Arguing with parents*	10							
4 *Staying out past curfew*	35							
5 *No studying or homework*	20							
6								
7 **Extra Penalty**								
TOTAL TOKENS LOST								

STEP 3: Rewards and Privileges

Select appropriate rewards and privileges that you think will motivate your teenager. Since kids differ widely in the activities they enjoy, it is important to involve your child in the selection of rewards and privileges.

Sample rewards and privileges are listed below. This list contains common rewards and privileges adolescents find appealing. After reviewing this list with your teenager, decide which rewards and privileges should be included on the Home Behavior Chart. It is good practice to have at least six to eight rewards and privileges listed on the chart. Your teenager should have some latitude in deciding what rewards and privileges he would like. Many of the privileges on the chart will be activities that he or she may normally have been allowed to do, but will now have to earn (e.g., television time, staying up past a certain hour, use of the telephone, etc.).

As a general rule, the list should include rewards and privileges that the teenager could exchange for tokens fairly often, perhaps one or more times per day. For younger adolescents, avoid listing many privileges that can only be used once a week or once a month. For example, it might be better to offer a reward such as "1/2 hour of television time" (which can be given one or more times a day) than "money to go out on Saturday night."

The final decision about a specific reward or privilege is left to the parents. They must consider the practicality of the rewards and privileges considering time, expense, and overall well-being of the adolescent.

Next, assign a token value to each of the items in the Rewards and Privileges section. Determining the value of each item can be tricky. Costs should be low enough to give the teenager an opportunity to earn one or more rewards and privileges each day, yet high enough so that the child cannot earn privileges too easily. If s/he is earning a lot of tokens, it is usually a sign that the program is working well. Don't be reluctant to give frequent opportunities to exchange tokens for rewards and privileges.

Sample Rewards and Privileges

- sleep until   o'clock on weekends
- use of telephone for half-hour
- chooses restaurant for dinner
- permission for friend to sleep over
- trip to clothing store
- stays out until   o'clock
- allowed to visit a friend
- earns extra $
- able to use the car

- can buy a new CD
- ticket to see a movie
- permission to sleep at friend's house
- free chore day
- ride to school/from school
- extra half-hour video games
- extend curfew on Sat. night
- chooses activity with dad
- go fishing

REWARDS/PRIVILEGES	Value	Su	Mo	Tu	We	Th	Fr	Sa
1 *Out on Friday night*	25							
2 *Buy a CD at store*	35							
3 *Free make bed pass*	20							
4 *Extra 1/2 hr on curfew*	25							
5 *Tickets to ballgame*	75							
6 *Sleep over at friend's*	35							
7 *Order a pizza*	25							
8								
TOTAL TOKENS SPENT								

STEP 4: Explain the Program to Your Teenager

Introduce the behavior management program to your adolescent in a positive manner. Explain that you have learned a method by which he might be able to earn rewards and privileges by behaving appropriately. Review the sample rewards and privileges list with the child and try to determine which items on the list are appealing. Add any other rewards and privileges you or your adolescent can think of and then decide which ones should be written on the chart.

Review the behaviors you have selected for the Start Behaviors section. Explain each one and briefly tell the teenager why you have considered putting this behavior on the list. Explain the behavior's reward value in tokens and discuss as necessary.

Review the behaviors you have marked down in the Stop Behaviors section. Explain each one and briefly tell the teenager why you have considered putting this behavior on the list. Explain the behavior's penalty value in tokens and discuss as necessary.

Once again, review the rewards and privileges that can be earned by accumulating tokens. With the adolescent's input, modify this list (if necessary) to reflect your child's ideas as to what will motivate him/her to behave more positively. Explain the cost of each privilege and when privileges can be exchanged for tokens.

Go over the sample charts included in this chapter and explain how tokens are tabulated each day based on payoffs, penalties, and rewards and privileges used.

Set up a convenient time each day to review the adolescent's performance for the day and tabulate the tokens earned, lost, and spent by the child. Put the total in the Total Tokens Remaining space.

Older children and teens will understand the concept quickly. Some may object at first to the idea of having to earn tokens for privileges (some of which they may already receive automatically), but they usually agree to try out the program. Be positive when introducing the program to older children and teens. Encourage cooperation. Avoid threatening or arguing about the merits of the program. Simply explain the features of the program in a firm, positive way but make yourself available for discussion.

Helpful Tips for Using a Token Program

- Verbally reinforce positive behavior as often as possible. Aside from the reinforcement the child earns by receiving rewards and privileges, praise and recognition are also powerful motivators for good behavior. Parents should take every opportunity to praise the child.

- Provide reinforcement immediately. Behavior that is reinforced immediately has the best chance of being repeated. Recognize and reinforce a start behavior right after it occurs, especially if it is a behavior which has been recently added to the chart.

- Avoid nagging and prompting. Parents should avoid nagging and should not repeatedly prompt the child to exhibit a specific start behavior. The adolescent should not be given any tokens for start behaviors which occur after repeated prompting by the parent or other family member.

- Provide opportunities to spend tokens. Parents should think of success whenever their child is spending tokens and should, therefore, provide the opportunity for the adolescent to cash in and earn rewards or privileges.

- Don't give second chances. Fine the adolescent anytime he or she exhibits a stop behavior is on the chart. Giving a second or third chance to someone who is misbehaving only weakens the overall program.

- Don't engage in prolonged discussions or arguments. Teenagers will often try to talk the parent out of giving them a fine for misbehavior and when this is unsuccessful, they may become argumentative. Avoid arguing. Record the fine on the chart with no further discussion.

- Don't allow hoarding. Some adolescents prefer to save their tokens rather than spend them. Unless the teen is cashing in tokens to earn certificates (which can be earmarked for a larger reward or privilege) tokens can lose motivating value if not exchanged regularly.

- Don't give loans. Parents may not loan tokens so that the teenager can receive a reward or privilege.

- Total tokens once a day. Set aside a time to total up the tokens earned, lost, or spent each day. Usually the best time to do this is in the late afternoon or early evening.

Summary

A home token economy program can be successfully used by parents and teens together to clearly define expectations at home and encourage responsibility. A token economy is essentially a contact between the parents and the adolescent, which provides privileges and consequences if the adolescent behaves in a certain way.

Parents and teens should construct the token program by listing Start Behaviors, Stop Behaviors, and rewards and privileges on the token economy chart. Rewards and privileges should be established based on points earned or lost for behavior. Try to keep the program as positive as you can by providing frequent opportunities to reward appropriate behavior.

12 Helping Adolescents with ADHD Succeed in School

Adolescents with ADHD typically experience many problems in school. They often rush through their work and pay little attention to instructions or details. They have trouble completing tasks, become bored easily, and school work which may have been tolerable in the past seems dull and irrelevant. They have other things on their minds! Driving, dating, dressing, appearance, and friends compete with schoolwork for the teenager's attention.

Complicating the situation further, adolescents face different challenges in middle school and high school than they did in elementary school. In secondary school, they have more teachers to cope with, more work to finish, and a busier schedule to organize. Class schedules can vary daily. The student must juggle long-term projects and short-term assignments. Good notetaking skills, reading comprehension, writing, and memory are required to read textbook chapters and assignments with speed, comprehension, and adequate recall. Focus, drive, and persistence are required to manage this work. For many adolescents, especially those with ADHD, responsible planning and good intentions are overtaken by the mood of the moment.

Middle school and high school teachers expect their students to show independence and responsibility. Teachers, who are typically responsible for more than one hundred students a day and who are pressed each year to get through their subject's curriculum, argue that they cannot easily meet the special needs of individual students. Many consider this the job of special educators, who have smaller classes and additional training, to teach students with special needs. However, most students with ADHD are in regular education because they don't need the intensive assistance that smaller, special education programs offer. However, they do need a little more of their teacher's time and attention.

To accomplish their difficult task, teachers will need the support of parents and the cooperation of their students. Everyone must work together to identify the appropriate accommodations to take some of the pressure off the student and still enable him to learn. They can identify the student's strengths and capitalize on those areas so the student can be successful in school.

**To best help adolescents in
school, parents and teachers
must work together with the student.**

CH.A.D.D. published an article entitled, "Adolescents with ADD: The Transition from Childhood to Adulthood." It reviews strategies parents and teachers can use to help secondary school students succeed. Several of the following suggestions come from ideas in this article, which is the work of Pam Cook, Rae Hemphill, and Pat Edney with the assistance of Marlene Snyder and Maureen Gill.

Watch for Warning Signs of Trouble

Early detection of a problem in school is very important. We can prevent problems from building and getting out of control if we can step in early and provide help to the student. Parents can often detect if their teenager is having a problem with school even though their son or daughter may not tell them directly. Parents should be on the lookout for the following warning signs of trouble:

- frequent complaints of boredom
- excessive absenteeism from school
- drop in grades
- lack of interest in doing homework
- frequent tardiness
- talk about dropping out of school
- resentment expressed toward teachers
- no books or papers brought to or from school
- reports from teachers that the student is not completing work
- disorganization—books and papers not appropriately cared for
- work done sloppily or incorrectly
- doesn't seem to care about school attitude
- low self-esteem
- teacher complains of frequent inattention in class
- hyperactivity
- teacher reports student doesn't do in-class assignments
- teacher notes the student is hanging out with other students who are doing poorly in school
- student doesn't seem to comprehend assignments when trying to do them
- school reports unauthorized absences from class

Develop a Plan and Take Action

Parents should support their struggling teen by taking action when they notice warning signs of school problems. Teachers generally welcome input from parents. Parents who work closely with their child's school will be in a position to be informed of how they can help their son or daughter. To stay informed and to develop an action plan, follow these steps:

- request a meeting with teachers to review concerns
- prepare written information for the meeting
- encourage the student's participation at the meeting
- schedule future follow-up meetings
- encourage systematic evaluation of the student's difficulties
- prepare a plan of interventions, implement the interventions, and monitor their effectiveness.

200 Accommodations to Help Students

Teachers can make accommodations in the secondary school classroom environment to assist the teenager with ADHD. Parents can also make accommodations at home to provide structure, support, and help with academic work. Accommodations at school and at home can help the student who has problems in a variety of areas. Below are a list of accommodations that teachers, parents, and students have found to be helpful.

Attention

If the student is having problems paying attention:

- seat student in quiet area
- increase distance between desks
- seat student away from distracting stimuli
- allow extra time to complete assigned work
- shorten assignments/work periods, use timer
- break long assignments into smaller parts
- assist student in setting short-term goals
- give assignments one at a time
- require fewer correct responses for grade
- reduce amount of homework
- encourage student to ask questions when information is not understood
- provide instruction in self-monitoring so student can keep track of their own behavior
- pair written instructions with oral instructions
- provide peer assistance in notetaking

- give clear, concise instructions
- increase saliency of lesson to student
- look at student when talking
- seek to involve student in lesson presentation
- provide written outline of lesson
- pair students to check work
- cue student to stay on task with a private signal
- schedule class earlier in school day
- evaluate effectiveness of medication
- preferential seating (front and center or away from distractions)
- simplify/repeat/reword complex directions
- provide both oral and written instructions

Organization and Planning

If the student is having problems with organization and planning:
- encourage parents to help with organization
- provide rules for getting organized (i.e., deadlines for papers), types of notebooks, work arranged in specific ways, etc.)
- encourage student to have notebook with dividers and folders for work
- provide homework assignment book
- supervise writing of homework assignments
- check homework daily
- send home daily/weekly progress reports
- encourage neatness rather than penalize sloppiness
- allow student to have extra set of books at home
- provide peer assistance with organization
- give assignments one at a time
- set short-term goals in completing assignments
- do not penalize for handwriting if visual-motor deficits or organizational deficits are present
- encourage learning of keyboarding skills
- allow tape recording of assignments
- write main points of lessons on chalkboard
- use visual aids in lesson presentation

Academic Skill Problems

If the student is having problems with academic skills:
- if skill weaknesses are suspected refer for academic achievement assessment
- if reading is weak: provide additional reading time, use "previewing" strategies, select

text with less on a page, shorten amount of required reading, avoid oral reading, allow use of "Cliff Notes" when appropriate to gain an understanding of subject matter prior to reading the complete document, use books on tape to assist in comprehension of book, use highlighters to emphasize important information in reading selection

- if oral expression is weak: accept all oral responses, substitute display for oral report, encourage expression of new ideas or experiences, pick topics that are easy for student to talk about
- if written language is weak: accept non-written forms for reports (i.e. displays, oral, projects), accept use of typewriter, word processor, tape recorder, do not assign large quantity of written work, test with multiple choice or fill-in questions, instruction in "brainstorming" to generate ideas
- if spelling is weak: allow use of Franklin Spellers (headphone if speller talks) or other spell check tools, overlook spelling errors when appropriate on assignments where spelling is not the focus of the assignment
- if math is weak: allow use of calculator, use graph paper to space numbers, provide additional math time, provide immediate feedback and instruction via modeling of the correct computational procedure, teach the steps needed to solve a particular math problem, give clues to the process needed to solve problem, and encourage use of "self-talk" to proceed through problem-solving

Behavior

If the student is having problems complying with the rules:
- praise good behavior
- post class/school rules in conspicuous place
- provide immediate feedback about behavior
- ignore minor inappropriate behavior
- use teacher attention to praise positive behavior
- use "prudent" reprimands for misbehavior (i.e. avoid lecturing or criticism)
- supervise closely during transition times
- seat student near good role models or teacher
- set up behavior contract
- implement behavior management system
- instruct student in self-monitoring (i.e. following directions, raise hand to talk)
- encourage parental cooperation and support of teacher
- keep parents informed
- identify cause of behavior problems
- if depressed, get appropriate treatment
- arrange for a parent-teacher-student conference
- evaluate medication for type and dosing
- change seat

- determine antecedents of problem behavior (i.e., what triggers it)
- establish location where student could "chill out"

Activity

If the student has difficulty controlling activity level:
- allow student to stand sometimes while working
- provide opportunity for "seat breaks"
- provide short break between assignments
- supervise closely during transition times
- remind student to proofread work product
- give extra time to complete tasks

Mood

If the student is having problems with mood:
- provide reassurance and encouragement
- compliment positive behavior and work
- speak softly in non-threatening manner if student shows nervousness
- review instructions when giving new assignments to make sure student comprehends
- look for opportunities for student to display leadership role in class
- focus on student's talents and accomplishments
- conference frequently with parents to learn about student's interests and achievements
- assign student to be a peer teacher
- make time to talk alone with student
- encourage social interactions with classmates if student is withdrawn or excessively shy
- reinforce frequently when signs of frustration are noticed
- look for signs of stress and provide encouragement or reduced work load
- spend more time talking to students who seem pent up or display anger easily
- train anger control: encourage student to walk away and use calming strategies

Socialization

If student is having a problem socially:
- praise appropriate social behavior
- monitor social interactions to gain clearer sense of student's behavior with others
- set up social behavior goals with student and implement a social skills program
- prompt appropriate social behavior either verbally or with private signal
- encourage student to observe classmate who exhibits appropriate social skills
- avoid placing student in competitive activities

- encourage cooperative learning tasks
- provide small group social skills training in-class or through related services
- praise student to increase esteem to others
- assign special responsibilities to student in presence of peers to elevate status in class
- pair students instead of letting students choose
- encourage participation in after school "clubs" and activities
- social exposure through activities outside of school

Impulsivity

If the student has trouble with impulsivity and self-control:
- ignore minor, inappropriate behavior
- increase immediacy of rewards or consequences
- supervise closely during transition times
- use "prudent" reprimands for misbehavior (i.e., avoid lecturing or criticism)
- reinforce positive behavior with praise, etc.
- seat student near good role model or teacher
- set up behavior contract
- instruct student in self-monitoring of behavior (i.e., hand raising, calling out)
- call on student only when hand is raised appropriately
- ignore calling out without raising hand
- praise student when hand raised
- implement behavior management system
- implement home-school token system

Writing Assignments

If the student does not write assignments down:
- use a structured outline/a teacher using an overhead
- use a daily, weekly, monthly planner
- post assignments on chalkboard in same location each day
- provide time to copy down assignments at start of class rather than at end of class
- teacher sign-off in an assignment book
- use a reward or incentive program for writing assignments
- train in use of an automated homework hotline if available
- parents and teacher communicate re: assignments by e-mail, if available
- teacher posts assignments for students on Internet web site

Bringing Materials Home

If the student does not bring necessary materials home:
- having a second set of books at home
- use a checklist for materials to be brought home in locker or notebook
- color code book covers, workbooks, and notebooks
- use notebooks with colored pockets for homework to be done, work returned, papers and tests graded, etc.

Homework

If the student does not complete homework assignments on time:
- request flexibility on late work turned in and receive credit
- maintain list of other students phone numbers to get work
- provide long-term outline of assignments and due dates
- mail home assignments for next several weeks or use e-mail or Internet web site
- parents have access to teacher's school phone number and free period
- prepare a written contract with student to complete work
- evaluate effectiveness of medication
- frequent progress reports between school and home
- keep track of grades—give immediate feedback about test scores
- check homework each day and collect at start of class
- encourage student to put completed work in specific folder
- have student check school work that is due the evening before
- teacher calls parent if (3) assignments are missing

Long-Term Projects

If the student has difficulty with long term projects:
- break projects into smaller parts and prepare time line for each part
- work with parents at home to organize when work segments are to be completed
- use a "month-at-a-glance" calendar to track long-term assignments

Scheduling Difficulty

If the student's schedule causes difficulty:
- schedule academic classes when the student is most alert
- alternate academic classes and electives
- find teachers with right personality for student
- find teachers who are very structured in their teaching methods
- consider medication schedule when scheduling classes or vice versa

Handwriting Difficulty

If the student has difficulty with handwriting:
- allow printing instead of cursive
- encourage use of keyboard (i.e., typewriter or computer)
- allow for use of a notetaker
- tape record, especially review sessions, with prior teacher approval
- shorten assignments (odd or even problems, etc.) so as not to assign too much hand-written work
- allow extra time to copy assignments, complete tests worksheets, etc.

Notetaking

If the student has poor notetaking skills:
- instruct how to make an outline or mind-mapping
- allow use of notetakers
- teacher supplies copy of notes
- portable computers
- supply copy of another student's notes
- allow use of a tape recorder

Test-Taking

If the student has poor test taking skills:
- review methods of studying for different types of tests
- give test in quiet place
- provide a reader to read test aloud for student with reading disability
- allow student to dictate answers to a scribe
- change format of test (multiple choice, true/false, essay, fill in the blank)—use format easiest for student
- allow choice of how to present knowledge of information
- allow student to write answers directly on test instead of "scantron sheet" answer sheet

Unhappy in School or Elsewhere

If the student seems unhappy with school, talks about dropping out, or seem unhappy in general:
- be supportive and encourage positive thinking
- emphasize student's strengths and abilities

- provide frequent praise and recognition of success
- find ways the student can succeed
- assign student to be peer teacher or assist with younger students
- praise in public; reprimand in private
- be aware of stress and reduce work load if appropriate
- mark correct responses on tests/assignments, not errors
- prohibit any humiliation or teasing from other students
- arrange for meeting with parents and other teachers to find ways to help student feel better about school and/or self
- consider possibility of depression and refer for help

Accommodations are Rights, Not Favors

The accommodations listed above can be tremendously beneficial to students with ADHD. Often they don't require extra teacher time, and teachers are generally willing to provide extra help to students who need it. They are especially interested in helping when the student's parents make an extra effort.

While many of the accommodations listed earlier can be implemented in school informally, it is often best to have a formal accommodation plan written for the student. If your child's ADHD impacts upon his performance in school to the extent that he is considered disabled, he may be entitled to special services under Section 504 of the Rehabilitation Act. This act requires the school to provide accommodations for students with documented disabilities. Usually schools will develop a 504 plan for the student, which contains a list of accommodations and services the school will provide.

Going through the procedures required to develop a formal 504 plan rather than just having an informal agreement with one or more teachers has several advantages:
- all of the student's teachers will be knowledgeable about the student's disability and accommodations that can be provided to help him;
- a case manager will be assigned to monitor the student's progress in school and to see if the accommodations in the plan are effective;
- periodic meetings with teachers, parents, and the student will be scheduled to monitor progress;
- the student may be eligible for additional services once classified as having a disability;
- the school is required by law to follow certain procedures that safeguard your child and ensure he receives appropriate services.

Fortunately, with a combination of support, parent and teacher cooperation, and the identification of a student's strengths and weaknesses, teens with ADHD can indeed find success in school. Furthermore, if the student plans to go on to higher education, colleges and universities will also work with the student to provide accommodations as well.

Summary

Accommodations at school can greatly benefit students with ADHD. Accommodations can be made by teachers to helps students who are having difficulty with attention, organization, activity level, academic skills, mood, behavior, completing homework, etc. A list of over 200 accommodations was provided. Many of these are fairly easy to implement in the classroom and at home.

Teachers are generally more than willing to provide additional help to students who need it, especially if the student and the parents are cooperative and supportive. Parents need to take appropriate steps to initiate help for their adolescent. Meetings with teachers and school administrators may result in an evaluation of the student for disability services based on his having ADHD. If the school determines that the student is disabled, a 504 plan may be developed, which outlines specific accommodations the school will provide to the student.

Parents are encouraged to work closely with the school to monitor the student's progress and to provide their input and support.

13 Study Strategies To Improve Learning

"True education is to learn *how* to think, not *what* to think."…Krishnamurti

This chapter reviews several study strategies which can help students understand *how* to learn more effectively in school. While parents may benefit from the information presented, you should encourage your teenage son or daughter to look over the strategies presented in this chapter. For more detailed information about study strategies, students are referred to the book, *Study Strategies Made Easy* by Leslie Davis, Sandi Sirotowitz, and Harvey C. Parker.

Organization

Students who organize their work, their time, and their belongings often do well in school. Whereas, students who have trouble with such things as keeping track of assignments, scheduling their time, procrastinating, and cramming instead of regular studying are going to be at greater risk for academic trouble.

Disorganization is often cited by secondary school teachers as the biggest problem their students face. This is especially true in high school where many students have several classes, a busy after school schedule, and even a part-time job to manage. Students who are not well organized can easily lose track of what they are supposed to do and when.

This strategy involves organization of school supplies, time management, and planning for long-term projects and assignments.

Organizing School Supplies

Let's start with the basics. The student should have adequate school supplies available for them to study properly and complete assignments. Below is a list of the minimum supplies a serious student should have on hand. Encourage your teenager to look over this list to determine whether anything is needed.

School Supply Checklist

NOTEBOOKS
- ❏ one three-ring notebook (2" or 3" rings) for all subjects
- ❏ spiral notebooks, one per subject
- ❏ dividers with pockets, a different color for each class
- ❏ a case for highlighters, pens, pencils, etc.

ASSIGNMENT BOOKS
- ❏ a student planbook
- ❏ an appointment book
- ❏ a calendar to schedule work on assignments
- ❏ electronic organizer

RESOURCES
- ❏ a dictionary
- ❏ a thesaurus
- ❏ an atlas
- ❏ access to an encyclopedia or to the Internet

INFORMATION STORAGE SYSTEMS
- ❏ index cards and a box to put them in
- ❏ a three-ring notebook with dividers
- ❏ folders for each class to store papers
- ❏ a crate to hold file folders for each class

OTHER SUPPLIES
- ❏ writing tools—pens, pencils, colored pencils, crayons, and erasers
- ❏ a pencil sharpener
- ❏ a ruler, compass, protractor
- ❏ markers and highlighters
- ❏ glue stick, scotch tape
- ❏ scissors, hole punch,
- ❏ stapler and staples
- ❏ hole punch
- ❏ paper clips
- ❏ rubber bands
- ❏ reinforcers for notebook paper

Time Management

In a perfect world, we would all plan our days in advance so we would know exactly what we had to do and when. However, most of us are slaves to time rather than masters of time. We either run out of it or waste it. If time were money (as the saying goes), maybe we would be more careful about how we spend it.

People with ADHD, in particular, have a hard time managing time. They don't seem to judge time well and they don't seem to plan well. Therefore, time management is an extremely important strategy for adolescents with ADHD to learn.

Daily, Weekly, Monthly Planning

As a first step in managing time, it is useful to plan for the immediate future (daily planning), short-term future (weekly planning) and long-term future (monthly planning). Most time management programs encourage people to use planners, organizers, calendars, appointment books, or some such system to keep track of how their time will be used.

Daily Planning

Adolescents should be able to prioritize their activities and responsibilities for the day. They should be encouraged to write daily assignments and activities on a "do list" each day.

1. List the things that are necessary to be accomplished first.
2. Prioritize each item on the list by assigning it a number (1 most important to 5 least important).
3. Cross off each item on the list as it is completed. This will give you a sense of accomplishment.
4. Try to complete the "do list" each day. What doesn't get done should be put on the "do list" for the following day.
5. Look over the "do list" each evening and make a new one for the next day.

Today's Do List		
Date: *November 6th*		
Priority	Activity or Asssignment	Due
1	*Work on history paper*	*11/9*
1	*Do math homework pages 125-7*	*11/7*
1	*Report to work by 5:30*	*11/6*
2	*Review notes for English test*	*11/12*
3	*Go shopping after school*	*11/6*
4	*Call Mike to make plans for Fri.*	*11/6*

Weekly Planning

A weekly planner can be use to map out time commitments for the week. Fixed activities scheduled for the week should be written down. These could include class time and time set aside for homework and studying, work time, or any other set appointments. Add changeable activities such as appointments, errands, or special events to the schedule as needed.

Weekly Planner

Time	Monday	Tuesday	Wednesday	Thursday	Friday
8:00					
8:30					
8:00					
9:30					
10:00					
10:30					
11:00					
11:30					
Noon					
12:30					
1:00					
1:30					
2:00					
2:30					
3:00					
3:30					
4:00					
4:30					
5:00					
5:30					
6:00					
6:30					
7:00					
7:30					
8:00					
8:30					
9:00					
10:00					
10:30					
11:00					
11:30					
12:00					

The Weekly Planner could be scanned to indicate blocks of free time that could be used for study, recreational activities or other jobs that need to be accomplished. A copy of the Weekly Planner can be found in the Appendix and may be reproduced for personal use.

Monthly Planning

A monthly calendar with daily squares large enough to write notes is an ideal way to keep track of activities, assignments, study times, tests, deadlines, and appointments that are planned throughout the month. Items should be transferred from the weekly planner to the monthly calendar and vice versa. This will provide an excellent way to scan a month's activities at a glance.

Other Time Management Tips

- Make good use of waiting time.
  It is estimated that people spend as much as an hour a day just waiting for something to happen. Use this time effectively. Carry a book, class notes, make calls, or catch up on homework while waiting.

- Traveling time can be time well spent.
  Most people spend a considerable amount of time each day traveling from one place to another. When driving or taking public transportation, listen to tapes that are important to your field of study, use the time for reading (if someone else is driving), or review study notes to better prepare for future tests.

- Spend most of the time you have on yourself. Saying "no" to others who request one thing or another from you will be necessary to stick to your personal schedule and reach goals which have been set.

- Stay out of the habit of procrastinating.
  Try not to waste time by procrastinating. Get in the habit of starting things right away. Stop making excuses for getting things done. Recognize times you say phrases such as: "I'll do it later," "soon," "when I can fit it in," "not now," "tomorrow," "next week," and so on. Those who are truly committed to doing something either do it right away if time allows or schedule it in their daily, weekly, or monthly planner to be done later. Procrastination just keeps things "hanging over your head" and creates unnecessary stress. Challenge the reasons why you procrastinate. Fear, avoidance, laziness, self-doubt are common reasons for procrastination. Once these issues are faced, there will no longer be a reason to procrastinate.

- Beat deadlines before they beat you.

  Be aware of deadlines. Set a deadline for tasks that need accomplishing and try to stick to it. Break complicated tasks down and set a deadline for completing each part. An example of how to do this can be found in the following section on organizing long-term projects.

Organizing Long-Term Research Projects

Organizing long-term research projects is difficult for most students, but it's especially hard for those with ADHD. When a term paper or project isn't due for a while, students tend to procrastinate and then panic as the due date approaches. By planning long-term assignments in advance the student can break large projects down into more manageable steps. In their book, *Study Strategies Made Easy,* Leslie Davis, Sandi Sirotowitz, and Harvey Parker explain a step-by-step program students can use to do long-term projects such as research papers. They discuss three main stages of preparing a research paper: the pre-write, the first write, and the home stretch

The Pre-Write

This stage involves choosing an appropriate topic. The student does preliminary research on the topic chosen to determine if there is enough information available to fulfill the requirements of the assignment. This is also a good way to see if the topic is interesting. Once a topic is selected, the student collects sources (i.e., books, magazines, on-line information, periodicals, etc.)

The First Write

In this stage the student brainstorms more specific topics that she or he would like to include in the research paper. Then a thesis statement—a sentence that states the central theme of the paper is written. Next, the student decides the order in which facts should be presented and a rough outline of the paper is written. Notecards are prepared from the sources that were selected earlier. These note cards are sorted according to the outline. The student is now ready to prepare a rough draft of the paper.

The Final Write

In this stage the student reviews and revises the rough draft to make sure it contains all the points the student wants to make and backs those points up with facts taken from sources. The student makes certain the order of information is correct, the paper reads fluently, and the information is presented in a way that will be easy for the reader to understand. The paper is checked for mistakes in spelling, grammar, and word usage. Then the rough draft is rewritten, edited by someone other than the writer to check again for spelling, grammar, and word usage, and a final copy is prepared.

Knowing Your Best Learning Style

Some students learn best by listening, others learn best by watching, and still others learn best by doing. These three learning styles are called auditory, visual, and kinesthetic. It is helpful for a student to know which style or combination of styles he prefers and use this when learning.

For example, if your adolescent was given a list of words and their definitions to memorize, which approach would suit him or her best?

Visual Approach

- reads the words and definitions over and over.
- closes his eyes and "sees" them mentally.
- forms pictures of the words and their meanings.

Auditory Approach

- recites words and definitions to self.
- tapes words and definitions and listens to them repeatedly.
- listens as teacher or parents explain meanings.

Kinesthetic Approach

- writes the words and definitions.
- draws pictures to remember meanings.
- walks or moves around the room while concentrating on words and definitions.

It is also a good idea for students to be aware of the study environment in which they concentrate best. Most people become accustomed to studying in certain settings, at a specific time of day, and in a way that they feel most comfortable. Educators used to believe that ADHD students were more distractible than non-ADHD students and recommended they study in quiet, distraction-free environments. For some ADHD students this is true, for others it isn't. In fact, many people with ADHD say they concentrate better when there is background noise (i.e., music or television in the background). Some say they are more productive studying in the morning while others prefer evening. They may vary in the way they study as well (e.g., sitting up in bed and reading, sitting at a desk and writing notes, etc.).

Your Biological Clock

Part of knowing your learning style is also realizing when your mind and body learn best. Determine the time of day you study most effectively. For some people this is in the morning, while others have their peak times of alertness and concentration at night. Once you've figured out which time of the day is your best learning time, take advantage of this information. Study during your most alert time. If possible, try to schedule your most difficult classes when your mind is working the best.

Reading Comprehension Strategies

Reading comprehension is vitally important to success in school. In high school, students must be able to read and understand textbook chapters, reference material, novels, and other sources of information with reasonable speed and accuracy. There are several strategies that students can use to improve reading comprehension. These strategies are fully described in *Study Strategies Made Easy* and are summarized below.

Read to Understand

This strategy emphasizes the importance of picking out the topic, main idea, and supporting details of a reading passage. By organizing this information, the reader will be able to answer questions of where, when, why, and how about the passage and writes the topic, main idea, and supporting details down for notetaking.

Topic: _____

Main Idea: _____

_____

Supporting Details:

1. _____
2. _____
3. _____

Practice Paraphrasing

After reading a passage, the student tries to paraphrase what the author is trying to convey. In his own words, the student should be able to recite the topic, main idea, and supporting details of the passage.

Identify Signals in a Passage

Authors use certain words, punctuation, and type styles to signal something important in the passage. By understanding the signals authors use, students can extract information more quickly. For example, phrases that signal that an idea is an overall concept or result are:

in conclusion   thus
in summary   because
the major point   consequently
as a result   therefore

Authors provide cues in their presentation of information that signal important information. Some presentation cues are:

words in bold print
words in italics
<u>words underlined</u>
words printed in larger type

Learn New Vocabulary

Reading comprehension relies heavily on one's understanding of the vocabulary in a passage. Students encounter many new words in subjects such as social studies, science, English, math and foreign language. The student should have a system of writing down new words and their definitions for study later.

In one system for learning new vocabulary words described in *Study Strategies Made Easy,* the student divides a notebook paper into three columns. The vocabulary word is written in the first column, the definition in the second column, and the third column is folded over the second so the student can test himself on the definitions.

In a second system, the student uses index cards and illustrations of word definitions to memorize meanings. The index card system is shown below.

Index Card

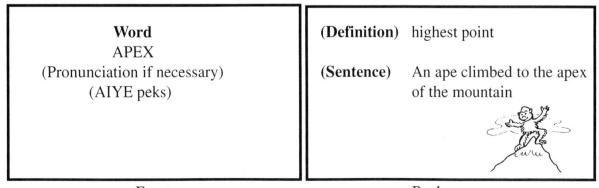

Front   Back

Learn New Words Through Reading

Reading is a sure-fire way to build a wider vocabulary. When reading, try to figure out the meaning of new words by the context of the sentence in which they are used. Keep a dictionary close by to look up definitions. Don't rely on context alone to figure out the meaning of an unfamiliar word.

• Write the dictionary definition of the word on an index card and keep a file box of new vocabulary words.

• From the dictionary definition make up another definition in your own words. Add this to the index card.

• Take a moment and memorize the definition.

• Review the vocabulary index cards each day until the words have been memorized.

Get into the habit of reading well-written magazines and newspapers such as *The New York Times, The New Yorker, Time, Newsweek* and others.

Use the SQ4R Method for Reading Comprehension

The SQ4R method for reading comprehension is frequently taught by teachers to improve reading comprehension. SQ4R stands for Survey, Question, Read, "Rite" (write), Recite, Review. Follow these steps when using SQ4R:

1. Survey the entire reading selection. Get an overview of the material to be read by looking over the main headings and subheadings.
2. Make up questions about the information surveyed.
3. Read the sections entirely.
4. "Rite" (write) answers to the questions you made up in step 2.
5. Recite the information (to yourself and out loud, if possible).
6. Review your work.

Notetaking Strategies

It is just not possible for a student to remember everything a teacher says during a class period. Even attentive listeners can recall the main ideas of a lecture for only a few days and details are forgotten even sooner. Taking good notes in class or from material read from a textbook or other source can be key to successful learning.

Some general rules to keep in mind for notetaking follow below.

• Keep your notes well organized. Maintain all notes for a particular class in a spiral notebook or section of a looseleaf binder dedicated to that class only.

• Write only information that is important in your notes. Listen for clues the instructor may give to signal important information.

• Organize your notes by main topics and supporting ideas and details.

- Highlight or underline any new vocabulary words or terms.
- Review notes as soon after class as possible. Fill in any gaps.
- Look over notes each day and again before the next class session.
- Ask permission to tape record a class lecture if notetaking is too difficult.

In *Study Strategies Made Easy*, the authors discuss eight different notetaking strategies a student can use when taking notes in class or from reading material. These strategies include simple outlining, mind mapping, combo notes, using abbreviations for speed writing, using recall questions to turn notes into study sheets, improving listening power, taking notes from lectures, and adding textbook notes to lecture notes. Several of these strategies are described below.

Simple Outlining, Mind-Mapping, and Combo Notes

Students may choose to organize their notes in either a simple outline format, in a more informal format known as mind-mapping, or in a combination outline/mind-mapping format known as combo notes.

Most students know how to outline, but they often need to learn how to find the main idea, supporting details and sub-details of information in a chapter or lecture.

When they use mind-mapping, students can create a "visual map" of how supporting details relate to main ideas. Mind maps are often more fun to use than outlines and offer the student the freedom to organize information in a personalized way. A sample mind map is shown on the opposite page.

A student can use combo notes to organize information in notes. The combo note is a combination of a simple outline and a mind-map. It is also constructed from main ideas, supporting details, and sub-details found in a passage or lecture. Main ideas may be boxed, supporting details starred, and sub-details checked.

Use Abbreviations for Speed Writing

Using abbreviations in notetaking increases speed. A student should become familiar with commonly used abbreviations and should be encouraged to develop his or her own system of abbreviations.

#	number	≥	equal to or greater than	cont	continue
%	percent	≤	equal to or less than	def	definition
$	money, dollars	→	to or toward	eg.	example
+	plus, and, more	∴	therefore	govt	government
−	negative, not, no	±	about, more or less	pp	pages
=	equal	@	at, per, each	re	regarding
≠	unequal	amt	amount	w/	with
>	greater than	asso	association, associate	w/o	without
<	less than	bio	biology, biography	intro	introduce

Use Recall Questions

A student can turn his notes into study sheets by making up recall questions in the margins. Recall questions ask who, what, where, when, why, and how. They can be valuable aids in studying and helping the student remember factual information. Recall questions can be used with simple outlining, mind-mapping, or combo notes.

Improve Listening Skills

Students can improve their listening skills in class and take more accurate notes if they prepare ahead of time. Students should preview the textbook chapter the night before the lecture so they have an idea of what to listen for and what to write down. Taking notes will actually help students focus on the lecture. In this way, students become active participants instead of passive observers. Students should also pay attention to the lecturer's verbal, presentation and body language cues to determine if a piece of information is important.

Memorization Strategies

Getting good test scores can depend a great deal on the student's ability to memorize. Information is usually stored in our memory for immediate recall, short-term recall, or long-term recall.
*   Immediate memory enables us to recall information for a brief time that we have just seen or heard (e.g., when you ask information for a telephone number).
*   Short-term memory enables us to briefly retain facts for a few hours or a few days.
*   Long-term memory enables us to retain and recall information much later.

Although we don't purposely direct information into one of these storage systems, our brain seems to know how we intend to use the information we are remembering and the period it will need to be stored for recall.

An important strategy to improve recall on tests is to make sure memory is not overloaded with unnecessary facts. Some students take a "shotgun" approach to memorizing information for a test. They don't pay attention to cues a teacher may give about what information is most important, and they don't distinguish between important and unimportant information in a chapter. They try to memorize just about everything. This usually doesn't work well because our capacity for memorizing information is limited, and we don't want to use valuable memory space for unnecessary facts.

Study Strategies Made Easy reviews nine different memory techniques to improve recall: acrostics, acronyms, charting, visual emphasis, visualization, association, word linking, story linking, and rehearsal. A few of these are briefly described below.

Acrostics

Acrostics refers to the use of mnemonics to improve recall. A mnemonic is a trick that helps you remember something specific. For example, the mnemonic to remember the planets in order—Mercury, Venus, Earth, Mars, Jupiter, Saturn, Uranus, Neptune, and Pluto—My Very Educated Mother Just Served Us Nine Pickles. Or, to memorize the order of mathematical operations—Parentheses, Exponents, Multiply, Divide, Add, Subtract—Please Excuse My Dear Aunt Sally.

Acronyms

An acronym is a short version of an acrostic. An acronym just uses the first letter of each concept to be learned to form one word. For example, to remember the Great Lakes—**H**uron, **O**ntario, **M**ichigan, **E**rie, **S**uperior—use the acronym **HOMES.**

Visualization

We can improve recall by forming a mental picture of something we want to remember. To remember a word and its definition, look at the word and its meaning and try to think of a picture that would convey the meaning and the word together. For example—**insuperable** means "unable to overcome." A student could picture a soup can trying to jump over a wall. The soup can could not <u>come over</u> the wall. This is reflected in the following picture.

Note: From Leslie Davis, Sandi Sirotowitz, and Harvey C. Parker (1996), *Study Strategies Made Easy.* Florida: Specialty Press, In.c. Copyright 1996 by Leslie Davis and Sandi Sirotowitz. Reprinted by permission.

Association

Another strategy to improve recall is association. Try to find a connection between separate facts. The more silly the connection, the better the chance of remembering it. Look at the examples below which illustrate this strategy which is more fully explained in *Study Strategies Made Easy.*

Hartford, Connecticut   **Connected hearts**

Helena, Montana   **Helen** climbs a **mountain**.

Columbus, Ohio   **Columbus** said, **"Oh, Hi!"**

Test-Taking Strategies

Throughout middle school and high school, a student will take different tests in many different forms. Good test grades are essential to making a high final grade in most subjects. There are a number of strategies a student can use to improve the way he prepares for tests and answers test questions.

Read Instructions Carefully

Probably the most basic strategy, but the one that is most important, is to make sure that all instructions are read carefully before answering test questions. This is particularly important for students with ADHD who tend to rush through tests without carefully reading the instructions. It may be good practice to encourage the student to underline the instructions while reading them to ensure they are fully read.

Learn from Old Tests

Another useful test-taking strategy is to make good use of old tests. One of the most valuable study tools a student has is an old test returned by the teacher. Students who analyze their mistakes on past tests will likely improve their scores on future tests. If information was important enough for a teacher to ask about it once before, they are likely to ask about it again. Performance on past tests can also tell a student the areas that need further reviewing in notes or in a book chapter.

Avoid Cramming for a Test

Pacing your study for tests rather than cramming the night before is usually an effective strategy for test-taking—especially if the test is a mid-term or final exam. When a student crams for a test, they literally try to stuff as much information into their brain as they can the night or morning before a test. Unfortunately, cramming only works for very brief periods of time and for very small amounts of information, so it is not a very useful way to study. Students will do much better if they get a head start in studying by trying to cover some of the test material a week or two in advance.

Summary

Knowledge of study strategies can be a great asset in learning. Unfortunately, schools rarely have a separate curriculum that teaches study strategies. Students incidentally learn these skills throughout school.

A number of different strategies to improve organization, reading comprehension, notetaking, memorization, and test-taking were discussed. By learning these strategies, students with ADHD may be able to improve school performance. Encourage your adolescent to develop the habit of using these strategies for homework, test preparation, and projects. A more detailed description of these and other study strategies can be found in the text, *Study Strategies Made Easy* by Leslie Davis, Sandi Sirotowitz, and Harvey C. Parker.

14 Social Skills Training

Jennifer is a 15-year-old high school sophomore. She gets good grades in school and is respected by her teachers and liked by her friends. However, Jennifer is extremely timid and her parents feel she is missing out socially because of her shyness. Jennifer has been shy all of her life. In elementary school, her teachers would tell her parents she was the perfect student, but too quiet. She had a few close friends while growing up, but since she started high school, it seems that her friends met new people, and they now spend less time with Jennifer. Jennifer rarely calls friends on the phone to make plans, and she is alone most weekends.

David is anything but quiet. He is loud and boisterous and can easily get on your nerves if you're with him for more than 10 minutes. He never seems to notice when others are irritated with him. His parents say he was born with a megaphone in his mouth. They often go to another room when David is home just to get some peace and quiet. Unfortunately, David usually finds them and keeps right on talking. His parents hoped that when he got into high school he'd become more aware of his behavior and would quiet down. No such luck!

Frank's biggest problem is his temper. He can't ever seem to control his anger. When he gets mad, his younger brother and sister run for cover. In elementary school he frequently visited the principal's office. In high school he was disciplined twice for fighting. Now he has a job at a service station after school, and he's on probation for arguing with a customer.

Jennifer, David, and Frank are all having problems with social skills and might benefit from social skills training. Social skills training involves educating youth about social skills and teaching them to use learned skills in their social interactions. As children enter adolescence, they must become more assertive, more comfortable interacting with the opposite sex, and must develop skills to negotiate with parents, teachers, and others. They will have to advocate for themselves in different situations, deal with authority figures appropriately, maintain control over their behavior, and show empathy and compassion for others to make friends.

Social skills training may be particularly important for children and adolescents with disabilities such as ADHD. For example, people with ADHD may have more trouble holding conversations because they may not be able to listen attentively to a speaker or they may interrupt others too often. They may have difficulty waiting their turn in games or in organized activities which require giving others a chance at equal participation. They may not be able to control their temper when they feel they have been wronged, causing them to lash out inappropriately. Social skills training may help them recognize when their behavior is inappropriate, and they may benefit by learning more appropriate, prosocial behavior.

During the past 20 years, social skills training was not taught in school. Teaching social skills was regarded as the parents' job rather than one for teachers. However, with the increase in child and adolescent aggression and violent behavior in our nation's schools and communities, programs were developed for educators to work with youth to improve self-control and social behavior. Youth now can receive group training to help them learn social skills. There are a number of social skills training programs available.

Dr. Hill Walker and his colleagues developed a social skills program called *ACCESS* or the *Adolescent Curriculum for Communication and Effective Social Skills*. It was designed to teach 31 social skills in three areas: relating to peers, relating to adults, and relating to yourself. Specific skills across these areas include listening, greeting, offering assistance, getting an adult's attention, disagreeing with adults, following classroom rules, taking pride in your appearance, being organized, and using self-control.

Arnold Goldstein and Ellen McGinnis, in their training model to teach social skills to adolescents known as *Skillstreaming the Adolescent*, identified 50 social skills within six different categories.

Group 1: Beginning Social Skills
1. Listening
2. Starting a conversation
3. Having a conversation
4. Asking a question
5. Saying thank you
6. Introducing yourself
7. Introducing other people
8. Giving a compliment

Group II: Advanced Social Skills
9. Asking for help
10. Joining in
11. Giving instructions
12. Following instructions
13. Apologizing

14. Convincing others

Group III: Skills for Dealing
with Feelings
15. Knowing your feelings
16. Expressing your feelings
17. Understanding the feelings of others
18. Dealing with someone else's anger
19. Expressing affection
20. Dealing with fear
21. Rewarding yourself
22. Asking permission
23. Sharing something
24. Helping others
25. Negotiating
26. Using self-control
27. Standing up for your rights
28. Responding to teasing
29. Avoiding trouble with others
30. Keeping out of fights

Group V: Skills for Dealing with Stress
31. Making a complaint
32. Answering a complaint
33. Being a good sport
34. Dealing with embarrassment
35. Dealing with being left out
36. Standing up for a friend
37. Responding to persuasion
38. Responding to failure
39. Dealing with contradictory messages
40. Dealing with an accusation
41. Getting ready for a difficult conversation
42. Dealing with group pressure

Group VI: Planning Skills
43. Deciding on something to do
44. Deciding what caused a problem
45. Setting a goal
46. Deciding on your abilities
47. Gathering information
48. Arranging problems by importance

49. Making a decision
50. Concentrating on a task

The core training procedures involved in the *Skillstreaming* program are modeling, role-playing, performance feedback, and generalization training. Trainers lead individuals in the group through nine steps to learn a skill, practice using it, and receive feedback from group members during role-play exercises.

A program called *Job-related Social Skills (JRSS)* covers a number of skills: prioritizing job responsibilities, understanding directions, giving instructions, asking questions, asking permission, asking for help, accepting help, offering help, requesting information, taking messages, engaging in a conversation, giving compliments, convincing others, apologizing, accepting criticism, and responding to complaints. Skills are taught using direct instruction, active participation of the students, rehearsal, modeling, and role playing.

Training Programs You Can Use at Home

Dr. Berthold Berg has developed a series of games and workbooks that are designed to train social skills in older children and adolescents. His programs can be used with the guidance of a health care professional, educator, or parent. Similar to the social skills programs described above, Dr. Berg identifies specific social skills and provides an inventory to assess the individual's current use of these skills in social interactions.

These are introduced to the adolescent in a game-like format and reinforced with a workbook the adolescent can write in to strengthen skill knowledge. Through playing the game and completing the exercises in the workbook, children learn to identify the things they say to themselves during social interactions. They identify what Berg refers to as "negative self-talk," which he believes mediates behavior and causes us to act in negative ways to others or to ourselves. The games and exercises encourage children to replace negative self-talk with "positive self-talk," which is more constructive and likely to lead to self-confidence, better self-control, and positive interactions with others. His games and workbooks also focus on teaching children to say things to themselves that make them feel competent, expect success in what they try to do, not worry, accept making mistakes, give themselves credit, and compliment themselves.

In the *Social Skills Game* and the *Social Skills Workbook,* Berg lists four categories of skills containing specific behaviors under each:

1. Making friends
   Asking a question
   Giving a compliment
   Introducing yourself
   Listening
   Starting a conversation

2. Cooperating with peers
   Following rules
   Joining in
   Sharing
   Suggesting an activity
   Taking turns

3. Responding positively to peers
   Accepting a compliment
   Helping peers in trouble
   Offering help
   Showing concern for peer
   Standing up for peers

4. Communicating needs
   Asking for help
   Asking to borrow another's property
   Expressing negative feelings
   Expressing positive feelings
   Getting attention appropriately

In the *Anger Control Game* and the *Anger Control Workbook*, Berg lists six skills for anger control.
1. Knowing when others are being aggressive
2. Knowing feelings related to anger
3. Knowing how victims feel
4. Knowing how others view aggression
5. Talking to yourself to control anger
6. Looking for alternatives to aggression

Generalization of Skill Training to the Real World

Teaching adolescents social skills is not difficult. Getting them to apply what they have learned and to use these skills in the real world is another matter. The results have been very disappointing.

Linda and Nick Elksnin explain that to be socially competent, a person must be able to determine when a social skill would be appropriate to use in a given social situation and <u>must be motivated to use it</u>. The Elksnins differentiate between a social skill problem being the result of an acquisition deficit or a performance deficit. Social skills problems may be the result of a person not knowing what to do within a social situation—an acquisition deficit. Or, social skills problems may be the result of a person not doing what they know—a performance deficit.

After receiving social skills training, an adolescent may know what skill to use and how to use it within a given social situation, but may fail to use the skill correctly, if at all. If they have ADHD, they may not be able to regulate their behavior sufficiently to use the social skill, even if they know what it is.

An ADHD adolescent may know the appropriate negotiation skill to use to ask his parent for permission to stay out past his curfew. He ,may not, however, be capable of controlling his frustration if his parent doesn't grant permission. At the slightest sign of a negative response, the ADHD adolescent's emotions may erupt into an aggressive attack. The parent may respond aggressively, and the conversation erupts into an argument. Instead of getting permission to stay out later, the parent may punish the teen by grounding him that night.

Many social skills training programs try to build into their programs ways to increase the likelihood that a trainee will use the social skill in their daily life. In the *Skillstreaming the Adolescent* program, Arnold Goldstein and Ellen McGinnis provide training to parents as well as the adolescents. Parent training groups meet separately from the adolescent group. Parents are instructed to use the trained social skill in the presence of their adolescent son or daughter. They strengthen the skill for their adolescent by modeling. Parents are also trained to provide positive reinforcement to the adolescent when they observe a social skill being used properly.

Parents can help their adolescent learn appropriate social skills by:

1. Serving as good role models and behaving in socially appropriate ways themselves. Children and adolescents learn what they live. Parents who model appropriate social behavior are more likely to promote appropriate social behavior in their children. This is particularly true when a specific social skill is targeted for learning. Make an effort to model use of the social skill as much as possible.

2. Recognizing when their adolescent is using a social skill well and providing positive reinforcement to the adolescent. This will strengthen the use of the social skill in the future.

3. Calmly and constructively pointing out inappropriate social behavior and suggesting a more appropriate replacement behavior. Reminding your teenager about appropriate social behavior may precipitate annoyance from your son or daughter. It is important to couch reminders in a positive, non-condescending way.

4. Encouraging their adolescent to use problem-solving strategies. Through use of the problem-solving strategies discussed in Chapter 10, adolescents could learn to successfully resolve potential conflicts with peers in an appropriate manner.

Summary

Many adolescents with ADHD would benefit from learning and using appropriate social skills. Social behavior is often inappropriate in those with ADHD. Hyperactive-impulsive people tend to interrupt others, shift topics in conversations frequently, intrude into other's "space," and have difficulty controlling behavior and emotions. Other people notice this behavior within a short time of meeting someone with ADHD and quickly form a negative impression. People with ADHD—inattentive type, tend to be more quiet and passive. They would benefit from learning and using social skills that would enable them to be more assertive in their communications with others.

There are a number of social skills training programs available. These programs are usually run in small social skills groups and are offered in schools or in counseling settings. There are some programs available for adolescents to use at home, guided by a therapist, teacher, or parent. Parents can reinforce the use of social skills by appropriately modeling skills to their child and by praising their adolescent's positive behavior.

15 Parents as Advocates: Legal Rights of Students with ADHD

Every parent of a child with a disability must be an advocate for their child in school and elsewhere. To be an effective advocate in school, it is important that a parent:

- know about their child's disability and how it affects their education;
- . understand the system of laws that exist to protect children with disabilities;
- be familiar with how schools function and the steps that are involved in accessing appropriate services; and
- communicate effectively with others.

Being your child's advocate doesn't mean you are the school's adversary. Educators are advocates for students as well. The parents and the school should work together to achieve results that are in the best interests of the child.

Your Adolescent's Legal Rights

Getting an appropriate education in our country is a right, not a favor. Laws such as the Individuals with Disabilities in Education Act (IDEA), Section 504 of the Rehabilitation Act of 1973, and the Americans with Disabilities Act (ADA) exist in the United States to protect people with disabling conditions from discrimination and to improve educational and other services available to them.

These federal laws ensure that disabled persons, regardless of the nature and severity of their disability, be provided a free appropriate public education (FAPE). The laws also mandate that disabled students be educated with non-disabled students to the maximum extent appropriate to their needs. Furthermore, they stipulate that state and local educational agencies must take steps to identify and locate all unserved disabled children and must evaluate such individuals to avoid inappropriate education stemming from misclassification. The laws also require that procedural safeguards are established so parents and guardians can take an active role regarding the evaluation and placement of their children.

The Individuals with Disabilities Education Act (IDEA)

IDEA has its roots in the Education for All Handicapped Children Act of 1975. IDEA has been amended various times, most recently in 1997. The purpose of IDEA is to provide financial aid to states to ensure adequate and appropriate services for disabled children ages birth to 21.

To be eligible for special education under IDEA, the child must meet the criteria for eligibility contained in one of the eligibility categories in the law. These categories include serious emotional disturbance, learning disabilities, retardation, traumatic brain injury, autism, vision and hearing impairments, physical disabilities, and other health impairments. If the child meets the criteria of one or more of these categories, requires special education or related services, and his or her disability adversely affects educational performance, the child may be eligible to receive services.

Section 504 of the Rehabilitation Act of 1973

In 1973, the Vocational Rehabilitation Act became law. As part of the act, Congress enacted Section 504, which provided that individuals cannot be discriminated against solely on the basis of their disability. Section 504 became the first federal civil rights law to protect the rights of persons with disabilities.

Section 504 applies to all divisions of state government and all public or private agencies, institutions, and organizations that are the recipients of federal financial assistance. All local school systems in the United States are subject to Section 504 regulations if they receive federal aid through grant programs such as vocational education, Chapter 1, special education, and food/nutrition programs.

To be eligible for protection under Section 504 an individual with a disability means any person who (1) has a physical or mental impairment that substantially limits one or more of such person's major life activities, or (2) has a record of such an impairment, or (3) is regarded as having such an impairment.

The Americans with Disabilities Act of 1990 (ADA)

The ADA guarantees disabled people access to employment, transportation, telecommunications, public accommodations and public services. The ADA expands on the concepts and protections introduced by Section 504 of the Rehabilitation Act of 1973. It provides comprehensive federal civil rights protections for people with disabilities in the private and public sectors.

ADHD and Federal Law

ADHD has never been listed as a discreet disability category under IDEA and as a result students with ADHD have always had a difficult time accessing appropriate educational services. The U.S. Department of Education agreed that there was significant confusion among state and local education agencies about whether children with ADHD were covered under the IDEA at all. To rectify this, the Department of Education issued a memorandum in 1991, which clarified the department's policy on ADHD to chief state school officers around the country. This policy clarification explained that ADHD was a condition that could be covered under IDEA under the category of "Other Health Impaired" in instances where the "ADD is a chronic or acute health problem that results in limited alertness, which adversely affects educational performance." It emphasized state and local education agencies' responsibility to address the needs of children with ADHD both within general and special education.

The policy clarification also indicated that even if a child did not qualify for special education and related services under IDEA, the requirements of Section 504 of the Rehabilitation Act of 1973 could apply. Section 504 provided that individuals cannot be discriminated against solely on the basis of their disability. This federal law requires public school districts to provide a free, appropriate public education to every "qualified handicapped person" residing within their jurisdiction. The school must conduct an evaluation to determine whether or not the child is "handicapped" as defined by the law. If the child is found to have "a physical or mental impairment, which substantially limits a major life activity (e.g., learning)," then the local education agency must make an "individualized determination of the child's educational needs for regular or special education or related aids or services." The Office of Civil Rights (OCR) is the federal agency within the Department of Education that enforces Section 504. OCR has ruled that ADHD children are "qualified handicapped persons" under Section 504 if their ability to learn or to otherwise benefit from their education is substantially limited due to ADHD.

Section 504 also states that the child's education must be provided in the regular classroom, "unless it is demonstrated that education in the regular environment with the use of supplementary aids and services cannot be achieved satisfactorily." The department encouraged state and local education agencies to take necessary steps to make accommodations within the regular education classroom to meet the needs of students with ADHD. The policy clarification emphasized the important role that teachers in regular education have in providing help to students with ADHD. It also emphasized that steps should be taken to train regular education teachers and other personnel to develop their awareness about ADHD.

Thus, regardless of whether an ADHD child meets eligibility guidelines to receive federally funded special education programs (under IDEA), Section 504 of the Rehabilitation Act of 1973 guarantees the child, who is disabled by virtue of having ADHD, the right to receive a free, appropriate public education.

IDEA, Section 504, and the ADA all have a similar purpose, to protect disabled persons from discrimination, but they differ in many respects. The following chart provides a comparison of all three laws.

Differences Between IDEA, Section 504, and the ADA

IDEA	Section 504	ADA
Purpose		
To provide financial aid to the states in their efforts to ensure adequate and appropriate services for children with disabilities.	A civil rights law to protect the rights of individuals with disabilities in programs and activities that receive federal financial assistance from the U.S. Department of Education.	A federal statute that requires businesses and other entities to provide reasonable accommodations to individuals who are protected by the Act.
Who is Protected?		
All children ages birth through 21 who are determined to be eligible within one or more of 13 categories and who need special education and related services.	All school-age children who meet the broader definition of qualified handicapped person; i.e., (1) has or (2) has had a physical or mental impairment which substantially limits a major life activity or (3) is regarded as handicapped by others. Major life activities include walking, seeing, hearing, speaking, breathing, learning, working, caring for oneself, and performing manual tasks.	Same broad definition as 504.
Responsibility to Provide a Free Appropriate Public Education		
Both IDEA and Section 504 require the provision of a free appropriate public education (FAPE) to eligible students covered under them. IDEA requires a written IEP document with specific content and required number of specific participants at the IEP meeting.	Section 504 does not require a document such as an IEP, but does require a plan. It is recommended that a group of persons knowledgeable about the student convene and specify the agreed upon services.	ADA does provide for FAPE to eligible students. The ADA has two provisions and services for eligible students with a disability. First, the ADHD applies its protections to cover nonsectarian private schools. Second, the ADA provides an additional layer of protection in combination with actions brought uner Section 504. and IDEA.
Funding		
IDEA provides additional federal funding for eligible students.	No additional funds are provided by Section 504.	No additional funds are provided by the ADA.
Regular vs Special Education		

A student is eligible for services under IDEA if it is determined that the student is disabled under one or more of the specific qualifying disabilities and requires special education and related services.
 	
    The student must be provided services within the least restrictive environment. Special education and related services included within the IEP must be provided at no cost to parents. In addition, a full continuum of placement alternatives, including the regular classroom must be available for providing special education and related services required in the IEP.
	A student is eligible as long as he or she meets the definition of a broadly defined qualified person. It is not required that the disability adversely affect education performance, or that the student need special education in order to be protected.
	
	    The student's education must be provided in the regular classroom unless it is demonstrated that education in the regular environment with the use of aids and services cannot be achieved satisfactorily.
		ADA does not address the provision of services within the regular or special education classroom. It broadens the policies set forth in Section 504. The public schools must provide appropriate accommodations. Related aids and services may be appropriate modifications.

IDEA	Section 504	ADA
Program Accessibility		
Requires appropriate modifications for eligible students.	Has detailed regulations regarding building and program accessibility.	Requires modification be made if necessary to provide access to FAPE.
Procedural Safeguards		
IDEA and 504 require notice to the parent or guardian with respect to identification, evaluation, and/or placement. Requires written notice with specifies required components of written notice. Requires written notice prior to any change of placement.	IDEA and 504 require notice ot the parent or guardian with respect to identification, evaluation and/or placement. Written notice is not required. Requires notification only before a "significant change" in placement.	Does not specify procedural safeguards for special education.
Evaluations		
A comprehensive evaluation which assesses all areas related to the suspected disability is required. The child must be evaluated by a multidisciplinary team or group. Informed consent required before an initial evaluation is conducted. Re-evaluation to be conducted at least every 3 years. Re-evaluation may be necessary before a significant change in placement. Provides for independent educational evaluation at district's expense if parents disagee with evaluation obtained by school and hearing officer agrees.	Evaluation must draw on information from a variety of sources in the area of concern. Decisions made by a group knowledgeable about the student, evaluation data, and placement options. No consent from parent or guardian required—only notice is required. Requires periodic re-evaluations. Re-evaluation is required before a significant change in placement. No provision for independent evaluations at district's expense.	Does not delineate specific evaluation requirements. However, appropriate modifications must be provided during an evaluation such as modifying entrance exams or providing readers or interpreters.
Procedures for Placement		
IDEA and 504 require districts when interpreting evaluation data and making decisions regarding placement to: • Draw upon information from a variety of sources. • Assure that all information is documented and considered. • Ensure that decisions regarding eligibility are made by persons who are knowledgeable about the child, the meaning of the evaluation data, and placement options. • Ensure that the student is educated with his/her non-disabled peers to the maximum extent appropriate (least restrictive environment).	IDEA and 504 require districts when interpreting evaluation data and making decisions regarding placement to: • Draw upon information from a variety of sources. • Assure that all information is documented and considered. • Ensure that decisions regarding eligibility are made by persons who are knowledgeable about the child, the meaning of the evaluation data, and placement options. • Ensure that the student is educated with his/her non disabled peers to the maximum extent appropriate (least restrictive environment).	No specific placement procedures are required. However, appropriate modifications are required.

IDEA	Section 504	ADA
Enforcement		
Enforced by the U.S. Department of Education, Office of Special Education Programs (OSEP). The districts response is monitored by the Staate Department of Education and OSEP. Potentially, federal funding could be withheld or a payback required should the district not be in compliance.	Enforced by the U.S. Department of Education, Office of Civil Rights. Potentially, all federal funding could be withheld should a state education agency or district not come into compliance.	Enforced by the Equal Employment Opportunity commission and the Department of Justice.
Grievance Procedures		
Does not require a grievance procedure nor a compliance officer. Citizen complaints, however, may be filed with state department of education.	Districts with 15 employees required to (1) designate an employee to be responsible for assuring district is in compliance with Section 504 and (2) provides a grievance procedure for parents, students, and employees.	Does not require specific grievance procedures related to education.
Due Process		
Parents have the right to participate in all IEP meetings and to receive notice of all procedural safeguards when the school district intends or refuses to take action or when a proposed change of placement or services is considered. Districts are required to provide impartial hearings for parents or guardians who disagree with the identification, evaluation, and/or placement, or any change of placement. The parent or guardian has the right to an independent hearing officer, present testimony and cross examine witnesses, and exclude evidence not presented by the opposing side at least five days prior to the hearing. The parent or guardian also has the right to be represented by counsel, and the right to a written decision within 10 days. IDEA has a "stay-put" provision. When the parent requests an impartial due process hearing, the child must remain in the current educational placement until all administrative and legal proceedings are finished. Suspensions or expulsions of a chid from school may trigger the "stay-put" placement provision if the parent requires a due process hearing to challenge the proposed suspension or expulsion. There is no similar "stay-put" provision in Section 504.	Section 504 requires notice to the parent or guardian with respect to identification, evaluation, and/or placement. Such notification does not have to be written. Notice is required before a "significant change" in placement is being made. Allows for the school district to appoint an impartial hearing officer. Requires that the parent or guardian have an opportunity to participate and be represented by counsel. Other details are left to the discretion of the local school district.	Does not delineate specific due process procedures. Individuals with disabilities have the same remedies which are available under Title VII of the Civil Rights Act of 1964, as amended by the Civil Rights Act of 1991.

Section 504 or IDEA! How Should My Child be Served?

Section 504 provides a quicker procedure for obtaining accommodations and services for children with disabilities than with IDEA. The eligibility criteria are broader, less information is usually required to determine eligibility, and less bureaucratic "red tape" exists to get services for the child. This may be quite satisfactory for children who have less serious disabilities.

The more formal and rigorous procedures under IDEA, although time-consuming, offer better protections and safeguards for families than Section 504. Under IDEA parent or guardian participation is required at each step of the evaluation, placement, or change of placement. These safeguards with respect to due process and discipline are particularly important, especially when a change in placement of the child is being considered. The ADA provides an extra layer of protections for persons with disabilities in addition to those outlined in IDEA and Section 504.

For children whose disability is less serious, many school districts will encourage the use of Section 504 rather than IDEA. It is quicker, more flexible, and the district has greater latitude and less accountability for decision-making and enforcement. Many parents find that districts are reluctant to place children with ADHD in special education under IDEA within the Other Health Impaired category. Parents and guardians must evaluate their individual child's situation, the track record of the school and district in providing services under a 504 plan, and then determine the best option for their child.

How the Process Works

Step 1: The Referral

If your adolescent has been identified as having problems in school, which suggest that he might be disabled and in need of special education services, the rules and regulations of your local and state school system require that a referral be made to determine whether he is indeed disabled and what kind of special education programming and related services might be needed to educate him appropriately. This process begins with a written referral to the principal of the school the child is in or would attend if he were in a public school. Any of your child's teachers can make such a referral or you can, as well, if you think your child needs special education services.

After the referral is made, the principal will call a committee meeting to consider the referral. Committee members usually include the child's teacher(s), the person making the referral, other specialists involved with the child or the school, the principal, or someone designated by the principal. The name given to this initial committee varies from district to district, but is sometimes referred to as the "school screening committee," "child study team," or "educational management team." The committee's purpose is to review your child's progress in school, to assess his learning and school performance, and to determine whether these problems warrant a formal evaluation by the school psychologist or other specialist. Prior to obtaining such an evaluation, the committee might gather data from other sources, may make suggestions about adapting the child's current school program to better meet the needs of the child, or may suggest strategies to the classroom teacher that might help the child. If members of the committee recommend that the child receive a full evaluation, the child may be referred to a school psychologist or other specialist for that purpose. You must be informed in writing of the committee's decision.

Depending on the district, parents may not even be aware that their son or daughter has been referred to the committee for consideration. Some districts are careful to notify the parents of any meetings held to make a decision about a child's educational needs; others only notify the parent if they want to obtain consent for a formal evaluation. Whether or not you are invited to this meeting, if you are aware that your child is being referred to the committee for consideration, you should contact the school and ask to be involved in this initial meeting. If the screening committee does not recommend that your child receive an evaluation, you can dispute this decision through a formal procedure called a due process hearing. Due process procedures will be discussed later.

If you did not have prior knowledge of the committee meeting, the first you might hear of it is when you receive a letter requesting permission for the school to evaluate your child. The school should notify you of its wish to evaluate your child. It should review with you what the purpose of the evaluation is and what tests will be administered to your child.

Step 2: The Evaluation

The evaluation process can become rather complex depending on the nature and severity of the problem your child may have. On the permission slip, the school may ask for your consent to give your child tests of educational achievement, learning ability, intelligence, psychological functioning, hearing, and speech and language skills. If this is the first time you have been notified that an evaluation has been recommended for your child, or if you have any questions about why these tests have been chosen, you should contact the school and ask to have a meeting to discuss the reasons for the evaluation and the tests and procedures to be used.

Under IDEA it is required that the evaluation be conducted by a multi-disciplinary team of professionals with expertise in different areas. Usually evaluations are comprehensive in scope and include assessments of more than one of the following areas:

1. Academic achievement may be evaluated by tests that measure reading, math, and written and oral language.

2. Medical tests or reports may be required to determine the medical history of the child and whether or not any current medical problems exist, which could affect learning.

3. Social history is taken to determine family background, developmental history, previous academic history, and other social factors, which might be relevant to the child's learning or adjustment.

4. Psychological testing and observation of the child may be done to evaluate the child's intellectual ability, social skills, perceptual functioning, behavior, attention, and emotional development. Clinical psychologists or psychiatrists may be called upon to do additional evaluation of the child in these areas if needed.

5. Speech and language development may be assessed to evaluate the child's communication skills.

6. Tests of hearing and vision may be done to determine whether hearing or vision impairments affect the child's learning or academic performance.

Under Section 504, the guidelines for doing evaluations are broader than under IDEA. The evaluation must draw on information from a variety of sources in the area of concern. Many school districts have set up procedures to do 504 evaluations for students suspected of having ADHD. Information from parents, teachers, and other sources is obtained to determine whether there is evidence of ADHD. A full, comprehensive psychoeducational evaluation may not be done as required under IDEA.

Step 3: Determining Eligibility

Under IDEA, after the evaluation of your child is complete, written reports are prepared and sent to a committee to review to determine whether your child is eligible for special education services. The job of the committee is to determine if your child meets criteria for eligibility based on having a qualified disability and the child's need for special education and related services. In some cases, the child may be found to meet criteria for eligibility for more than one disabling condition, (e.g., specific learning disability and other health impairment, such as ADHD). Usually the eligibility committee will try to identify the primary handicapping condition—the one most responsible for inhibiting the child's educational growth. If both conditions contribute equally to the child's problems, the committee may declare the child multi-handicapped and eligible for special education.

Once the eligibility committee determines whether the child is eligible for special education, parents should be notified of the committee's decision. There are typically two points of contention that can arise between parents and the school about eligibility. The committee may decide that the child is not eligible for special education and the parent may disagree, or the committee may decide that the child is eligible for special education, but determines that the child's disability is something different from what the parent believes it is. For example, the committee may conclude that the child is primarily emotionally disturbed, but the parent may believe the child is disabled because of having a specific learning disability or ADHD. In either case, parents have a right to contest the committee's decision by filing an appeal.

If your child has undergone an evaluation to determine eligibility for services under Section 504, a 504 committee will convene to discuss evaluation results. The job of the committee is to determine if your child meets criteria for eligibility based on having a disability as defined under Section 504. This is a broader definition of disability than under IDEA.

Step 4: Determining a Program of Services

The Individualized Education Program (IEP)

If your child is deemed eligible to receive special education under IDEA, he must have an Individualized Education Program (IEP) designed specifically to meet his needs. The IEP is at the heart of the whole process of special education because it specifies the services and programs that the adolescent will receive as a result of his disability.   It is the school's commitment that your child will receive specific programs and services. The IEP is individualized in that it meets the adolescent's unique identified educational needs rather than those of the group.

The IEP specifies the educational placement or setting in which your child will receive instruction, lists specific goals and educational objectives for your child to reach, and designates the related services that your child will receive to enable him to reach those goals and objectives. The IEP also contains dates when services will begin, how long they will last, and the method by which your child's progress will be evaluated. The IEP will be reviewed periodically and modifications will be made as needed.

The 1997 IDEA Amendments added some new requirements in the development of IEPs, which are of particular concern to students with ADHD. The IEP team must consider the strengths of the child and the concerns of the parents for enhancing the education of their child. The IEP must take into account the results of the initial evaluation and most recent evaluation of the child In the case of a child whose behavior impedes his or her learning or that of others, the IEP must take into account the appropriate strategies, including positive behavioral interventions and strategies that address this behavior.

The 1997 IDEA Amendments also promote the inclusion of disabled students and requires statements in the IEP concerning how the child's disability affects the child's involvement and progress in the general curriculum.

The IEP team is comprised of the following people:

*   at least one regular education teacher of the child (if the child is participating in regular eduction;

*   at least one special education teacher;

*   a representative of the district who is knowledgeable about the instruction necessary to meet the unique needs of the child with a disability;

- other individuals who are knowledgeable or special expertise regarding the child;

- an individual who can interpret the evaluation results;

- the child's parents;

- whenever appropriate, the child with a disability.

The 504 Plan

If your child is deemed eligible to receive services under Section 504, he must have a 504 Plan. This plan must be designed to meet the individual educational needs of the child. Implementing an IEP in accordance with IDEA is one way to meet the standard of individual education needs under Section 504. However, more commonly, a 504 Plan is prepared which takes into account the child's education needs. The 504 Plan lists the accommodations (i.e., specialized instruction or equipment, auxiliary aids or services, program modifications, etc.) the 504 committee recommends as necessary to ensure the child's access to all district programs. In deciding on such services, the committee must recognize that the child is entitled to be educated in the least restrictive environment.

The majority of children who have 504 Plans are receiving accommodations within the regular education environment. Examples of such accommodations for secondary school students can be found in Chapter 12. A case manager is assigned to monitor the child's progress under the 504 Plan. Future meetings of the 504 committee, the parents, and the child can be scheduled to review progress and make modifications to the 504 Plan.

Step 5: Due Process Procedures

Obviously, parents don't always agree with their school system on issues regarding the education of their children. Both IDEA and Section 504 provide a due process mechanism to protect the child from being denied appropriate services.

The primary purpose of the due process procedure is to provide for an impartial third party, called a hearing officer, to examine the issues on which you and the school system disagree and to arrive at an unbiased decision. Federal law requires that all state education agencies must have due process procedures described by state statute, regulation, or in the written policy of the state education agency, but it does not go into detail about the procedures states must follow in providing due process. Procedures adopted by the state education agency are followed by local districts within the state. Parents and the school system have a right to appeal to the state education agency any local due process decisions.

Conflicts between parents and school systems fall under the province of due process. Examples of conflicts which are most frequently brought to due process hearings are disagreements:

    a.   over evaluation results and/or eligibility findings (i.e., school's evaluation indicates eligibility under the disability of emotional handicap, but parents feel the child has ADHD and should be eligible under the other health impaired category of disability);

    b.   over whether a child should receive related services (i.e., should the child receive speech and language therapy, physical therapy, or occupational therapy);

    c.   over issues involving least restrictive environment (i.e., placement in a self-contained classroom, resource room, etc.).

    d.   over whether the child should be educated in a private school at public expense);

    e.   over the suitability of certain tests done in an evaluation;

    f.   over whether the IEP is being followed (i.e., is the child being provided the educational programs and services specified in the IEP).

Due process does not cover all types of conflicts that may surface between a parent and a school system. For instance, you are not entitled to a due process hearing if you want to attend all meetings where your child's eligibility for special education will be discussed if state law does not require your presence. You may not use due process to change your child's teacher if the school system feels the teacher is qualified to teach your child. Nor may you use due process to modify the teacher's behavior if you feel he or she does not understand your child, or if you don't care for the school psychologist assigned to evaluate your child and would like another one to do the testing. To solve these disagreements, parents are urged to speak informally with school officials or find additional support for your concerns in your local PTA or from professionals within the community.

The decision to settle a dispute by going through a due process hearing should be well thought out. Such hearings often involve a great deal of time and effort on the part of parents and the school system. Before requesting a due process hearing, parents and school officials should make every effort to deal with conflicts in a less formal way through meetings and negotiations. You might get additional perspectives on the issue by discussing the problem with other parents, local professionals, or parent advocates in your community. Brainstorm potential solutions and bring them to the attention of school officials. Try to see the problem from all angles and see if you can come up with workable solutions. If the disagreement persists, even after you have exhausted all other avenues of resolving the conflict, ask the school system to provide a mediator or to have an administrative review of the issues. If you're still at an impasse with the school system, you may want to request a due process hearing.

Summary

Parents and teachers play important roles as advocates for children with disabilities. To be an effective advocate, parents need to have an understanding of how their child's disability affects educational performance, what laws exist to protect disabled students, and how they can communicate effectively with their child's school. Parents familiar with the rights of their child and the responsibilities of the school are in a better position to act as advocates for their child.

Federal laws such as IDEA, Section 504 of the Rehabilitation Act of 1973, and the Americans with Disabilities Act of 1990 ensure protections for children with disabilities. These laws require schools to provide programs and services for disabled students. These laws differ in terms of how they each define who is eligible for such programs and services, how evaluations should be conducted to determine such eligibility, procedures for providing services, and safeguards for parents and guardians upon which to rely.

Parents play an important role in ensuring that their child receive an appropriate education and they should establish a productive relationship with their child's school.

16 ADHD, Delinquency, and the Juvenile Justice System

Are adolescents with ADHD at greater risk for delinquent behavior? What are the warning signs parents can watch for to signal that their child is on a course for delinquent behavior? What can parents do to prevent their ADHD child from becoming delinquent? What can parents do to help ADHD youth who are delinquent? How do ADHD adolescents fare in the juvenile justice system?

These are extremely important questions for parents of adolescents with ADHD who are uncertain where the hyperactive-impulsive behavior of their children will lead. Although there is some comfort in the fact that the vast majority of youth with ADHD will not end up in the juvenile justice system for acts of criminal behavior, ADHD is a risk factor for delinquency. In fact, emotional and behavioral disorders, learning disabilities, and ADHD are all risk factors for delinquency among youth. It may be that more than half to as many as 90 percent of youth in the justice system meet the diagnostic criteria for one or more of these disorders.

Minor, usually infrequent acts of delinquency are fairly common among adolescents. The percentage of youth who commit offenses such as shoplifting, forgery, experimental use of drugs, illegal purchase of alcohol or cigarettes, truancy, violations of curfew, and running away is quite high. Most adolescents will stop this behavior on their own as adolescence ends and they enter their adult years. Some adolescents, however, will continue to exhibit serious problems with conduct, which will inevitably lead them into involvement with the juvenile justice system.

Are Adolescents with ADHD at Greater Risk?

The research done in this area has followed fairly large groups of ADHD subjects who were initially diagnosed as children and tracked as adolescents and adults. The rate of arrest and incarceration was greater in the ADHD group than it was in a normal control group. Most of the difference between the ADHD and control group was related to the presence of conduct disorder. ADHD by itself without the presence of conduct disorder does not lead to delinquency.

Warning Signs

ADHD youth who show signs of conduct disorder before 10 years of age are at greatest risk for delinquent behavior in adolescence and antisocial behavior in adulthood. Oppositional behavior in early childhood, aggressive behavior toward other people or animals, destruction of property, deceitfulness or theft, and serious violations of rules such as staying out at night despite parental prohibitions, running away from home, or truancy from school are characteristics of youth with conduct disorder. ADHD youth who first display these characteristics in adolescence are less likely to have as severe and persistent problems as those whose pattern of antisocial behavior started in childhood.

Parents should be on the lookout for warning signs such as early sexual behavior, drinking, smoking, use of illegal drugs, poor academic performance, school truancy, aggression toward others, destruction of property, reckless behavior, and risk taking.

The Path to Delinquency

The typical path of development of conduct disorder is found in the young preschool or elementary school-age child who is tough to manage at home because of severe problems with oppositional behavior. This is the child who is strong-willed, refuses to obey parental requests, stubborn, and loses his temper easily. Parents are worn down by this type of child. Normal parental responses of warning to behave, scolding, or punishment are ineffective, which causes parents to escalate their control over the child's behavior. They become more coercive and negative towards the child. Family life is marked by frequent arguments with the child and disagreements between the parents about how to best manage the child's behavior. The child becomes isolated from siblings and parents within the family and gradually grows angry and resentful.

Oppositional behavior leads to conduct disorder, which can lead to delinquency.

Defiant behavior continues at school. Other children notice the child's unusual, aggressive behavior and stay away from him. He is excluded from social activities in which the other children are invited to participate. His negative behavior in school causes teachers to respond negatively in turn. Gradually, interest in learning lessens, grades worsen, and the child stops trying in school. Parents receive negative reports from teachers and apply more pressure at home. This only reinforces the destructive cycle that has been going on for years and contributes to further deterioration of relationships at home. Those parents who exhibit antisocial behavior themselves are likely to continue to pull away from their child and spend less time trying to teach their child mainstream values in a positive, productive way.

Frequently, the child finds acceptance from other children who have similar problems. They cluster together and reinforce one another's negative view of other people, school, and family. Reckless and risky behavior is accepted in their peer group and acts of defiance, aggression, and petty delinquency may win approval with other children whose behavior is also deviant. As the child gets older, the negative cycle gets stronger with greater frequency of misbehavior leading to further social isolation and growing distance from mainstream values. With progression to middle school and high school, the adolescent's circle of friends widens. New, more deviant forms of behavior are tried and learned. Acts of mischief and misbehavior in the past escalate into more serious problems of substance abuse, school truancy, shoplifting, lying, and aggressive behavior. Eventually, this estranged child turns into a hostile adolescent who will come into contact with the juvenile justice system. By this time, they have a well established pattern of antisocial values and delinquent behavior. They have few, if any, solid adult relationships they trust, and they are highly likely to continue offending.

Most ADHD adolescents do not take the path into delinquency.

Thankfully, most ADHD children do not take this path into delinquency. However, enough do so any parent of an ADHD child needs to be concerned. As many as 60 percent of ADHD children will exhibit oppositional behavior. About half of that group, or as many as one quarter to one third of the ADHD group as a whole, can end up on this delinquent path. ADHD children who have made it into adolescence without problems fighting, stealing, lying, or destroying other people's property, will not likely take this path of delinquency through adolescence. Even if they get into some trouble with law-breaking during their teenage years, there is a good chance that they will improve with help and eventually learn from their mistakes. If your ADHD child has shown early signs of serious misbehavior (particularly before the age of 10) and continues to show these problems in adolescence, the outlook is less optimistic, and you will have to do everything you can to turn this child around as soon as possible.

Here are some things you should consider:

*   Get professional help. Treatment for ADHD can include parent training, medication, behavior management, and counseling for you, your ADHD adolescent, and for other family members.

*   Get in touch with your adolescent's school. If your child is performing poorly in school, find out what steps can be taken to help him succeed. Are there special education programs that can help? Will a change in the academic program more suitable to your son's or daughter's interest help? Is peer counseling available? If your child is considering dropping out of school, does your district offer any dropout prevention programs?

*   If your adolescent son or daughter is involved in serious behavior problems such as stealing, lying, destruction of property, aggression, or substance abuse, take action right away. Don't get caught in denial by minimizing or ignoring these problems. They will only get worse unless you deal with them. Confront your child and explain the reasons for your suspicions. Provide more close parental supervision. Set limits on behavior, provide a curfew, and make certain you know your child's whereabouts as best you can.

*   Become acquainted with your child's friends and if any seem to have a negative influence on your child, discourage or prohibit the relationship. Although your son or daughter will complain mightily about this, your should remain steadfast and not allow them to associate with undesirable friends.

*   Set a good example yourself. ADHD adolescents who develop delinquency problems frequently have parents who exhibit inappropriate, antisocial behavior as well. If you break the law, lose your temper with others, and act irresponsibly and antisocially—so will your child.

*   Try to build on your child's talents. If they have a special ability or show an interest in something wholesome and appropriate, you should cultivate and encourage them to pursue it. For instance, if your child is athletic, encourage participation in sports as a way of building self-discipline and pride.

*   Try to put an end to negative communication at home. Avoid arguing, lecturing, accusing, nagging, and threatening. Encourage positive communication by listening to your child's thoughts and feelings and trying to understand his behavior.

- Make every effort to be a strong, yet positive parent. Recognize the things your child does well and give frequent praise. Try to spend as much time with your child as you can so that you have a better chance to influence his thinking.

ADHD Adolescents
in the Juvenile Justice System

Adolescents with ADHD come to the attention of juvenile justice authorities in one of three ways:
- as abused or neglected children, by frustrated caretakers;
- as children in need of supervision because their disruptive and defiant behavior cannot be controlled by parents or school officials; or
- as children who break the law.

Gerald E. Rouse, a county judge in Nebraska, has had many juvenile's with ADHD come before him. He emphasizes that while ADHD does not excuse a juvenile who breaks the law, it should be factored into the decision-making process of the juvenile justice system. He is a strong advocate for improved treatment of ADHD offenders and more training for juvenile justice professionals about the impact of ADHD on juvenile offenders.

> **Kids with ADHD who come into the juvenile justice system sink further and faster into the system than those without ADHD.**

Judge Rouse is concerned that adolescents with ADHD who come into the juvenile justice system go further, faster into the system than children without ADHD. He contends that right from the start, ADHD youths may lack the social controls and skills that are needed to make a good impression on decision makers in the system. Rouse is concerned that judges may be tougher on ADHD children who show a lack of eye contact, poor grooming, and who say impulsive things in the courtroom. He adds that ADHD juveniles, who are prone to impulsive behavior and poor judgement, frustrate supervisors and judges to such an extent that quicker motions to revoke probation and more restrictive dispositions may be recommended. Without proper education and understanding about ADHD, juvenile justice system professionals (social workers, probation officers, guardians ad Litem, judges, and juvenile court services) will not be aware of the steps that can be taken to assist ADHD youth who come before them.

The Pacer Center of Minneapolis, Minnesota has prepared a handbook for professionals working with youth with disabilities in the juvenile justice system entitled *Unique Challenges, Hopeful Responses*. The authors of this enlightening handbook emphasize that it is extremely important that juvenile justice professionals recognize the impact that a developmental disability (emotional or behavioral disorder, learning disability, ADHD, mental retardation, autism, etc.) may have on juvenile offenders and this needs to be considered as the juvenile goes through the justice system. The Pacer Center contends that:

- If a youth's behaviors are characteristic of a disability, an evaluation of the youth may be required to determine the presence of or impact of the disability on the youth;

- If a youth's disability interferes with his or her capacity to participate in the justice process, the proceedings should be adapted to meet the needs of the person stemming from the disability;

- If the presence of a disability is confirmed, a youth may be entitled to specific services relative to the disability while in a correctional program and in aftercare.

The Pacer Center encourages juvenile justice system professionals to be ever mindful of their mission—to ensure that youth are judged in a way that recognizes and considers each person's unique culpability and rights. The goal of the system is rehabilitation of the youthful offender. To accomplish this mission and this goal correctly, individuals with disabilities must be identified and accommodated appropriately.

What can parents do to help their child go through the juvenile justice system?

Parents typically provide emotional support and hire legal representation for their adolescent son or daughter who is involved in the juvenile justice system. However, parents can also play an important role in helping the system understand their child's disability and their child's specific needs that require attention as he proceeds through the justice system.

- Depending on the seriousness of the offense and the risk the juvenile poses to society, a youth may be incarcerated in a juvenile detention facility before a final disposition of the case is made. Parents should be involved in the assessment of their child as soon after they are admitted to a detention facility as possible. They can alert the facility staff that their child has ADHD so this can be considered during the juvenile's stay at the facility.

- Impulsive, reckless behavior of ADHD youth may cause some of them to get into more trouble while in a detention facility. If your child takes medication and needs that medication to help control behavior and attention, parents should request that the medication be administered at the detention facility. Detention facilities have policies regarding administering medication to juveniles. If your child is taking medication to treat his ADHD, he may be entitled to have that medication continued while in detention.

- Some detention facilities provide for a continuation of the juvenile's education. Parents could make certain that the facility is aware of any special education needs of their child—for example, if an individualized education plan (IEP) has been in place in school.

- Parents may have some unique understanding of how their child's ADHD may have impacted on the intent of the juvenile in commission of a crime or with respect to how the juvenile responds during adjudication (trial) proceedings.

- Parents can play a particularly important role in the evaluation that is requested by the court after the juvenile has been adjudicated. This evaluation examines different aspects of the juvenile's life, which aids the judge in forming an appropriate disposition. Dispositions can be quite complex and could involve various degrees and modalities of treatment for the juvenile's disability and punishments for the offenses he is found guilty of committing. Parents can provide vital information to evaluators, which could lead to a disposition that makes the most sense for the juvenile with respect to treatment, punishment, and restitution.

- If the court requires that the juvenile and family members seek treatment for ADHD, parents should make certain there is full compliance with the court's order. Parents should make every effort to be part of the treatment.

- After the juvenile returns home, parents should provide close supervision to reduce the probability of additional wrongdoing.

Summary

ADHD youth who show signs of conduct disorder before age 10 are at greatest risk for delinquent behavior in adolescence. Parents should be alert to signs that may warn them their child is on the wrong path. Early sexual behavior, smoking, drinking, use of illegal drugs, poor academic performance, school truancy, aggression toward others, and destruction of property are among the types of behavior associated with the development of delinquency.

Parents who find their adolescent is heading in this direction should consider getting professional help. Early treatment for ADHD may prevent behaviors from worsening. Parents should also stay in close contact with the student's school to find opportunities for success. Confront serious misbehavior head on and provide close parental supervision if you suspect your child is involved in wrongful behavior. Parents should also set a good example themselves for appropriate behavior.

If an adolescent enters the juvenile justice system, parents can play an important role in helping the system understand the teenager's disability and their specific needs that require attention as they proceed through the juvenile justice system.

17 Substance Abuse in Adolescence
Alan Goodstat, L.C.S.W. and Harvey C. Parker, Ph.D.

Who Uses Drugs?

Drug use and abuse occurs at all ages, across all ethnic groups, among all races, and among the rich and the poor. However, some people are at higher-than-average risk for substance use. The likelihood of an individual becoming a substance abuser or substance dependent varies from substance to substance. Each substance has its own addictive characteristics, some more than others. It is estimated that one out of every 10 individuals who experiment with a substance will become addicted. The main characteristics of someone addicted to alcohol or substances are loss of control, preoccupation with the substance, and continued use despite negative consequences.

Being male is one risk factor in substance use, although sex differences in substance use are decreasing. Another risk factor is being an adolescent or young adult and being exposed to illicit drug use among peers or family members. Approximately six out of ten individuals who come from a substance abusing home end up substance abusers. Higher drug use rates are found in youth who come from a single-parent family, or whose mothers failed to complete high school, or for those who are disinterested in school and do not do well academically. Higher drug use rates are also found in risk taking personality types. People who drive too fast, who don't wear seat belts, and who see themselves as invincible are in this group. People like this often enjoy the excitement associated with a drug use lifestyle and ignore warnings of danger about using drugs.

Non-drug users also share similar characteristics. Drug use is less frequent among youth who attend school regularly, do well academically, are religious, have good relationships with parents and family members, and are confident in themselves and less able to be influenced by peer pressure. Being raised in a family that has a no-drug use policy and where problem-solving and conflict is dealt with constructively is another characteristic of non-drug use youth.

**Families with a "no-drug" policy
have fewer problems with substance use.**

Fortunately, the majority of adolescents who use drugs do not advance to higher levels of substance abuse or substance dependence. However, episodic use of drugs can cause immediate problems such as automobile crashes, violence, school failure, and high-risk sexual activity. This can lead to unwanted pregnancy, contracting the HIV virus, or other sexually transmitted diseases.

Why Do People Use Drugs?

The reasons for drug use are varied. Some use drugs to fit in with a peer group. Others like the excitement of doing something illegal, others do so to imitate adult models in their life. Most people's use of drugs is done on an experimental basis—usually trying out the drug one or more times, but not continuing to use it regularly. Some people use drugs to cope with difficulties they are having in life. They use drugs to alter their mood and to cope with depression, anxiety, low self-esteem, or other psychological problems. In this group are people who use drugs to escape from day-to-day pressures.

Some people use drugs for recreation. They drink alcohol or smoke marijuana with friends when they go out socially. For them, the mood altering allure of the drug is what they seek. It becomes a form of entertainment.

Familial factors may also make children vulnerable to substance use. Parents who use substances are more likely to have substance using offspring. This may be a combined genetic and environmental effect. Parents who suffer from depression or anxiety, or families wherein there is a great deal of stress, violence, and negative parenting styles, may contribute to substance use in children.

**An adolescent's peer group
can be a great persuader in drug use.**

Influence of others in the adolescent's peer group may result in substance use. Most adolescents want to be accepted and have an identity within a peer group. Peer pressure is a major cause of drug use in adolescence and leads teenagers to experiment with different substances. This experimentation is dangerous. Research has shown that drug use begins with the gateway drugs—alcohol, cigarettes, and marijuana—and is reinforced by an adolescent's peer group. Use of the gateway drugs are strong indicators that an increased pattern of substance abuse may occur.

ADHD in Adolescents and Substance Use

Children at higher risk for substance use show problems with self-regulation of behavior and difficulties with planning, attention, reasoning, judgement, and self-monitoring of their actions. In addition, these children show higher levels of aggressive behavior. They also tend to be sensation-seeking. In clinical evaluations these children are frequently diagnosed with ADHD and conduct disorder.

**Having ADHD, in itself, does not
put a person at higher risk of substance abuse.**

However, several researchers have shown that the rate of substance use was *not* higher than normal in adolescents with ADHD alone. Those ADHD adolescents who did exhibit substance use problems also had a diagnosis of conduct disorder. Thus, the relationship between adolescent substance use and ADHD is largely due to the presence of conduct disorder. ADHD is found in 30 to 50 percent of adolescents with substance use disorder and conduct disorder. The presence of ADHD in this group of adolescents has been associated with more severe substance dependence.

What is Substance Abuse?

Substance abuse is defined by the American Psychiatric Association as a "maladaptive pattern of substance use, leading to clinically significant impairment or distress, as manifested by three (or more) of the following, occurring at any time in the same 12-month period:

(1) recurrent substance use resulting in a failure to fulfill major role obligations at work, school, or home (e.g., repeated absences or poor work performance related to substance use; substance-related absences, suspensions, or expulsions from school; neglect of children or household)

(2) recurrent substance use in situations in which it is physically hazardous (e.g., driving an automobile or operating a machine when impaired by substance use)

(3) recurrent substance-related legal problems (e.g., arrests for substance-related disorderly conduct)

(4) continued substance use despite having persistent or recurrent social or interpersonal problems caused or exacerbated by the effects of the substance (e.g., arguments with

spouse about consequences of intoxication, physical fights)

Drug addiction experts define abuse as the chronic use of any substance despite adverse social, psychological, or medical effects. This pattern of abuse may be intermittent or continuous with or without physical dependence. For example, a person who drinks excessively once every few weeks and then drives is abusing alcohol even though he is not physically dependent on alcohol. Similarly, a teenager who smokes marijuana a few times a week after school and can't function at night to do homework is abusing the drug.

What is Substance Dependence?

Substance dependence or drug addiction is defined by the American Psychiatric Association as a "maladaptive pattern of substance use, leading to clinically significant impairment or distress, as manifested by three (or more) of the following, occurring at any time in the same 12-month period:

(1) tolerance, as defined by either of the following:
   (a) a need for markedly increased amounts of the substance to achieve intoxication or desired effect
   (b) markedly diminished effect with continued use of the same amount of the substance.
(2) withdrawal, as manifested by either of the following:
   (a) the characteristic withdrawal syndrome for the substance
   (b) the same (or a closely related) substance is taken to relieve or avoid withdrawal symptoms.
(3) the substance is often taken in larger amounts or over a longer period than was intended.
(4) there is a persistent desire or unsuccessful efforts to decrease or control substance use.
(5) a great deal of time is spent in activities necessary to obtain the substance (e.g., visiting multiple doctors or driving long distances), use the substance (e.g., chain smoking), or recover from its effects.
(6) important social, occupational, or recreational activities are given up or reduced because of substance use.
(7) the substance use is continued despite knowledge of having a persistent or recurrent physical or psychological problem that is likely to have been caused or exacerbated by the substance (e.g., cocaine use despite recognition of cocaine-induced depression, or continued drinking despite recognition that an ulcer was aggravated by alcohol consumption).

Substance dependence usually follows a pattern of repeated drug use, which results in tolerance, withdrawal, and compulsive drug taking.

Is Drug Use on the Rise Among Adolescents?

Data from the University of Michigan 1996 Monitoring the Future (MTF) Study revealed that drug usage is very prevalent among adolescents. The MTF study found that nearly one-third of high school seniors reported having been drunk in the past month and one-fifth of 10th graders and seniors reported using marijuana in the past 30 days of being surveyed. The table below shows the rate of use of selected substances by adolescents in 8th, 10th, and 12th grades. Nearly 5 percent of high school seniors reported using marijuana on a daily or almost daily basis within the past 30 days of the survey.

Percentage of Students Reporting Use of Selected Substances in the Past 30 Days

Substance and Pattern of Use in Past 30 Days	Grade		
	8th	10th	12th
Cigarettes—any use	20.1	30.4	34.0
Cigarettes—1/2 pack or more per day	4.3	9.4	13.0
Alcohol—any use	26.2	40.4	50.8
Alcohol—"been drunk" at least once	9.6	21.3	31.3
Any illicit drug—any use	14.6	23.2	24.6
Marijuana—any use	11.3	20.4	21.9
Cocaine (including crack)— any use	1.3	1.7	2.0
Hallucinogens—any use	1.9	2.8	3.5
Stimulants (excluding medical use)—any use	4.6	5.5	4.1
Inhalants—any use	5.3	3.3	2.5

Source: Monitoring the Future Study (Johnston, 1996).

Tobacco and alcohol are the most frequently abused drugs in the United States. They are readily available and widely promoted in the media directly through advertisements and indirectly through exposure and association with adolescent role models.

Although substance use is widespread among adolescents, only a subset of adolescent drug users meet the criteria outlined above for substance abuse or substance dependence. According to research done a few years ago, marijuana **abuse** rates for youth ages 10 through 13 years was .2 percent, for youth ages 14 through 16 years was 1.4 percent, and for youth ages 17 through 20 years was 2.9 percent.

Stages of Alcohol and Substance Abuse in Adolescence

The adolescent moves through four stages of substance use, which is usually consistent with their peer group. The stages move from experimental use to substance dependence.

Stage One

This stage begins with experimental use of various substances. The average age when adolescents begin experimenting is 13. The substance used is greatly determined by access and the peer group. The majority of use is done on weekends. For many peer groups it is assumed normal to use the gateway drugs—alcohol, cigarettes, and marijuana—with no understanding of the risks involved. During this stage there are no remarkable symptoms or behavioral changes.

Stage Two

In stage two, behavioral changes are evident due to increased use and lifestyle changes. The adolescent realizes the enjoyment of the substance and looks forward to becoming high or intoxicated. Lifestyle changes include change of friends, decrease in grades, change in appearance, increased isolation from the family, increased difficulties with authority, and lack of motivation. Due to symptoms being present, the first intervention usually occurs at this stage.

Stage Three

Substance use increases to almost daily during this stage. The adolescent is preoccupied with the substance and the lifestyle it brings. An increase in depression, rebelliousness, impulsive behavior, problems with the law, and family conflicts increase. Due to the impact these issues have on the adolescent, thoughts of suicide are common. The adolescent begins to feel that he cannot function without the chemical and can lose his sense of self and purpose.

Stage Four

During this stage the adolescent believes he needs the substance to feel normal. In many cases, this is due to the physical dependence characteristics certain substances have. He may become totally isolated from the family and usually distances himself from the peer group where he first began the use. Physical signs such as increased skin problems, weight loss, unexplained injuries, fatigue, and sore throat are common. The risk for overdosing is higher due to the increased amount and potency of the substances being used.

Signs of Substance Use

Adolescents who experiment with drugs don't start out addicted and don't show symptoms. For many, nothing will seem out of the ordinary and parents often won't be able to discern experimental drug use. The teen looks healthy and generally behaves normally. Adolescents who have reached the level where regular use or addiction is a problem will often tell you that they have used drugs casually for quite some time without anyone noticing. Their parents never had a clue.

Substance abuse is a progressive illness. Most addiction starts with experimental use and progresses to regular use as the adolescent goes through the stages described earlier. After the first stage or second stages, behavioral changes and signs of regular use can be much more noticeable.

Guillermo D. Jalil provides some suggestions for parents to detect clues of casual drug use. The following are some examples from his book, *Street-Wise Drug Prevention.*

- Hug your child when he comes home. Smell any residual odor of marijuana use, alcohol, or cologne or chewing gum used to cover up an odor.

- Be suspicious if your child walks straight to his room when he comes home without stopping to say hello or talk with anyone. Go up to them and start a conversation. Be aware of speech, balance, and coordination.

- Stay awake and keep the lights on until your child comes home.

- Don't give permission for your child to sleep away from home if you suspect drug use.

- Be unpredictable with your schedule.

- Get involved with the parents of your child's friends. They may have concerns as well they would like to share.

- Don't rely on report cards to tell you what is happening at school. Contact your child's teachers to get more information.

- Try to meet your child's friends when they come over. If they never do, tell your child to bring them home so you can meet them.

- Get to know your neighbors. You can't be all the time. Neighbors can sometimes alert you when they think there may be a problem going on at your house.

When experimental drug use turns into more regular drug use signs can become more obvious. These signs could be in the area of behavior change, changes in friendships, deterioration in school performance, greater interest in drug culture, physical signs of drug usage, evidence of drug paraphernalia, or possession of drugs. These warning signs are explained in more detail below:

- Changes in behavior—mood swings, staying out later than usual, irritability, defensiveness, lying, stealing money, making excuses for responsibilities not being done, isolation from the family, sleeping longer than usual, difficulty falling asleep.

- Changes in friends—dropping old friends, making new friends, reluctance to provide information about their friends or to talk about what they and their friends are doing.

- Deterioration in school performance—tardiness to school, less time spent on schoolwork or homework, lack of motivation to achieve good grades, absenteeism from school

- Interest in drug culture—magazines, newspapers, videos, or music CDs and tapes that are drug related, frequent talk of drugs in conversation with friends, jokes about drugs, or frequent references made to drugs.

- Physical signs of drug usage—bloodshot eyes, pupil dilated, lapses in memory and attention span, trouble sticking to a task, difficulty concentrating, poor grooming, unhealthy appearance, changes in appetite, slurred or incoherent speech, poor motor coordination, chronic runny nose or sneezing.

- Drug-related paraphernalia found in adolescent's possession, in their room or car. This could include rolling papers, pipes, "joint" clips, eye drops.

- Possession of drugs or signs of drugs such as pills, drug residue, glass vials, hypodermic needles, marijuana plants or small amounts of marijuana leaves or seeds in pockets. Odor of drugs or use of incense or room deodorizers to cover up drug smells.

It is important to listen to others who might be telling you that your child is having a problem. Sometimes your child's friends, worried for your child, will confide in you. Other parents, teachers, or neighbors might have suspicions that they will share. Take them seriously. Get details from them—who, what, where, when, and why? These details will be important when you take the next step—confronting your child. Make sure you write them all down with reference to who said what.

Confronting the Adolescent

Parents who notice these warning signs should confront their child calmly at a time when the adolescent is not under the influence of drugs. Before confronting your child make a list of all the reasons you have for suspecting your child is using drugs. Refer to the notes you took when others (your child's friends, teachers, relatives, neighbors) informed you of their concerns. Your list should also include any of the warning signs listed above with specific references to time and place. Collect any documentation of behavior change (i.e., report cards, traffic tickets, etc.).

Deal with suspicions of drug use firmly and directly.

Confronting your child with your suspicions could be done one-on-one, but it may be more effective if both parents are present. In some instances, all members of the immediate family should be present. The more support you have for your suspicions and the more concern expressed by those close to your child, the greater the impact on your child.

Start the meeting out by expressing your love for the child and the concern you have for his health and welfare. For example, *"We want to talk to you today about an issue that we all feel is very important for your health and safety. We love you very much and we want to make sure you are alright. We believe there is a problem we have to deal with head on."*

First ask your child if he is using drugs. Some children will tell you the truth. Give your child a chance to explain. Confront your child with the facts that made you concerned. Be specific. Ask for detailed explanations. Don't look for answers you want to hear. Look for the truth.

Always be supportive of the adolescent during this time. Never demean him. Criticize the behavior, not him personally. There is a strong tendency at this time to get angry and condemn the child for his behavior. Always tell the child you love him and that you are here to help him with his problems. Your message should be clear—you will not tolerate any drug use. Each person in the meeting should make this no-tolerance statement.

After the confrontation and discussion, an action plan must be formulated. This may involve professional treatment by a specialist in the area of adolescent substance abuse. The plan may include supervision of the child's behavior. Restrictions on behavior may be imposed with curfews, no overnight stays away from home, more structure with respect to use of free time, and random urine testing to determine if there is continued use. Write down details of the action plan. Don't negotiate, don't get over emotional, don't become a victimized parent and lay a guilt trip on the child, and don't assume that everything will be fine now that you have had this discussion.

Be available for your adolescent for support and direction.

Adolescent substance abusers can be very manipulative, and parents need to be prepared to deal with this. Follow the suggestions below to manage manipulative behavior:

- Formulate an action plan and stick to it. Don't be talked out of your behavioral expectations and don't accept excuses from your child. Be persistent and follow through. Apologies are important, but they shouldn't excuse behavior and replace a consequence. Accept the apology, but follow through.

- Act, don't yak! Psychologist, Dr. Sam Goldstein points out that parents often talk too much instead of taking action. Don't sermonize, lecture, demean, or try to induce guilt.

- Don't waver on important issues. Negotiation is food for the manipulative adolescent. The more they talk and get you to talk, the greater the likelihood someone will start negotiating and compromising. Some negotiation may be okay for small issues, but not on issues that have to do with core values. Stand firm in your no tolerance for drugs position. Kids will try to persuade you that it is alright for them to do a little drugs (i.e., beer at a party with their friends, smoking a cigarette now and then, etc.). They are just testing limits to see how serious you are. Stand firm.

- Bring others to the discussion to provide support. If you are the type of parent who can be easily persuaded, call in the troops (e.g., another parent, sibling, relative, etc.) to provide support.

- Don't be intimidated by threats your child might make. Deal with threats immediately. Your child needs to respect the authority in your home or you can help him find alternative living arrangements.

- Take threats of suicide seriously—especially if backed up by behavior that makes you believe your child is depressed. Stress can build in some adolescents to the point they may become suicidally depressed. Seek professional assistance if you believe your child has reached this level.

Drug Slang

Substance abuse brings with it a specific culture and vocabulary. It is important that parents know the language to identify if drug us is occurring by their child.

Alcohol:	booze, brain grenade, hooch, paint
Marijuana:	pot, grass, dank, smoke, buds, trees, Mary Jane, weed, Colombian, reefer, joint
Cocaine:	coke, snow, nose, flake, blow, line, C, powder
Rock Cocaine:	crack, rock, base, Roxanne
Amphetamines:	crank, bennies, splash, peaches, crystal, meth, speed, water, black beauties,
Heroin:	Big H, smack, brown sugar, tar, mud, thing, horse
LSD:	acid, barrels, blue sugar, blotter, acid, tabs, squares, windowpanes

Drugs That are Abused

Alcohol

Alcohol is a "gateway drug" and the most accepted drug of choice in the adolescent peer group. It is also the most accessible drug. Alcohol is mood altering and causes changes in the body. Alcohol is physically addicting and once an individual is dependent, physical withdrawal will occur. It depresses the central nervous system, which produces a slowing down of the body in all areas. Alcohol use can cause damage to the brain, liver disease, impotence, stomach problems, and high blood pressure. Of all fatal car accidents involving young drivers, nearly half are alcohol related.

Opiates

Opiates, commonly referred to as narcotics, are natural or synthetic drugs that reduce pain, cause drowsiness, and induce euphoria. This group includes such drugs as opium, morphine, heroin, methadone, codeine, meperidene, and fentanyl. Opiate use often leads to dependency. The euphoria associated with opiates is the primary reason for their abuse. They are frequently injected under the skin, into the muscles, or directly into the veins, however, they may also be absorbed from the stomach and intestine (by swallowing), the nasal membranes (by snorting), or the lungs (by smoking).

Central Nervous System Depressants

CNS depressants are sedative type drugs that slow down the overall activity of the nervous system. This group includes alcohol, barbiturates (Seconal, Nembutal, Amytal, and Tuinal), anti-anxiety agents or tranquilizers (Xanax, Valium, Librium) and others such as methaqualone (Quaalude) and Placidyl. Drug users refer to barbiturates as "downers" or "downs." The primary reason for use of barbiturates is the mood altering effect and calmness that results from their use. People usually first use CNS depressants prescribed by physicians for insomnia or anxiety or they are introduced to barbiturates by drug abusing peers. Chronic use of barbiturates can lead to dependency and larger, more frequent doses are required after repeated use. Accidental deaths can occur when people use two or more CNS depressants together such as barbiturates and alcohol.

Central Nervous System Stimulants

CNS stimulants speed up the nervous system resulting in acceleration of heart rate, increase in blood pressure, constriction of blood vessels, dilation of the pupils and bronchial tubes, and increase of gastric and adrenal secretions. In small doses the user feels more awake and alert and may have an increase in motor activity. This group includes cocaine, amphetamine, nicotine, and caffeine.

Cocaine, known as "coke," produces a feeling of euphoria, and it is a popular recreational drug. Cocaine is usually snorted or injected intravenously. The cocaine can also be heated with ether or other chemicals and then its vapors are inhaled. This practice is known as "free-basing." Crack is a form of free-base cocaine, which is smoked in glass pipes or sprinkled on tobacco or marijuana. Use of cocaine produces an intense, but short-lived feeling of euphoria which is followed by irritability, anxiety, and depression. Sudden death from cocaine is usually the result of excessive CNS stimulation that causes convulsions and respiratory collapse, cardiac arrhythmias, excessive constriction of the arteries to the heart resulting in ischemia (lack of oxygen to the heart muscle), and potential heart attacks or strokes.

Amphetamines are synthetic chemicals that stimulate the central nervous system. The group includes dextroamphetamine (Dexedrine), *d-l*-amphetamine (Benzedrine), and methamphetamine (Methedrine). On the street they are referred to as "speed," "crystal," "meth," and "ice," which is a smokeable form of methamphetamine. In small doses, amphetamines usually cause people to become more alert, less tired, and less bored. They are sometimes used to reduce appetite, but this effect lasts only a few weeks before higher doses are required for appetite reduction. Amphetamine abuse often starts as a way for someone to improve their performance on a task. For example, students use it to study more or truck drivers use it to stay awake longer. If large doses of amphetamines are injected, they can produce euphoria, which is replaced by irritability and depression when the effect wears off. Long-term use of "ice" can result in paranoia, hallucinations, and delusions.

Caffeine

Caffeine is a commonly used and abused drug. It is found in coffee, tea, cocoa, soft drinks, and over the counter drugs such as No-Doz. Caffeine stimulates the heart and respiratory system, increases muscle tension, and in small doses it increases alertness and may produce a feeling of well-being. In large doses caffeine can cause nervousness, irritability, headaches, difficulty with sleep, and stomach distress.

Marijuana

Marijuana has had widespread use in the United States with more than 30 percent of Americans having tried it at least once. Marijuana comes from the Indian hemp plant, *Cannabis sativa*. THC or tetrahydrocannabinol, is the main active ingredient in marijuana. Hashish is also prepared from this plant. Marijuana is usually smoked, but it can also be swallowed. The primary effect of marijuana in small doses is euphoria, exaggerated sensory experiences, slowing down of time sense, a deep feeling of relaxation, and impaired motor coordination. In larger doses marijuana can cause significant memory impairment, disturbances of thought processes, impaired attention, and out-of-body experiences. The long-term effects of marijuana are not well understood. Chronic bronchial irritation is one of the few widely agreed upon long-term effects of chronic use. Other possible negative effects include long-term memory impairment, gum disease, and increased risk of cancer around areas of the mouth and lungs.

Tolerance to marijuana develops with chronic use. Physical dependence as marked by significant symptoms of withdrawal has not been well established. The chronic marijuana user often expands their use of mind-altering drugs to other drugs, and marijuana is considered by many to be a gateway drug leading to further abuse.

Psychedelics

Psychedelics are a group of drugs whose primary effect is the alteration of perception, feelings, and thoughts. Because of this they are frequently referred to as hallucinogens. They include LSD (lysergic acid diethylamide), mescaline, psilocybin, STP (dimethoxy-methyl-amphetamine), DMT (dimethyl-tryptamine), and many others. They are usually swallowed or smoked.

LSD has a very powerful effect on the user even in very small doses. These effects include alterations in sensory modalities of vision, hearing, sense of time, and perceptions of one's body. In large doses there are often strong feelings of depersonalization or out of body experiences. Users quickly develop tolerance to the effects of many psychedelics after using for a few days and no physical dependence or withdrawal symptoms occur with discontinued use. Among the adverse effects of psychedelics are severe panic reactions, which can be horribly frightening to the user. These can occur with any dose of LSD, and they are impossible to predict. Even after the chemical effects of the drug have worn off, the user may experience spontaneous flashbacks or other psychological disturbances.

Most of the other psychedelics have similar mind-altering effects as LSD. Mescaline, also known as peyote, supposedly results in a different experience than LSD. DMT does not last as long as LSD while STP, in contrast, lasts longer. Mind-altering, psychedelic effects can also be induced by eating certain mushroom, certain morning glory seeds, nutmeg, jimson-weed, and other botanical products, but dizziness and other adverse effects have diminished their popularity.

Deliriants

This group of drugs causes severe, temporary impairment in brain functioning, which results in abnormal behavior or toxic psychosis. The symptoms can include inability to maintain attention, mental confusion, hallucinations, emotional dyscontrol, and delirious behavior. More severe adverse reactions can include convulsions, memory impairments, coma, and occasionally death.

PCP or phencyclidine, known as "angel dust," is a synthetic drug that can cause these severe alterations of brain functioning. Its use was popular in the mid-1960s and its use has continued to the present.

Inhalants are chemicals that are readily available to the public, which cause users to get "high" when inhaling fumes. There are three groups of inhalants: (1) volatile solvents—including adhesives and aerosols; (2) nitrites—found in room odorizers and in street drugs butyl nitrite and amy nitrite; and (3) anesthetics—including nitrous oxide or "laughing gas." For people under age 18, use of inhalants is increasing. Obviously, because of the availability of many inhalants, the use is difficult to control. Most of the inhalants produce effects that slow down bodily functions, cause users to feel less inhibited and in less control. Some inhalants can cause loss of consciousness, heart failure, or even death. High doses can cause replacement of oxygen in the lungs and central nervous system with the inhaled substance resulting in suffocation. This likelihood is increased when inhaling from a bag or in a close area. Other potential adverse effects from inhalants include impairments in thought processes, memory, perception, and coordination as well as hearing loss, and damage to the liver, kidneys, and bone marrow.

Designer Drugs

Designer drugs refers to substances that are produced synthetically in laboratories by modifying the chemical make-up of an existing drug. The result is known as an analogue drug. MDA, known as the "love drug," is an analogue of methamphetamine and mescaline. It produces a mild euphoria, but it can be fatal. MDMA, known as "ecstacy," causes hallucinogenic effects, elevates mood, and increases feelings of well-being and intimacy with others. It can also have adverse effects causing panic, anxiety, paranoid thought processes, increased heart rate, and involuntary muscular movements. An overdose can cause seizures, disturbances in heart function, and high blood pressure.

Treatment of Adolescent Substance Abuse and ADHD Combined with Substance Abuse

One of the most common treatments for adolescent substance abuse is family therapy and counseling for the adolescent abuser. This type of treatment involves all members of the family with the assumption that substance abuse is often closely linked to dysfunctional family interaction patterns. This approach also usually takes into account other social influences including peers, teachers, neighbors, and law enforcement officials who potentially can have an impact on the adolescent's substance use. An important part of the family therapy is training parents how to set limits, how to manage behavior appropriately, how to provide positive reinforcement, and how to improve communication and use problem-solving negotiation skills within the family.

**Counseling and family
therapy is an important part of the
treatment for adolescents with substance abuse.**

Less well studied have been the effects of adolescents attending 12 step Alcoholics Anonymous (AA) or Narcotics Anonymous (NA) programs or inpatient programs and the impact these programs have on substance abuse. 12 step AA or NA programs can have a dramatically positive effect on adult substance abuse. Inpatient programs often offer many components to treatment starting with detoxification. They also use individual counseling, family therapy, drug education, and incorporate 12 step AA or NA programs in their treatment.

Adolescent substance abusers, who have other psychiatric disorders such as anxiety disorders, depression, or ADHD, may be treated with medications to address these other conditions. Improvement in these other areas may have a positive impact on the adolescent's substance abuse. Dr. Paula Riggs points out, however, that child and adolescent psychiatrists are often reluctant to prescribe medication to treat the ADHD component of the ADHD adolescent substance abuser fearing that the use of a psychoactive medication such as a stimulant may worsen the substance abuse problem. Therefore, they may delay treatment of the ADHD until the substance abuse problem has improved. Dr. Riggs questions the wisdom of this, stating that treating the ADHD may enable the adolescent to take full advantage of the treatments for substance abuse by enhancing concentration, improving academic performance, etc.

Although there have not been many reports of children and adolescents with ADHD abusing prescribed stimulants, such abuse of stimulants may be more likely in ADHD adolescents with a history of substance use. The media have also reported Ritalin being sold by students to other students. For this reason, Dr. Riggs recommends that physicians may prefer to treat the ADHD with medications such as Cylert (pemoline) or buproprion with careful monitoring. She warns against using tricyclic antidepressants, which may be too dangerous to use with impulsive, substance abusing youth because of the adverse drug interaction effects these medications can have with illicit substances.

Treatment Settings

There are various types of treatment for the substance abusing adolescent. It is imperative that the family is involved for treatment to work. In addition, the adolescent must remain abstinent during this process to have maximum benefit and prognosis. These approaches also usually take into account other social influences including peers, teachers, neighbors, and law enforcement officials who potentially can have an impact on the adolescent substance abuser. The majority of professionals working with the adolescent in the following settings are in recovery themselves. This seems to be increasingly helpful in developing relationships with the adolescent. The adolescent feels understood and seems to open up more.

Outpatient Treatment

Outpatient treatment can either consist of a structured program or individual therapy with a private counselor. A structured outpatient treatment program includes group therapy, family therapy, education, and individual therapy. The amount and time involved in the program is determined by the treatment team providing the service. The treatment team works closely with other resources (psychiatrist, case manager, school social worker) in the community that the adolescent may be participating in. The majority of the time is spent in group therapy. Group therapy seems to benefit the adolescent most due to having peers in the group who can identify. The group becomes the adolescent's surrogate family and provides a safe place to share feelings.

Inpatient Treatment

Inpatient treatment is indicated when the adolescent cannot or will not stay abstinent while attending outpatient treatment. Many of the treatment interventions are the same as outpatient, however, it allows the adolescent to be separated from the drug lifestyle and environment. There are different types of inpatient programs that can meet the individual's needs. They include therapeutic communities, psychiatric-based facilities, medical-based facilities, and residential facilities. Each model has its own philosophy and style regarding treatment. Therapeutic communities and residential programs are usually longer in duration with an emphasis on education, structured activities and group therapy. The adolescent is introduced to the "12-step model," which is followed in both Alcoholics Anonymous and Narcotics Anonymous. The psychiatric and medical based facilities are less confrontational in nature and look to provide crisis intervention services. In addition, medication and individual therapy is most likely utilized.

Family Therapy

Family therapy is crucial for any type of treatment to work. During the family therapy process the family is identified as a system, where all members of the family have a role in the adolescents life. This setting provides a safe atmosphere for family members to share feelings related to not only the adolescent's substance abuse but how the family functions on a daily basis. An important part of the family therapy is training parents how to set limits, how to manage behavior appropriately, how to provide positive reinforcement, and how to improve communication and use problem-solving negotiation skills with their child. Enabling and communication are major areas targeted during this process.

12-Step Support Groups

As drug and alcohol use increases, so does increased participation by adolescents in the 12-step programs. The 12-step programs provide continuing support for individuals with drug and alcohol problems. The only requirement to join these groups is a desire to stop using drugs and alcohol. Groups are held daily in almost any city in the country. The goal of 12-step programs is total abstinence through acceptance of the illness and fellowship with other individuals with alcohol and drug problems. There is no charge for these groups. The adolescents can develop new peer groups while attending meetings, which will help in the recovery process. Examples of 12-step groups are Alcoholics Anonymous, Narcotics Anonymous, and Cocaine Anonymous. In addition, groups for family members are offered based on the same principle. The family members identify their role in the illness and are able to share and learn coping skills.

What Can Parents Do to Prevent Drug Use or Abuse?

Parents can do a great deal to prevent drug use or abuse in their children.

1. Parents should begin at an early age to teach their children appropriate behavior and standards of right and wrong. Parents should make a strong effort to instill these values in their children by their teachings and their behavior. Parents should communicate these values by:

    a.   Teaching children from early on that drug use is wrong and can be harmful to one's health.

    b.   Setting a good example by not using drugs themselves.

    c.   Letting their children and teenagers know clearly and emphatically that drug use is against the law.

    d.   Encouraging their children to be responsible for schoolwork, chores at home, proper behavior toward others, and making certain that they are held accountable for their behavior.

    e.   Setting limits on behavior through the establishment of house rules and street rules that promote responsibility to one's self and others in the family and community.

    f.   Following through with action when their child violates a rule or when behavior falls below the standard set by the parent or school.

2. Parents should be available to their children and adolescents to guide them in dealing with stress and pressure, which could lead to substance abuse. This could be done by:

    a.   Taking an active interest in the child's whereabouts, activities, and friends. Know what your child is doing and with whom. Parents who show an interest in their kids, as children and teenagers are less likely to find them in trouble when they get older.

    b.   Keep channels of communication open with your child. Allow your son or daughter to express feelings to you and encourage them to talk about their day. Try to be nonjudgemental at these times so that your child will feel free to discuss sensitive topics such as drug use at school, in the neighborhood, and among their peers.

c.   Encourage your son or daughter to ask questions about drugs and supply them with drug education information.

d.   Develop a relationship with the parents of your child's friends. You can often fill in missing gaps of information about your child's activities and the nature of their friends by talking with other parents.

e.   Be sensitive to what your child is watching on t.v., reading, or listening to. Consider restricting your son or daughter from exposure to media that glorifies drug usage.

3. Parents should be alert to early warning signs of drug usage and should be familiar with the steps they can take should they recognize these signs in their child or adolescent. Parents should:

a.   Look for warning signs of drug use in their child.

b.   If these signs are recognized, parents should be ready to take action. They should discuss their concerns calmly with their son or daughter.

c.   If their suspicions are confirmed, parents should move to restrict the child from any activities which might lead to further drug use. This might mean setting limits on where they could go, when, and with whom.

d.   Seek professional advice from a drug counselor or from school officials with experience in working in the area of substance abuse.

e.   Encourage the entire family to become involved in the helping process.

4. Parents should get involved in school and community activities that focus on alcohol and drug abuse. Parents should involve themselves in organizations/groups such as:

a.   School-parent groups where a consistent policy is developed regarding sub stance abuse in the school. Parents need to know how schools are educating their children and what measures are in place to intervene at the earliest occa sion.

b.   Parent support groups are an important intervention tool in the fight for drug free communities. Parents share mutual experiences and ideas to prevent drug abuse and together have increased resources to get things done.

c.   Resource groups provide information and direction for parents and families that are dealing with drug or alcohol abuse. These groups can be set up through the PTA in your community.

d.   Coalitions are developed as a partnership between the business community, provider community and residents in the community. Resources are combined to facilitate an organized effort to fight substance abuse. *The Miami Coalition for a Safe and Drug Free Community* is an excellent example of this effort.

The Miami Coalition was developed 10 years ago to help in the fight for a drug free Miami. Areas where they have played a major role in this fight include law enforcement, neighborhoods, schools, workplace issues, treatment, media and organization of community resources.

Prevention and education is the best solution to the drug abuse problem. Prevention programs focus on education about drug use and on government regulation and control of the drug supply. Education programs are present in most school systems from kindergarten through 12th grade. They focus on all areas related to substance abuse. The "decision-making model" seems to work with children. It provides a three part identification process of why we use drugs (motivation), the information we know about drugs (education), and the values that are threatened by using drugs. In addition, informing people about the harmful effects of drugs and the different reasons people have for using drugs is important.

What Your Children Should Know

The U.S. Department of Education's, *A Parent's Guide to Prevention*, describes certain information that a child should obtain throughout the schooling experience.

By the end of the third grade a child should understand;
- What an illicit drug is, why it is illegal, what it looks like, and what harm it can do;
- How medicines can help when prescribed by a doctor and how they can hurt when they are misused;
- Avoid unknown containers and substances;
- Which adults the child should rely on for information;
- What the school and home rules are about alcohol and drugs; and
- How using alcohol and drugs are illegal for all children.

By the end of sixth grade the child should know:
- Ways to identify specific drugs and alcohol;
- The consequences of drug and alcohol use;
- The effects drugs and alcohol have on your body; and
- The consequences drugs and alcohol have on your family's life, society, and the user.

By the end of ninth grade your child should know:
- The characteristics and nature of specific drugs;
- The physiologic effects drugs and alcohol have on specific organs of the body;

- The stages of chemical dependency and symptoms;
- The way drugs and alcohol affect motor activity, such as driving a car;
- Family history of chemical dependency due to genetic nature of illness.

By the end of the 12th grade the adolescent should understand:

- Short and long-term effects of specific drugs;
- Possible fatal effects of combing drugs and alcohol;
- The relationship of drug use and other diseases;
- The effects of alcohol on a fetus during pregnancy;
- The effects drugs can have on society;
- The treatment resources available; and
- The legal implications involved in alcohol and drug use.

Resources Available to the Parent

The quickest way to find help is through the yellow pages in your area or a referral from your family physician. In the yellow pages you will find phone numbers for Alanon, Alcoholics Anonymous, Narcotics Anonymous, and local treatment programs.

Listed below are other resources available to you at no charge:

American Council on Drug Education	1-800-488-DRUG
Families in Action Drug Information Center	1-404-934-6364
National Clearinghouse on Alcohol and Drug Information	1-800-SAY-NOTO
National Council on Alcoholism	1-212-206-6770
Tough Love	1-800-333-1069
Cocaine Helpline	1-800-COCAINE
NIDA Hotline	1-800-622-HELP
PRIDE	1-404-577-4500
Mothers Against Drunk Driving	1-214-744-6233
Just Say No Foundation	1-800-258-2766

Summary

Substance use by adolescents is rising in the United States. Tobacco and alcohol are the most widely used drugs. Add marijuana and you have the three gateway drugs, which often lead to further substance use. Adolescents who come from families where parents use substances or where there is significant conflict within the home are at risk for substance use. Moreover, adolescents who show problems with self-regulation, attention span, low self-esteem, and who are sensation-seeking are more likely to develop a substance use problem. The presence of ADHD has been associated with adolescent substance use in adolescents with a conduct disorder. There is no evidence that the presence of ADHD in itself (without the presence of conduct disorder) increases an adolescent's risk for developing a substance use disorder.

Parents should look for warning signs of drug use in their child. Experimental or casual drug use is difficult to detect. Parents are often surprised how long their child has been using drugs, and they never had a clue. With regular substance use, warning signs sometimes become more noticeable. Caregivers should be knowledgeable about different types of psychoactive substances that are used and the early warning signs of drug use. Parents should gather as much information as possible detailing suspicions of substance use and confront their child. Express concern and love, but be firm and decisive in your handling of drug-related behavior. Emphasize a no tolerance position regarding drug use and set limits on behavior. Treatment of adolescent substance use may involve family therapy, use of medications to treat associated disorders, attendance at 12-step programs for the adolescent and family members, impatient programs when needed, and drug education literature.

18 College, Vocational Education, and the Workforce

After graduating from high school, students have many choices to consider for their next step. Whether your son or daughter chooses college, trade or technical school, or decides to go straight into the job market—issues with ADHD should be considered. This chapter will focus on the different options available to older adolescents with ADHD and any special factors that should be kept in mind when planning for their future.

Preparing for College

The College Search

Colleges and universities are enrolling many more students with disabilities today than ever before. The American Council on Education reports that learning disabilities represents the largest disability group of students in college. In 1994 approximately 32 percent of disabled college students had a learning disability. Individuals with ADHD are adding to the growing number of students who are claiming a disability and seeking accommodations.

There is no formula for picking the "right" college for a student with a disability. Students with disabilities, like other students, differ in their interests, preferences, abilities, and goals. Some prefer a large school with intercollegiate sports, a huge stadium, a diverse student population, and a broad range of majors from which to choose. Others may want a smaller college with a personal touch, small class sizes, and the opportunity to have closer contact with instructors. There are many institutions, both large and small, which can successfully meet the needs of students with disabilities.

Graduating high school seniors with ADHD will have a successful college search if they try to balance their preferences with their specific learning needs. They will need to understand how their ADHD affects their learning and performance in school and what accommodations they might need to help them. Then they will have to search through the institutions they prefer and find the ones that can realistically meet their needs. When they've narrowed down the list to five or six schools, they must learn as much as they can and visit the schools. On the visit, try to schedule a meeting with other students with disabilities. Arrange to meet a counselor at the Disabled Student Services (DSS) office. Arrange to meet with instructors in the student's area of interest. Encourage your child to stay overnight in a residence hall and get first-hand information from other students about school and campus life.

**Prospective college students
with ADHD should understand
how their ADHD affects learning and
what accommodations they may need in college.**

Rights of Students with Disabilities in Higher Education

The rights of students with disabilities in postsecondary education are protected under the law. Section 504 of the Rehabilitation Act of 1973 and the Americans with Disabilities Act (ADA) protect students who are qualified to participate academically and who meet the requirements of the postsecondary program they are attending. Institutions are required to provide accommodations to qualified students who disclose their disability to the college or university. A student is not required to disclose they have a disability during the admission process and generally, postsecondary schools do not inquire about one's disability on admission applications.

Many colleges and universities are well prepared to provide services for students with ADHD. Increasingly, ADHD students are taking advantage of these services to ensure that they have a successful college experience. For those students who have had an earlier diagnosis of ADHD, the same accommodations and study strategies that helped them in high school can often be provided in college. Recently diagnosed students will benefit from working with college faculty to receive the assistance they need.

Should You Keep Your Disability a Secret in College?

To be eligible to receive accommodations in college, a student must disclose their disability to the college or university. Jeanne M. Kincaid, a noted authority on disability law and education, cautions that students with a disability who choose to attempt college without accommodations do so at their own risk. She points out that students with learning disabilities or ADHD, who have been labeled during many years of school may want to try college without special assistance. Some do succeed without accommodations, but court and agency rulings have consistently placed the responsibility for securing disability-related accommodations on the student's shoulders and do not hold the school responsible if the student failed to disclose the disability.

The Disabled Student Services Office

The student and family should contact the college's Disabled Student Services (DSS) office to determine the types of services available for students with disabilities. Institutions differ considerably in the method by which they deliver programs and services to students with disabilities. In most cases, services for students with ADHD are an extension of the services developed for use with students with learning disabilities. Students should consult one of the excellent guide books for a listing of institutions that have programs and services for disabled students. *The K & W Guide to Colleges for the Learning Disabled: Fourth Edition* by Marybeth Kravets and Imy F. Wax is an excellent resource.

Documentation

Colleges will require documentation of a student's disability. Documentation establishes that the student has a disability and qualifies for protections under Section 504 and the ADA. In addition, documentation can provide information to the college as to the student's specific needs and can guide the college in providing appropriate services. Some colleges have developed guidelines regarding the assessment and documentation needed. Below is a list of the type of information The National Board of Medical Examiners requires in documentation:

- The documentation should contain a specific diagnosis of the disability. For ADHD, for example, the diagnostic criteria published by the American Psychiatric Association as listed in the DSM IV would be appropriate.

- The documentation should be current. In most cases, the evaluation should have been done within the past three years.

- The documentation should list the specific diagnostic criteria and or assessment procedures used, including dates when the tests or procedures were done, the results, and an interpretation of the results. A detailed educational, developmental, and medical history should be included.

- The documentation should describe in detail the individual's limitations due the diagnosed disability. That is, how the disability will impair performance.

- There should be specific accommodations recommended in the documentation with a detailed explanation of why these accommodations are needed and how they will lessen the impact of the functional impairment of the individual.

- The documentation should contain the professional credentials of the examiner, which qualify him to make the diagnosis. This should include information about license or certification in the area related to the diagnosis.

As you can see, a note from a student's doctor simply stating that the student has ADHD would most likely be regarded as insufficient documentation by many colleges. Families should check with the DSS office to see what documentation a specific college requires. Previous psychological or educational reports should be collected from health care providers or schools and sent to the DSS office to determine whether the existing documentation meets the criteria set by the college. If not, reports may need to be updated.

**Keep records of all past
medical and psychological
reports that may be needed for documentation.**

In grades K-12 school districts were required by law to identify students with disabilities and to do evaluations at no cost to the parents. In higher education, students are responsible for identifying themselves as disabled, and they must pay for their own evaluation. The DSS office may be able to do some of the assessment without charge.

Accommodations

The purpose of accommodations is to "even the playing field" for disabled students so they are not competing with non-disabled students unfairly. With this in mind, accommodations should be designed to reduce or eliminate the effect of a disability on a specific activity, such as learning.

Once it has been established that a student has a disability and the student will require accommodations, the DSS office, together with the student, will determine appropriate support services for the student. No two students with ADHD are exactly alike, therefore, support services are designed on a case-by-case basis to meet the student's individual needs. Examples of accommodations that may be arranged for the student are listed below:
- Extended test time to complete tests
- A notetaker or scribe
- Course substitution of nonessential courses
- A distraction-free test room
- Extended time to complete degree requirements
- Books on tape
- Tape recording of classes

- Use of calculator, dictionary, computer, spellcheck in exams
- Reduced course loads
- An alternate format for taking tests

Colleges differ in how teaching faculty are made aware of the accommodations they are required to provide for a student. In most cases, students are encouraged to be self-advocates. They may give a letter prepared by the DSS office to each of their instructors or the DSS office might send such a letter directly to the instructor. Students should practice self-advocacy from the very start of this process and throughout.

Self-disclosure of a student's disability is necessary to receive accommodations.

To receive accommodations, the students must self-disclose their disability and provide appropriate documentation. The students can become involved in the process by collaborating with the DSS office about the types of accommodations they will need and by meeting with instructors to facilitate the implementation of the accommodations. This last step is very important. While most college faculty know about Section 504 and ADA accommodations, some do not or are reluctant to make accommodations. In such cases, the student should promptly contact the DSS office and ask for them to intervene. It is the student's responsibility, not the college's, to let the DSS office know if an instructor is not providing the accommodations which were agreed upon.

Other Services

In addition to providing accommodations for students with disabilities, colleges may provide services (some at an additional charge) to such students. The DSS office can frequently arrange for assessment services, training in study skills, or tutoring, which the student may require. Counseling services are frequently available on many college campuses, and the DSS office may be able to arrange for priority registration for classes.

Mary McDonald Richard (1996), Coordinator of Services for Students with Learning Disabilities at the Office of Student Disability Services at The University of Iowa and a past president of CH.A.D.D., describes some of the services that a DSS office in college can provide for disabled students.

- Advocacy and Self-Advocacy

  DSS counselors may work with staff and/or faculty to advocate appropriate accommodations for students with ADHD. This could include training students in self-advocacy skills.

- Degree Requirement Substitutions

  If a student is prevented from completing degree requirements in such areas as mathematics or foreign language because of his disability, substitute courses may be approved.

- Alternative Examinations
  A frequent request by students with ADHD are accommodations for test-taking. Extended test time, distraction-free test environments, a reader or a scribe, or the use of a dictionary, computer, calculator, or proofreader are often requested.

- Notetaking Services
  Notetaking services may be required for an ADHD student. This could be supplied in various ways—supplying the instructor's notes to the student, making copies of another student's notes, and using the services of a paid notetaker.

- Recorded Reading Material
  Textbooks and reading assignments may be recorded on audiocassette tapes for students with print disabilities.

- Technological Tools and Auxiliary Aids
  Calculators, tape players and recorders, computers with word processing programs and spell checkers, time management systems, and personal organizers are examples of some of the tools that may assist a student with disabilities.

- Self-Management Instruction
  A student may benefit from instruction in how to regulate their attention and behavior. Strategies such as "self-talk," notetaking systems, and time management programs can be used.

- Individual Counseling
  Students with disabilities may experience more stress as they go through college than other students. Counseling to help them cope with this stress is often quite beneficial. The DSS office can provide a referral to the student for counseling. Through such counseling the student could get a better idea of their strengths and inner resources and learn self-advocacy skills to assist them in class and with campus life.

- Strategic Schedule Building
  With priority registration, students with disabilities have a better chance of selecting courses that fit better into their learning/study schedule. Many students with ADHD take medication to manage their attention and behavior. Courses taken in accordance with the use of such medication can make a difference in how well the student performs.

- Reduced Course Load
  Students with disabilities often take a reduced number of courses each semester. Mary

McDonald Richard recommends no more than 12 to 13 hours of credit per semester. If the student is doing well, the student may enroll in an additional course.

- Mentoring and "Anchoring"
  A mentor can be a positive role model for a student with disabilities. Mentors can encourage students who are striving to reach their personal goals in college.

- Assistance with Educational and Vocational Choices
  Programs that inform and guide students with ADHD in making decisions regarding college majors and career choices may be available through the DSS office. This can include assessment using career interest inventories, seminars, or internship experiences that provide the student with a slice of the real life career they are considering.

Tips for ADHD Students

In her book, *Succeeding in College with Attention Deficit Disorders,* Dr. Jennifer Bramer, a counselor at Lansing Community College, emphasizes that college students with ADHD should take advantage of as many programs and services as they need to help them succeed. She also stresses the importance of continued treatment for ADHD while in college, especially for management of medication. Dr. Bramer lists tips students with ADHD can use to make their college experience more successful.

Students' TIPS
(**T**ime management, **I**nterventions, **P**ositive attitudes, **S**upports)
for Getting the Most Out of College

Time management
- Arrange to live in a single dorm room or apartment
- Do not overload yourself --12 credits per term is probably enough
- Schedule classes with reasonably lengthy breaks between them
- Schedule classes so they vary in subject matter and intensity
- Keep your "prime time" in mind when scheduling
- Maintain a calendar of all events--assignments, appointments, social plans
- Break large assignments into smaller tasks to put on your calendar
- Make and prioritize a "to do" list daily
- Plan study time and consider it a serious commitment

Interventions
- Select a college that has the services and support you need
- Have a complete treatment plan in place: MEDICATION, COUNSELING, and EDUCATION

- Establish realistic goals
- Attend to physical well-being —exercise, nutrition, sleep
- Develop your spiritual well-being
- Know about your limitations and needed accommodations
- Obtain career counseling from someone familiar with your disabilities
- Share records of your disabilities with those providing assistance
- Request assistance —priority registration, course substitutions, taped textbooks, proctored tests, tutoring, note takers
- Register for developmental English and/or math classes, if needed
- Enroll in a study skills class
- Sit in the front of the room
- Experiment with various study environments until you recognize your best
- Invest in tutoring if it is not available free
- Organize and/or attend study groups
- Tape lectures and listen to them again while walking, jogging, or commuting
- Quiz yourself by taping questions, pauses, and answers; listen and respond to tapes while walking, jogging, or commuting
- Take medication as prescribed
- See counselor or therapist on a regular basis
- Increase structure and reduce distractions
- Educate yourself about ADD—strategies, legal rights, and advocacy

P ositive attitudes

- Advocate appropriately
- Participate in extracurricular activities you enjoy
- Celebrate small successes
- Remember that ADD is a neurologically based disorder
- Listen to or read the success stories of other students with ADD

S upports

- Seek accommodating instructors
- Develop a supportive relationship with a counselor or therapist
- Talk about problems with appropriate persons
- Participate in an ADD support group or start one
- Request an appointment with each instructor—discuss your needs, explain ADD if necessary
- Request accommodations—note taker, permission to tape, extended time, alternative testing conditions, permission to stand or take breaks, calculators or electronic spellers during exams, permission to hand in long assignments in stages

Closing Thoughts for Parents

Having experienced the college selection process with two daughters, I can tell you that the time between receiving college applications to the final selection of a college will be a mixture of emotions—confusion, anxiety, disappointment, and elation. It will all be worth it, however, provided that you and your child made the right choice. The search for the right college is just the beginning, and it is the time when you, as a parent, will probably have the most input. Afterward, whether your son or daughter attends school at home or out of town, you will have to let go and encourage them to develop the self-advocacy skills needed to take care of themselves.

College can be a difficult challenge for students with disabilities—but it is not an insurmountable one. With your support, their courage, and the school's help—they have a good chance of succeeding. Parents can contact the Association for Higher Education and Disabilities (AHEAD) for more information on college life for individuals with disabilities.

Vocational Education

Vocational training during high school or after graduation is essential in today's job market for students who are not going to college. In the past, unskilled jobs accounted for approximately 60 percent of the job market in the U.S. In the year 2000, unskilled workers will only make up 15 percent of the workforce. The School-to-Work Opportunities Act of 1994 (STOWA) emphasizes the importance of vocational education. The goal of STOWA is for every student upon completion of high school to be employed or receive training following graduation that would result in employment.

Vocational education can be divided into seven occupational areas:
1. agriculture
2. business and office
3   health occupations
4. marketing
5. family and consumer sciences (home economics)
6. trade and industry
7. technology and technical education (industrial arts)

Approximately 75 percent of the vocational education programs fall in the areas of business and office and trade and industry programs. Many high schools offer vocational instruction. Students typically attend vocational classes on the high school campus for up to a half day each day. They are provided with hands-on instruction and practice applying skills under supervision. Many communities have stand-alone vocational technical centers not located on the high school campus. On-the-job training programs offer another source of vocational education.

According to Robin Hawks, an instructor of special education at James Madison University, there are over 10,000 vocational-technical schools in the United States. Training is offered in more than 100 different careers such as cosmetology, automotive repair, computer training, truck driving, refrigeration and air conditioning, computer technology. Students receive hands-on training and experience. Students are taught by experts in their field of study, and they are often trained in the latest technology.

Rebecca Evers and Nick Elksnin, authors of *Working with Students with Disabilities in Vocational-Technical Settings,* stress the importance of vocational education for students with disabilities. Research data show that adults with disabilities, who have gone through some vocational education, do better in their employment than those who have had no vocational education.

Bias Against Vocational Education

Despite the importance of vocational education, it is believed to be a "second class" curriculum. It is often the choice of last resort for high school students in special education.

This is unfortunate. As our society becomes more technologically advanced the demand for skilled workers will increase. High school teachers, in general, have very limited experience with mainstream vocational education courses. Even teachers who specialize in teaching special education students are not prepared to direct their students into vocational education. High school guidance departments don't direct students into vocational education as much as the need warrants.

For high school students with ADHD who are receiving special education and have an IEP, planning for vocational education should be discussed during the IEP development and included in their Individual Transition Plan (ITP). Transition planning could also be part of the 504 Plan of a student with ADHD. Students with ADHD who are not receiving special education services or who do not have a 504 Plan may access vocational education in the traditional way.

Career Exploration

Students interested in vocational education can get information about different careers in several ways. High schools usually offer a general course in career awareness for all students. If such courses are not available, teachers and parents can provide career information through family-planned trips, school field trips, career days, class discussion, and independent reading.

Students wishing to explore various careers may get involved in a paid work experience program. Typically, the student attends school in the morning and is free in the afternoon to go to work. The high school provides credit for the work experience.

Another way to become familiar with a specific field is through job shadowing. Students follow skilled workers during their workday. They observe them in their workplace and become familiar with the worker's duties and responsibilities. Students can interview workers and obtain useful information about the particular field, how satisfied workers are in the field, and other benefits of the job. Job shadowing is a temporary placement. It serves only to introduce students to a field without providing any hands-on learning.

Students can also learn more about a career through voluntary service within the community. Some organizations and businesses have established volunteer programs wherein students can earn community service credits as well as become familiar with a field they may want to enter.

The Workforce

Some individuals prefer to go right into a job after high school. They may seek employment through state and local agencies, classified advertisements in newspapers, employment agencies, or through contacts among family, friends, and acquaintances. Unless the individual has a specific skill, most of the jobs they will get will be unskilled, entry level. Although an individual might start out on the ground level, he certainly doesn't have to stay there. Most employers reward good job performance with increases in salary and promotions.

People with ADHD often ask, "What is the right job for a person with ADHD?" There really is not "right" job for a person with ADHD. We have seen people with ADHD succeed in all types of careers and work environments. ADHD can pose similar challenges for the individual in the workplace as it did in school. Work, like school, places demands on the individual to perform. Employers, however, are much less likely than teachers to tolerate tardiness, inaccuracy, and poor performance. Chronic problems in these areas will usually lead to probation and eventual dismissal—especially if you are working in an unskilled job that is relatively easy for your employer to fill.

Dr. Kathleen Nadeau points out several areas of difficulty that people with ADHD may have in the workplace. These include problems with hyperactivity/motor restlessness, distractibility, organization, time management, procrastination, low frustration tolerance, interpersonal conflicts on the job, prioritization, and memory.   Below are some strategies to manage these challenges:

- Find a job that does not require long periods of time where you will be sitting in one place.

- Take frequent breaks (e.g., a walk to the water fountain once in a while, change the activity you are doing, stand up and stretch).

- Exercise before or after work if you have a sedentary job.

- Leave plenty of time in your schedule to get to work on time.

- If you leave your work area for lunch, take a walk.

- Set aside time during the day when you will be able to work quietly without being interrupted.

- Explain to your supervisor that you concentrate better in a distraction-free setting.

  - Frequently check whether you are paying attention to your work by asking yourself, "Am I on task?"

  - Learn to do one thing at a time and when finished, go on to the next project.

  - Try to work on a team with someone who is more organized.

  - Develop the habit of setting aside time each day for planning your work for the day.

  - Consider jobs that do not involve working on long-term, detailed projects.

  - Plan your day and follow your plan. Don't get distracted by events around you.

  - Learn to set reasonable limits by not taking on more work than you are able to do.

  - Don't get caught in "hallway conversations" that will last longer than you expect and take you away from your work.

  - Give yourself deadlines to complete work.

  - Avoid working in tense environments if you have a low frustration tolerance.

  - Pay attention to cues from others—you may be talking too much, intruding on other's space, interrupting too often.

  - Know when enough is enough and don't overstep your limits in work relationships.

  - Use lists to prioritize your work from "do it now" to "it can wait."

  - Take notes at important meetings.

  - Keep a notebook or pad by your workplace to write down important information.

Accommodations in the Workplace

The Americans with Disabilities Act (ADA) prohibits discrimination against people with disabilities in the workplace. To receive protection under the ADHD you must have a disability, you must be "otherwise qualified" to perform the job, you must have been denied a job or some benefit because of your disability, and the employer must be covered under the ADA.

The phrase, "otherwise qualified," means you have all the qualifications to do the job (i.e., education, experience, knowledge, and ability), and you would be able to perform the functions of the job if you were give certain reasonable accommodation. An accommodation is an adjustment in the employer's work or testing requirements that would allow an individual with a disability to meet the requirements of a job without putting an undue burden on the employer.

**Employers can make accommodations
for you at work to help you improve your performance.**

Attorneys Peter and Patricia Latham indicate that the federal law does not contain specific information concerning reasonable accommodations for individuals with ADHD. However they would consider that reasonable accommodations might include:

1.   Providing a structured learning/working environment.
2.   Repeating and simplifying instructions about work assignments.
3.   Supplementing verbal instructions with visual instructions.
4.   Adjusting class or work schedules.
5.   Modifying test delivery.
6.   Using tape recorders, computer-aided instruction, or work methods.
7.   Using other audiovisual equipment.

Should I Keep My Disability a Secret in the Workplace?

If a person with ADHD were to disclose they had a disability when seeking a job, the employer may not be as willing to hire them. Unfortunately, disclosure once an employee is hired may place that person's job at risk. It is usually best to try to obtain work place accommodations without revealing you have ADHD. Employers often understand that their employees have individual preferences in work habits. They are willing to make adjustments in the work setting or in work requirements to accommodate an employee, whether they have a disability or not. However, keep in mind that an employer is not required to make accommodations for a disabled employee who is qualified to receive accommodations unless the employer is informed of the need for such accommodations.

**Before you can receive
accommodations in the workplace,
you must disclose your disability to your employer.**

If you decide to disclose to your employer that you have ADHD, it is your responsibility to let your employer know what types of accommodations you will require. You or your employer can get help with determining appropriate accommodations through the Job Accommodations Network (JAN). JAN is a service of the President's Commission on the Employment of People with Disabilities. It is charged with providing accommodation information at no cost to businesses, rehabilitation professionals, and people with disabilities from in the United States. This information is then used by the caller to make appropriate accommodations in the workplace. From July 1994-June 1995, JAN received nearly 80,000 calls—the majority of which were from private or public employers of individuals with disabilities. JAN reports that within two to three months after calling, 38 percent of the employers who contacted JAN have implemented an accommodation based on the information provide to them. Of those employers who report having made an accommodation, 82 percent said that the accommodation was either extremely or very effective. Many of the accommodations were implemented at either no cost or very little cost to the employer.

Below is a small list of accommodations that may be useful for persons with ADHD in the workplace:
- Meet with supervisor more frequently for feedback.
- Write clear guidelines for job performance.
- Provide frequent job performance reviews.
- Provide less distractions in environment.
- Provide training in time management skills.
- Use headphones to reduce distractions.
- Provide work in smaller chunks instead of long-term projects.
- Use checklists to determine job priorities and set completion dates.
- Permit movement to manage hyperactivity or restlessness.
- Provide clerical help with paperwork.
- Use of an organizer or word processor.
- Post reminder notices of new procedures or work-related events.
- Simplify paperwork requirements.
- Make private office available when distraction-free environment is required.

Though many people have heard about ADHD, there is relatively little awareness of what it is and how it affects people in the workplace. Try to educate your employer or work supervisor about ADHD. Make an effort to establish a relationship with your employer/supervisor that respects one another's goals within the workplace.

Summary

Colleges and universities are enrolling more students with disabilities. Many institutions are well prepared to provide services for students with ADHD. The student will have to search through the institutions they prefer and find the ones that can realistically meet their needs. A visit to the college and a meeting with a counselor at the Disabled Student Services office is most helpful in determining what services a school can offer for students with ADHD.

Students may decide to obtain a vocational education rather than be on a college bound track in high school. As our society becomes more technologically advanced, there will be fewer employment opportunities for unskilled workers. Vocational education opportunities should be discussed with students in high school prior to graduation. Students with ADHD who are receiving special education and related services may wish to incorporate vocational education planning into their transition plans.

Individuals with ADHD who choose work as an alternative to school should be aware of how their ADHD might affect their work performance. Problems can occur with organization, meeting deadlines, dealing with others in the workplace, managing details, and setting limits on your time. If ADHD does affect performance at work, the employer may be able to make accommodations, provided the employee discloses his disability.

ADHD does not have to be a roadblock to success after high school. Many opportunities lie ahead for ambitious, bright, and talented people even if they have ADHD.

19 ADHD and the Military

I recently received this letter from a concerned parent.

My son was diagnosed with ADD during first grade. He has been under a doctor's care ever since and has taken Ritalin or Adderall since first grade. He has responded well to the medication, and maintained good grades throughout school. He even became part of the leadership program in high school and became a model student. He graduated from high school and hoped to enter the U.S. Coast Guard to continue his education. Unfortunately, his dreams were immediately shattered when advised by U.S. Coast Guard recruitment officer in Tampa that he would not be considered due to the medication he is taking. They went on to tell him that even if he was not taking it now, he would be rejected if he had taken medication for ADD since the age of 12.

I believe this is discrimination and would like to know what remedies are available to ensure that my chid is given every opportunity to succeed. This has not been an easy road for my son or our family, and I am appalled that the first door in his life was closed by the very government that passes laws to protect disabled persons. I would have expected such action from the private sector, but the government has no excuse for such discrimination.

Adolescents treated for ADHD with stimulant medication may be excluded from qualifying for service in the military. This comes as a complete surprise to many young men and women who have considered enlisting in a branch of the armed forces only to be turned down by recruitment offices because of their current or past history of ADHD and stimulant treatment.

In a recent edition of the *ADHD Report* (1997), William Hathaway, Ph.D. tried to unravel the details of military policy as it involves ADHD. He reviewed military documents and regulations and communicated with psychiatric consultants in several branches of the armed forces through telephone interviews. Much of the information that follows is extracted from Dr. Hathaway's investigation.

The Selective Service Act

Under the Selective Service Act, a diagnosis of ADHD can affect an individual's eligibility for military service (Latham & Latham, 1992). According to the act, individuals may be determined "unacceptable for service in the Army Forces" based on mental or physical conditions. Guidelines for determining when a physical or mental condition should be considered disqualifying for membership in the service are stated in a 1994 Department of Defense directive 6130.3 entitled *Physical Standards for Enlistment, Appointment and Induction.*

ADHD is considered under the category of *Specific Academic Skill Defects.* These are defects in which there is a chronic history of academic skills or perceptual defects resulting from organic or functional mental disorders that interfere with performance at work or school after age 12. The directive states that "current use of medication to improve or maintain academic skills (e.g., methylphenidate hydrochloride) is disqualifying."

**An earlier diagnosis of
ADHD or the current or past use of
stimulant medication to treat ADHD may
disqualify a person from serving in the military.**

Dr. Hathaway refers to a 1997 article in *Psychiatric Times,* by Joyce Baldwin, which clarifies the military's policy regarding an individual's past use of methylphenidate (Ritalin). Baldwin points out that individuals with a history of ADHD, who have been treated with Ritalin, may serve in the military. Their scores on the Armed Services Vocational Aptitude Battery must be acceptable, they must have a high school record demonstrating reasonable grades, and they cannot be taking Ritalin or a similar drug. Baldwin also refers to additional information from the military, which indicates that if a person was able to function at a normal level in high school without special accommodations or the use of medication, they may serve in the military.

It would appear then that military recruitment or enlistment is denied to persons with ADHD only if there has been a history of <u>recent</u> impairment in functioning, which would affect performance of military duty if <u>recent</u> treatment with medication was required.

The definition of <u>recent</u>, however, may vary from one branch of service to another, "depending upon the special personnel needs and operational environment of the respective services." Hathaway communicated with the chief of medical services at the Springfield,

Massachusetts Military Entrance Processing Station. He was informed that treatment with stimulant medication within the past year of taking the entrance exam would be considered too recent use of medication and would make a candidate ineligible to qualify for service in the U. S. Coast Guard. However, Hathaway points out that the Coast Guard is willing to look at individuals who have not used stimulant medication within the past five years, provided they can document suitability for military service through school and medical records.

Suitability for Duty

There are other regulations regarding what types of medical or mental difficulties render a member of the service as unsuitable to perform his duties. Suitability for military duty is at the core of the military's concern regarding any person with a physical or mental disorder. Put simply, is the person able to do the job required of him?

Hathaway interviewed some of the military's psychiatric consultants. They agreed that the presence of ADHD would not automatically make a member of the service unsuitable for duty. Obviously, ADHD affects people in different ways and depending on the individual's specific responsibilities within the military, ADHD symptoms may or may not significantly impair performance. Hathaway presents the following hypothetical example to illustrate this:

> Sargeant troop has had great difficulty completing his college degree due to problems with attention. He has been diagnosed with ADHD. He works as part of the staff in his unit's mobility section. The section's responsibilities include training all unit personnel in mobility readiness and documenting this training. Although he is somewhat inconsistent in completing his paperwork, his schedule is flexible enough to allow him to catch up when needed. Because he is well-liked by his coworkers and supervisors and because he does an outstanding job running exercises and doing briefings, his supervisors tolerate his inconsistent performance with the paperwork and more frequently task his other skills.

> Sargeant Troop's job is quite varied. On any given day he may be running briefings, attending an advanced training course, checking out the mobility inventory for his unit, or helping to plan the next mobility exercise. He finds this varied work fascinating and has little opportunity for boredom. His unit is aware of some of his ADHD related difficulties, but these do not significantly interfere with his job performance. His unit feels SGT Troop has proven to be an asset to the section.

Hathaway's point is well taken—suitability for duty must be made on an individual, case-by-case basis. Although the presence of a physical or mental disorder such as ADHD may heighten concerns about a person's suitability for duty, the diagnosis of ADHD alone may not be used to indicate whether someone is unsuitable. There must be evidence of impaired functioning in a specific area which is necessary for the person to sufficiently do his duty. The presence of ADHD may make a person at greater risk for unsuitability, but it does not guarantee that a member of the service will have a problem performing his assigned duties.

**Suitability for duty must
made on an individual basis.**

Hathaway discussed whether having ADHD would automatically exclude a service member from certain types of duties or clearances. The military's psychiatric consultants said that although the presence of ADHD might make it more difficult for someone to get assigned to certain specific duties or obtain clearances, the ultimate decision would be made on a case by case basis. Hathaway concludes this discussion by pointing out that there are substantial barriers within the wording of the regulations. This could make it very difficult for ADHD service members to get approval for certain types of duty or certain clearances.

Problems Arising from the Use of Stimulant Medication

As Hathaway states, "Although active duty members with ADHD are sometimes treated with stimulant medication, such treatment raises a host of management problems for the military…" (p. 4).   Methylphenidate, dextroamphetamine, and Adderall, common stimulants used to treat ADHD, are all Schedule II controlled substances. The military has strict rules regarding them. For example, a service member may have to be deployed to a ship or somewhere else in the world where access to medication may be difficult or impossible. In speaking with a consultant for the Navy, Hathaway reported that on Navy ships, all controlled substances must be maintained by the executive officer or a designated representative. It is left up to the executive officer of the ship to agree to maintain the stimulant medication for the member. Some do and some do not.

**Stimulant medication treatment
presents management problems for the military.**

Hathaway refers to a memorandum on ADHD issued in 1995 by the Surgeon General of the Air Force, Lt. Gen. Edgar Anderson, Jr., to illustrate ongoing concerns that the military has about the use of stimulants by active duty personnel. The directive in this memorandum stated that Air Force Medical Service, as well as the medical departments of the other services, require a psychiatric consultation on all active duty personnel who present with symptoms compatible with the diagnosis of ADHD prior to the prescription of psychostimulants. The psychiatric consultation would ensure required administrative actions are completed and would take into consideration the abuse potential of the stimulant medications.

Summary

Men and women who would like to enlist for service in one of the Armed Forces may find that their history of ADHD and prior or current use of stimulant medication could be a barrier to their acceptance. The Selective Service Act allows the government to deem a person "unacceptable for service" based on a physical or mental condition. ADHD is considered a mental condition, which could disqualify a candidate. Moreover, the earlier use of stimulant medication after age 12 could be another factor that makes a candidate ineligible for service. It seems that cases involving people with ADHD are being considered on a case-by-case basis. Factors that are taken into account are a person's prior ability to function at a normal level in high school without accommodations, the use of medication, or specific impairments that a person with ADHD has that could affect his ability to perform military duties.

Adolescents considering future service in the military must consider the potential problems a diagnosis of ADHD and a history of using stimulant medication may pose.

Resources

National Organizations
Association on Higher Education and Disability (AHEAD)
P.O. Box 21192
Columbus, OH 43221-0192
(614) 488-4972

Attention Deficit Disorders Association (ADDA)
9930 Johnnycake Ridge, Suite 3E
Mentor, Ohio 44060
(440) 350-9595
www.add.org

Children and Adults with Attention Deficit Disorders (CH.A.D.D.)
8181 Professional Place, Suite 201
Landover, Maryland 20785
(800) 233-4050
www.chadd.org

Council for Exceptional Children (CEC)
Eric Clearinghouse on Disabilities and Education
1920 Association Drive
Reston, Virginia 20191
(800) 328-0272
www.cec.sped.org

Learning Disabilities Association of America (LDA)
4156 Library Road
Pittsburgh, Pennsylvania 15234
(412) 341-1515
www.ldanatl.org

National Center on Addiction and Substance Abuse (CASA)
152 W. 57th St.
New York, New York 10019
(212) 841-5200
www.casacolumbia.org

National Clearing House for Alcohol and Drug Information (NCADI)
P.O. Box 2345
Rockville, Maryland 20847
(800) SAY NO TO
www.health.org

National Information Center for Children and Youth with Disabilities (NICHCY)
P.O. Box 1492
Washington, D.C. 20013-1492
(800) 695-0285
www.nichcy.org

Books and Videos
ADD WareHouse
300 N. W. 70th Ave., Suite 102
Plantation, Florida 33317
(800) 233-9273 • (954) 792-8100
www.addwarehouse.com

Newsletters
The ADHD Report
Guilford Publications
72 Spring St.
New York, New York, 10012
(800) 365-7006
www.guilford.com

Suggested Reading and Videos

Books for Parents and Teachers

Alexander-Roberts, C. (1995). *ADHD and teens: A parent's guide to making it through the tough years.* Dallas, TX: Taylor Publishing Co.

Barkley, R. A. (1995). *Taking charge of ADHD: The complete authoritative guide for parents.* New York: The Guilford Press.

Bramer, J. S. (1996). *Succeeding in college with attention deficit disorders: Issues and strategies for students, counselors, and educators.* Plantation, FL: Specialty Press, Inc.

Dendy, C. A. (1995). *Teenagers with ADD: A parents' guide.* Maryland: Woodbine House.

Fellman, W. R. (1997). *The other me: Poetic thoughts on ADD for adults, kids, and parents.* Plantation, FL: Specialty Press, Inc.

Fowler, M. C. (1992). *CH.A.D.D. educators manual.* Plantation, FL: CH.A.D.D.

Goldstein, S. & Goldstein, M. (1992). *Hyperactivity: Why won't my child pay attention?* Salt Lake City, UT: Neurology, Learning and Behavior Center.

Goldstein, S. & Mathers, N. (1998). *Overcoming underachievement: An action guide to helping your child succeed in school.* New York: John Wiley & Sons.

Gordon, M. (1991). *ADHD/hyperactivity: A consumer's guide.* DeWitt, NY: GSI Publications.

Hallowell, E. H. (1996). *When you worry about the child you love: Emotional and learning problems in children.* New York: Simon and Schuster.

Ingersoll, B. & Goldstein, S. (1993). *Attention deficit disorders and learning disabilities: Realities, myths, and controversial treatments.* New York: Doubleday.

Koplewicz, H. S. (1996). *It's nobody's fault: New hope and help for difficult children and their parents.* New York: Random House.

Latham P, & Latham, P. (1998). *ADD and the law* (2nd ed.). Washington, DC: JKL.

Nadeau, K. G. & Biggs, S. H. (1995). *School strategies for ADD teens.* VA: Chesapeake Psychological Services.

Parker, H. C. (1994). *The ADD hyperactivity workbook for parents, teachers, and kids* (2nd. ed). Plantation, FL: Specialty Press, Inc.

Parker, H. C. (1992). *The ADD hyperactivity handbook for schools* (2nd. ed.). Plantation, FL: Specialty Press, Inc.

Parker, H.C. (1992). *ADAPT: Attention deficit accommodation plan for teaching.* Plantation, FL: Specialty Press, Inc.

Phelan, T. (1993). *Surviving your adolescents.* Child Management, Glenn Elyn: IL.

Silver, L. (1993). *Dr. Larry Silver's advice to parents on attention-deficit hyperactivity disorder.* Washington, DC: American Psychiatric Press.

Wender, P. H. (1987). *The hyperactive child, adolescent, and adult.* New York: Oxford Press.

Videos for Parents and Teachers

Barkley, R. A. (1992). *ADHD—What do we know?* New York: The Guilford Press.

Barkley, R. A. (1992). *ADHD—What can we do?* New York: The Guilford Press.

Barkley, R. A. (1992). *ADHD in adults.* New York: The Guilford Press.

Barkley, R. A. (1997). *Understanding defiant behavior.* New York: The Guilford Press.

Barkley, R. A. (1997). *Managing defiant behavior.* New York: The Guilford Press.

Biederman, J., Spencer, T., & Wilens, T. (1997). *Medical management of attention deficit hyperactivity disorder—parts I and II.* Plantation, FL: Specialty Press, Inc.

Bramer, J. S. & Fellman, W. (1997). *Success in college and career with attention deficit disorders.* Plantation, FL: Specialty Press, Inc.

Brooks, R. (1997). *Look what you've done! Learning disabilities and self-esteem: stories of hope and resilience.* Washington, D.C.: WETA.

Lavoie, R. (1990). *How difficult can this be? The F.A.T. city workshop.* Washington, D.C.: WETA.

Robin, A. L. & Weiss, S. K. (1997). *Managing oppositional youth. Effective, practical strategies for managing the behavior of hard to manage kids and teens!* Plantation, FL: Specialty Press, Inc.

Books and Videos for Teenagers

Bramer, J. S. (1996). *Succeeding in college with attention deficit disorders: Issues and strategies for students, counselors, & educators.* Plantation, FL: Specialty Press, Inc.

Bramer, J. S. & Fellman, W. (1997). *Success in college and career with attention deficit disorders.* Plantation, FL: Specialty Press, Inc. (Video)

Davis, L., Sirotowitz, S. & Parker, H. (1996). *Study strategies made easy: A practical plan for school success.* Plantation, FL: Specialty Press, Inc.

Davis, L., & Sirotowitz, S. (1997). *Study strategies made easy: A practical plan for school success.* Plantation, FL: Specialty Press, Inc. (Video)

Goldstein, S. & Goldstein, M. (1991). *It's just attention disorder: A video for kids.* Salt Lake City, UT: Neurology, Learning and Behvior Center. (Video)

Gordon, M. (1993). *I would if I could: A teenager's guide to ADHD/Hyperactivity.* DeWitt, NY: GSI Publications.

Hallowell, E. & Ratey, J. (1994). *Driven to distraction.* New York: Simon and Schuster.

Nadeau, K. G. (1994). *Survival guide for college students with ADD or LD.* Washington, DC: Magination Press.

Parker, R. N. and Parker, H. C. (1992). *Making the grade: An adolescent's struggle with attention deficit disorders.* Plantation, FL: Specialty Press, Inc.

Quinn, P. O. (1994). *ADD and the college student.* Washington, DC: Magination Press.

Cited References

American Psychiatric Association. (1994). *Diagnostic and statistical manual of mental disorders* (4th ed., rev.). Washington, DC:Author.

Barkley, R. A. (1998). The prevalence of ADHD: Is it just a U.S. disorder? *The A.D.H.D. Report, 6, 1-6.*

Barkley, R. A. , Fischer, M., Edelbrock, C.S., & Smallish, L. (1990). The adolescent outcome of hyperactive children diagnosed by research criteria: An eight-year prospective follow-up study. *Journal of the American Academy of Child and Adolescent Psychiatry, 29, 547-557.*

Barrickman, L. L., Perry, P. J., Allen, A. J., Kuperman, S., Arndt, S. V., Herrman, K., & Schumacher, E. (1995). Bupropion versus methylphenidate in the treatment of attention-deficit hyperactivity disorder. *Journal of the American Academy of Child and Adolescent Psychiatry, 34, 649-657.*

Berg, B. (1988). *The social skills game.* Ohio: Cognitive Therapeutics.

Biederman, J., Faraone, S.V., Mick, E., Wozniak, J., Chen, L., Ouelette, C., Marrs, A., Moore, P., Garcia, J., Mennin, D., & Lelon, E. (1996). Attention deficit hyperactivity disorder in juvenile mania: An overlooked comorbidity? *Journal of the American Academy of CHild and Adolescent Psychiatry, 35, 997-1009.*

Biederman, J., Faraone, S.V., Keenan, K., Knee., & Tsuang, M. T. (1990). Family-genetic and psychosocial risk factors in DSM-III attention deficit disorder. *Journal of the American Academy of Child and Adolescent Psychiatry, 29, 526-533.*

Bramer, J. S. (1996). *Succeeding in college with attention deficit disorders: Issues and strategies for students, counselors, and educators.* Plantation, FL: Specialty Press, Inc.

Cantwell, D.P. (1985). Psychiatric illness in the families of hyperactive children. *Archives of General Psychiatry, 42, 937-947.*

Campbell, S.B., Szumowski, E.K., Ewing, L.J., Gluck, D.S., & Breaux, A.M. (1982). A multidimensinal assessment of parent-identified behavior problem toddlers. *Journal of Abnormal Child Psychology, 10, 569-592.*

Casat, C. D., Pleasants, D. Z., & Van Wyck Fleet, J. (1987). A double blind trial of buproprion in children with attention deficit disorder. *Psychopharmacology Bulletin, 23, 120-122.*

Castellanos, F. X., Giedd, J.N., Marsh, W. L., Hamburger, S.D., Vaituzis, A.C., Dickstein, D. P., Sarfatti, S.E., Vauss, Y.C., Snell, J.W., Rajapakse, J. C., & Rapoport, J.L. (1996). Quantitative brain magnetic resonance imaging in attention-deficit hyperactivity disorder. *Archives of General Psychiatry, 53, 607-616.*

Children and Adults with Attention Deficit Disorders. (1996). Why Educators and Parents Must Provide Care to Bridge the Gap. In *ADD in Adolescence: Strategies for Success* (pp 30-39). Florida: Children and Adults with Attention Deficit Disorders.

Cook, E. H., Stein, M. A., & Krasowski, M. D. (1995). Association of attention deficit disorder and the dopamine transporter gene. *American Journal of Human Genetics, 56, 993-998.*

Conners, C. K. (1980). *Feeding the Brain.* New York: Plenum Press.

Comings, D. E. & Comings, B.G. (1990). A controlled family history study of Tourette's syndrome. Attention-deficit hyperactivity disorder and learning disorders. *Journal of Clinical Psychiatry, 29, 667-668.*

Crook, W. G. (1991). *Help for your hyperactive child.* Jackson, TN: Professional Books.

Davis, L., Sirotowitz, S., & Parker, H.C. (1996). *Study strategies made easy: A practical plan for school success.* Plantation, FL: Specialty Press, Inc.

Elia, J., Borcherding, B. G., Rapoport, J. L., & Keysor, C. A. (1991). Methylphenidate and dextroamphetamine treatments of hyperactivity: Are there true nonresponders? *Psychiatry Research, 36 (2), 141-155.*

Evers, R. B. and Elksnin, N. (1998).*Working with students with disabilities in vocational-technical settings.* Austin, TX: Pro-Ed.

Faraone, S., Biederman, J., Weber, W., and Russell, R. L. (1998). Psychiatric, neuropsychological, and psychosocial features of DSM-IV subtypes of attention-deficity/ hyperactivity disorder: Results from a clinically referred sample. *Journal of the American Academy of Child and Adolescent Psychiatry, 37 (2), 185-193.*

Feingold, B. F. (1974). *Why your child is hyperactive.* New York: Random House.

Garfinkel, L. F., Kragthorpe, C., Jordan, D., Wright, B., Goldberg, P, and Goldberg, M. (1997). *Un ique challenges, hopeful responses: A handbook for professionals working with youth with disabilities in the juvenile justice system.* Minneapolis, MN: Pacer Center.

Goldstein, A. P. (1988). *The prepare curriculum. Teaching prosocial competencies.* Champaign, IL: Research Press.

Goldstein, A. P. & McGinnis, E. (1997). *Skillstreaming the adolescent.* Champaign, IL: Research Press.

Goldstein, M. & Goldstein, S. (1998). *Managing attention deficit hyperactivity disorder in children: A guide for practitioners.* New York: John Wiley & Sons, Inc.

Hathaway, W. L. (1997). ADHD and the military. *The ADHD Report, 5, 1-6.*

Hynd, G. W., Hern, K. L., Novey, E. S., & Eiopulos, D. (1993). Attention-deficit hyperactivity disorder and asymmetry of the caudate nucleus. *Journal of Child Neurology, 8, 339-347.*

Jalil, G. Street-wise drug prevention: a realistic approach to prevent and intervene in adolescent drug use.

Johnston, L. D. (1996). The rise in drug use among American teens continues in 1996. Press release from the Monitoring the Future Study, December 1996. Ann Arbor: University of Michigan.

Klein, R. G. (1987). Prognosis of attention deficit disorder and its management in adolescence. *Pediatrics in Review, 8, 216-222.*

LaHoste, G. J., Swanson, J. M., & Wigal, S. B. (1996). Dopamine D4 receptor gene polymorphism is associated with attention deficit hyperactivity disorder. *Molecular Psychiatry, 1, 121-124.*

Levy, F., Hay, D.A., McStephen, M., Wood, C., & Waldman, I. (1997). Attention-deficit hyperactivity disorder: A category or a continuum? Genetic analysis of a large scale twin study. *Journal of the American Academy of Child and Adolescent Psychiatry, 36, 737-744.*

Malhotra, S.,& Sontosh, P. J. (1998). An open clinical trial of buspirone in children with attention-deficit/hyperactivity disorder. *Journal of the American Academy of Child and Adolescent Psychiatry, 37, 364-371.*

Milich, R., Wolraich, M., & Lindgren, S. (1986). Sugar and hyperactivity: A critical review of empirical findings. *Clinical Psychology Review, 6, 493-513.*

Pauling, L. (1968). Orthomolecular psychiatry. *Science, 160, 265-271.*

Physician's Desk Reference. (1997). Oradell, NJ: Medical Economics.

Rehabilitation Act of 1973., P.L. 93-112. 20 U.S.C. 1412 (2).

Robin, A. L. & Foster, S. L. (1989). *Negotiating parent-adolescent conflict.* New York: Guilford Press.

Safer, D. J., Zito, J. M., & Fine, E. M. (1996). Increased methylphenidate usage for attention deficit disorder in the 1990s. *Pediatrics, 98, 1084-1088.*

U.S. Department of Education. (1992). *A parent's guide to prevention: Growing up drug free.* Washington, DC: Author.

Walker, H. M., Todis, B., Holmes, D., & Horton, G. (1988). *The Walker social skills curriculum: The ACCESS program.* Austin, TX: Pro-Ed.

Werry, J.S. & Quay, H.C. (1971). The prevalence of behavior symptoms in younger elementary school children. *American Journal of Orthopsychiatry, 41, 136-143.*

Zametkin, A. J., Nordahl, T.E., Gross, M., King, A.C., Semple, W.E., Rumsey, J., Hamburger, S., & Cohen, R.M. (1990). Cerebral glucose metabolism in adults with hyperactivity of childhood onset. *New England Journal of Medicine, 323, 1361-1366.*

Index

Additional Worksheets

Medication Effects Rating Scale
Family Communication Chart
Problem-Solving Flow Chart
Problem-Solving Worksheet
Home Behavior Chart
Weekly Planner

Medication Effects Rating Scale

Name_____   Grade_____

Date_____   School_____

Completed By_____   Physician_____

List name(s) of medication student is taking:

MEDICATION(S)	DOSAGE(S)	TIME(S) OF DAY TAKEN	DISPENSED BY
_____	_____	_____	_____
_____	_____	_____	_____
_____	_____	_____	_____

Mark any changes noticed in the following behaviors:

Behavior	Worse	No Change	Improved a Little	Improved a Lot
attention to task	_____	_____	_____	_____
listening to lessons	_____	_____	_____	_____
finishing work	_____	_____	_____	_____
impulsiveness	_____	_____	_____	_____
calling out in class	_____	_____	_____	_____
organization, fine motor	_____	_____	_____	_____
overactivity	_____	_____	_____	_____
restlessness, fidgety	_____	_____	_____	_____
talkativeness	_____	_____	_____	_____
aggressiveness	_____	_____	_____	_____

Mark any side effects noticed by you or mentioned by student:

Side Effects	Comments
appetite loss	_____
insomnia	_____
headaches	_____
stomach aches	_____
seems tired	_____
stares a lot	_____
irritable	_____
vocal or motor tic	_____
sadness	_____
nervousness	_____

Family Communication Chart
Behaviors Which Build Up or Break Down Communication

<u>Do</u>	<u>Don't</u>
Wait for the other person to finish speaking	Interrupt
Make brief statements without judging	Lecture, sermonize
Talk in a neutral voice	Talk sarcastically
Make eye contact, acknowledge you are listening by nodding head, etc.	Look away, act distracted
Sit in a relaxed position	Fidget, move around
Make brief statements, give others a chance to talk	Hog the conversation
Take other people's feelings seriously Recognize other's hurt, pain, anger	Discount feelings
Stay focused on one issue at a time	Change the topic
Make tentative rather than absolute statements, deal with specifics	Overgeneralize, catastrophize, exaggerate
Make suggestions instead of demands	Give orders or commands
Speak to others in a respectful tone	Call names
Stick with the current issue	Dwell on the past
Stay calm and look for an appropriate solution	Threaten
Express your feelings to others in an appropriate way	Keep feelings inside
Talk in a neutral voice	Yell or scream

Three Steps to Improving Communication

1. Identify common mistakes in family communication.

2. Practice communication skills with imaginary situations.

3. Practice communication skills with real situations.

Problem-Solving Flow Chart

The steps listed below will guide you through the problem-solving process. Follow the guidelines listed under each step.

STEP 1: IDENTIFY THE PROBLEM
Mother, father, and adolescent should take turns defining the problem as each sees it.
- Don't define the problem in an emotional way by exaggerating, blaming, and demeaning someone else.
- Limit your problem definition to just one issue.

STEP 2: THINK OF PLANS TO SOLVE THE PROBLEM
Brainstorm ideas to come up with possible plans to solve the problem.
- Take turns and think up as many plans as possible—anything goes here.
- Don't evaluate any of the plans until everyone has had a chance to share their ideas.

STEP 3: PICK THE BEST PLAN
Each person explains how the proposed plan would affect them personally, rates each plan with a plus or minus. Choose the plan with the most consensus.
- Be practical and think about how the plan would actually work if you tried it.
- Consider how each plan would affect other people's feelings.
- Pick the plan that is most agreeable with everyone.

STEP 4: TRY THE PLAN
Discuss how to put the plan into action and write an "action-plan."
- Define the behaviors to be targeted.
- Determine consequences (rewards/punishments) and how they will be administered.
- Make sure you have a way of keeping track of what is occurring.

STEP 5: EVALUATE THE PLAN
Within a week or so, meet again to discuss how the plan worked.
- Evaluate if the plan was effective.
- Consider if everyone is satisfied with how the plan is working.
- If the plan is working well, continue to use it. If the plan is not working well, use the problem solving process to come up with another plan.

Problem-Solving Worksheet

Date:_____

Instructions: Use this form to guide you through the steps of the problem-solving process. Write responses to each step in the spaces provided.

1. Identify the problem. As a family, decide how to define the problem situation and write it down here.

2. Think of some plans to solve the problem. Discuss different plans and write a few of them down here.

3. Pick the best plan. As a family, decide which plan is the best one to try.

Plus or Minus Ratings by
<u>Teen</u> <u>Mother</u> <u>Father</u>

Plan 1

Plan 2

Plan 3

Plan 4

4. Try the plan. Write down specifically what each member of the family will do to carry out the plan.

5. Evaluate the plan. Write down how the plan worked, what you could do to make it work better, what everyone thought of the plan.

Name _____ Week of _____ **Home Behavior Chart**

START BEHAVIORS	Value	Su	Mo	Tu	We	Th	Fr	Sa
1								
2								
3								
4								
5								
6								
7 Extra Credit!								
TOTAL TOKENS EARNED								

STOP BEHAVIORS	Value	Su	Mo	Tu	We	Th	Fr	Sa
1								
2								
3								
4								
5								
6								
7 Extra Penalty								
TOTAL TOKENS LOST (Minus)								

TOTAL TOKENS AVAILABLE								

REWARDS/PRIVILEGES	Value	Su	Mo	Tu	We	Th	Fr	Sa
1								
2								
3								
4								
5								
6								
7								
8								
TOTAL TOKENS SPENT								
TOTAL TOKENS REMAINING								

Weekly Planner

Time	Monday	Tuesday	Wednesday	Thursday	Friday
8:00					
8:30					
8:00					
9:30					
10:00					
10:30					
11:00					
11:30					
Noon					
12:30					
1:00					
1:30					
2:00					
2:30					
3:00					
3:30					
4:00					
4:30					
5:00					
5:30					
6:00					
6:30					
7:00					
7:30					
8:00					
8:30					
9:00					
10:00					
10:30					
11:00					
11:30					
12:00					